WINGS OVER GLOUCESTERSHIRE

Piccadilly Publishing
Unit A Inchbrook Trading Estate
Woodchester Stroud Gloucestershire 045383 5595

WINGS OVER GLOUCESTERSHIRE

BY

JOHN RENNISON

PICCADILLY PUBLISHING
1988

FIRST PUBLISHED 1988
© JOHN RENNISON
ISBN 0 9514047 0 9

Printed & Bound in Great Britain by
Dotesios Ltd. Bradford on Avon.
Typeset by Line One Studio
Cheltenham.

CONTENTS

Introduction & Acknowledgements

INTRODUCTION
&
ACKNOWLEDGEMENTS

There are those that would question the very idea that Gloucestershire played an important part in the historic events that occurred between the years 1935 and 1945. They would no doubt observe that the area was nothing more than a rural backwater during those momentous and hectic times. Nothing could be further from the truth, as will become all too obvious when you peruse the pages that follow. The Cotswold region (which was largely encompassed by the boundaries of the pre 1974 Gloucestershire) was very much in the thick of things.

This book attempts to chronicle the events of those years in order to record aspects of local history that may soon be forgotten or lost altogether. It details the history of air defence in the region and describes the air raids and other aeronautical activities that took place between 1935 and 1945, together with an account of the main events prior to those years. My hope is that it will serve to create a picture of the events and above all, the people that were involved. For history is most certainly about people and their activities. I have introduced as many individuals as I can into the narrative, though I fear I have done them less than justice.

If any single year could be said to be the point in time where it all began, then 1935 is probably that year. It was on February the 26th 1935, that Hitler announced to the world details of the reborne Luftwaffe. During that same year details of the RAF expansion scheme were finalised. On 1st April 1935 the ARP Department of the Home Office came into being. It was in that year also that the Defence Requirements Committee recommended the creation of a 'shadow' armaments industry. The die was indeed cast, although many were still unable to see it.

Like most works of its kind, this book would not have been possible without the help of many people. The initial persuasion to undertake the project came from my friends and fellow air enthusiasts in the Cotswold Aircraft Restoration Group, but I would also like to express my thanks to a number of others. I trust that I have not missed anyone out. If however, I have been remiss, please accept my apologies. Thanks are due to the following:

The staffs of the Public Records Office, Kew; the Air Historical Branch of MOD; Gloucester County Records Office; Gloucester and Cheltenham Libraries and the Echo newspaper.

The Severnside Aviation Society (Allan White and Barry Walding); the Cotswolds Aircraft Restoration Group (Tony Southern, 'Rog' Rogers, Harry Hodgson, Dave Mace, Geoff Lewis, Rod Smith) and many others for their help and consideration.

Fellow historians; Paul Aston, Brian Kedward, Ray Sturtivant, Ken Wixey, Dave Benfield (Airfield Research Group), Delwyn Griffith, Bart Rijnhout and Ken Wakefield.

Former and serving police officers; Ralph Wilkins, Ian Hughes, Roger Box and C. Taylor, and the following individuals; 'Sam' Masters, Agnes King, George Dennis, Alan Hartley, Phillipa Hodgkiss, Ben Legg, Jimmy Townsend, Andrew Bruce, Mike Denley, Peter Witts, Louisa Pearce, Robert Powell, G. Blythe, J.H. Johnstone, G.J. Jenkins, P. Dooley, G.R. Burr, Philip Sawyer, P. Willimont, Lila Hoskins, Peter Bolton, John Shaw, Jack and Nora Radford, W.G. Greenaway, Bill Sherwood, J.F. Lambert, E.O. Edwards and M.G.M. Weightman.

The majority of the photographs included have been as accurately credited as possible. (Any errors will of course be rectified in future editions). Many of the pictures have never been published before and have been uncovered through the tireless efforts of two dedicated individuals mentioned above, Paul Aston and Allan White.

A final vote of thanks must go to two ladies who have given freely of their time and understanding, my wife Pat and my 'demon' typist, and first line editor Angela. Thank you.

John Rennison
Cheltenham
1988.

Chapter 1

In the Beginning . . .

The threads that bind the county of Gloucestershire to the history of military aviation and the aerial battles of World War II have become much entangled over the years. The origins are, however, clearly rooted in a period of somewhat less than 30 years, leading up to the outbreak of the First World War. Of course, one should not discount the earlier aeronautical efforts of such pioneering balloonists as the intrepid Mr. Graham who first sailed aloft from Montpellier Gardens in Cheltenham during 1836. There were others not so far behind him, such as Charles Green, John Hampton and, indeed, Graham's wife. Laudable as they were, their attempts to get man into the air belong to another era of aviation.

Perhaps the first notable occurrence of that 30 year period was the birth at Cranham Villa, Kings Road, Cheltenham, of one Frederick Handley-Page in November 1885. Later knighted,

Frederick founded the famous Handley-Page Aircraft Company in 1909. One of the great early pioneers of aviation, he went on to build many famous aircraft that were to serve Britain well in both peace and war. Some seven years later, in April 1892, a second birth took place at Queen's Parade, Cheltenham, that was to have tremendous import for the history of military aviation in this country. It was that of Arthur Harris. Marshal of

Taken in 1943 this picture shows the then Air Marshal A. T. Harris, A.O.C. in C. Bomber Command consulting with senior colleagues.

the Royal Air Force, Sir Arthur Harris, as he was to become, was to lead RAF Bomber Command through a crucial period in its history during the Second World War. He was also destined to have a distinguished career in the First World War. (Plaques have been placed at both these addresses).

Yet another pioneer of military aeronautics also came upon the Gloucestershire scene at this time, Captain Clement Robert Wedgewood Allen. Although his fame is not a matter of public knowledge, "Bob" Allen played an important part in the development of military aviation and air reconnaissance. Born in Shanghai where his parents were missionaries, he was sent home to Stanton Court in Gloucestershire in 1883 to be brought up by his grandmother. Having learnt to fly at the famous Brooklands aerodrome (Royal Aero Club Certificate No.159), he joined the Royal Flying Corps four days after its formation in May 1912. While subsequently serving with No. 3 Squadron he was instrumental in perfecting many of the early reconnaissance techniques used later by the RFC in the 1914-1918 war. He was to die tragically whilst on a training flight in March 1914. Among the mourners at the funeral at Woodchester near Stroud were at least five of his contemporaries who were later to achieve high rank in the RAF, including Lieutenant, later Air Chief Marshal Sir Phillip Joubert de la Ferte.

One early airman still remembered in Cheltenham is Bentfield C. Hucks. He was to become famous for his "Hucks Starter", an ingenious device mounted on a "T" model Ford chassis which was used for starting high-compression propeller-driven engines. However, in the immediate pre-war years from 1910 onwards he was to become increasingly involved in the flying scene. He became the first Englishman to loop and fly upside-down. His

Two views of the Shuttleworth Trusts 'Hucks Starter' ready for action with the Trusts Hawker Hind.

Photos: R. Smith

favourite mounts were an early Blackburn Mercury and later a specially-strengthened Bleriot monoplane.

As a boy, George Dennis, a resident of Prestbury, had an encounter with Hucks when his flimsy machine forcelanded in the village due to lack of fuel. Petrol was provided by a local car

Bentfield Hucks in his Bleriot (note roundels on upper wings so that spectators could tell when the aircraft was upside-down.

owner and the village lads were recruited to hold the aircraft down as Hucks ran up the engine prior to take-off. He waved them away and the aircraft bumped over the grass and spluttered into the air. Within a brief space he had put down on his landing ground at nearby Whaddon farm enclosure. Needless to say, a starry-eyed George Dennis was, dare one say it, 'hooked' and went on to have a long career with the famous Gloster Aircraft Company.

Hucks visited Cheltenham in 1911 and again during the August Bank Holiday weekend of 1913. He gave flying displays that weekend over both Cheltenham and Gloucester with his 70hp open cockpit Bleriot monoplane. He offered "pleasure flights" for the then not inconsiderable sum of £5. In fact, only one person took this rather expensive chance to see Cheltenham from on high. The displays were poorly attended, only a few hundred people being in evidence at Whaddon enclosure. The more economically-minded majority had quickly discovered that you could equally well watch an air display from outside the enclosure and it cost nothing. Hucks was reported as being dangerously close to houses in the area when landing, apparently giving a rather close-up view of the wood-and-canvas Bleriot to some of the local householders.

The year 1910 marks a milestone in the aeronautical history of the county, for it was then that Sir George White formed the British and Colonial Aeroplane Company. He was already widely-known for setting up an electric tramway in Bristol, and indeed, it was in leased premises of the Bristol Tramways Company at Filton that the new firm was established. Frank Barnwell, a

The flimsy Bleriot monoplane flown by Bentfield Hucks during his visits to Gloucestershire was very similar to this example seen at Old Warden Bedfordshire
Photo: R. Smith

Bristol F2B fighter C4685. Most famous of the aircraft produced at Filton during World War 1, the 'Brisfit' as it was known, remained in production until 1926. The aircraft began it's operational service with No. 48 Squadron in 1917.
(Rennison Collection)

Scottish engineer, was taken on and things began to happen. By 1911 land had been acquired for an airfield near the workshops and a Government contract had been awarded for the production of Bristol Boxkite aircraft. The company established its position as a leading manufacturer of military aircraft with the Bristol Bullet fighter, production of which began in 1913. Probably the most successful of Barnwell's designs was the famous Bristol Fighter, but he was responsible for many other excellent designs.

The Gloucestershire connection with the fledgeling Royal Flying Corps was in evidence

Bristol M1c fighter aircraft C5017. The prototype of this monoplane design first flew in 1916. One hundred and twenty five of these aircraft were built by the British and Colonial Aeroplane Co. at Bristol. Its advanced streamlining and monoplane layout give a good indication of capabilities of the company designers during the early years of combat aircraft development.
(Rennison Collection)

once again during 1913. Lieutenant Lancelot Rogers-Harrison from Pittville Lawn, Cheltenham was killed when his aircraft plunged to the ground from some 400 feet at Farnborough. Rogers-Harrison, a Cheltenham College old boy, had been taught to fly by the famous American pilot, Colonel Samuel Franklin Cody. (Not to be confused with the well-known "Buffalo Bill", Col. William Frederick Cody). In fact, the aircraft involved in the accident was one of Cody's own designs. The resultant investigation established that the elevators had broken away, possibly due to over-energetic manipulation. The Lieutenant had been attached to the RFC from the 2nd Royal Warwickshire Regiment and, although his aeronautical career was brief, he ranks with Wedgewood-Allen as one of the early pioneers of military aviation. Tragically, Cody himself was to be killed in August of the same year when he fell from an aircraft near Fleet in Hampshire.

The Gloucestershire Aircraft Company came onto the scene somewhat later than the Bristol company. Its origins go back to 1915 when the directors of the Aircraft Manufacturing Company visited the Cheltenham-based firm of H.H. Martyn & Co. They were looking for a company skilled in wood-working to assist in the production of aircraft components. They liked what they saw at the Sunningend Works and Martyn's were given a contract for the manufacture of spare parts for Farman aircraft. The high standard of the finished work led to further contracts and within a short time the company was building fuselages for DH.4, DH.6, Nieuport and Bristol fighters. Other local firms began to undertake subcontract work for Martyn's, including the Gloucestershire Carriage and Wagon Co. Ltd. and Daniels & Co. of Stroud.

Both pictures show aircraft construction work taking place in the old Winter Gardens at Cheltenham during 1917. The aircraft are probably DH.6's intended for the Royal Flying Corps.   *Photo: Mrs. Pearce*

A large amount of the assembly work was also carried out in the Winter Gardens in Cheltenham (the site of the present-day Imperial Gardens). Whilst men were involved in the production and assembly of aircraft components and propellers, a large number of women were employed for the intricate and important work of putting fabric upon wings and fuselages. The Gloucestershire Aircraft Company (later and more widely known as the Gloster Aircraft Company) was formed in June 1917 to take over the aircraft work of Martyn's with nearly 800 employees. One of the youngsters taken on during the war expansion of the company was 18 year old George Dennis; unskilled as he was, the grounding he received with the company was to set the pattern for a large part of his working life. His encounter with Hucks those few years earlier had made it almost inevitable that the young George would seek a career in aviation. By the end of the hostilities Martyn's and its offspring GAC had been responsible for the construction of hundreds of DH.6's, DH.9's, Bristol F2B's, FE.2B's and various Nieuport aircraft, an invaluable contribution to Britain's war effort.

The British and Colonial Aircraft Company was also greatly expanded with the outbreak of war in 1914. New premises were constructed at Filton and the number of staff rose dramatically. The Ministry established the South-West Aircraft Acceptance Park on the airfield with some 18 hangars at its disposal, necessary because of the large amount of aircraft being produced. By the end of the war, the company had a work force of over 3,000. Filton was, of course, used extensively by the Royal Flying Corps from 1915 onwards, a number of units taking over their new Bristol Fighters at the base and "working up" before departing for France. Large numbers of second-hand aircraft became available with the end of the fighting and thus military orders tailed off. As a result of this, both GAC and Bristols were to have a lean time for some years post-war but both firms established good reputations and were to go on to greater things.

Needless to say, there had also been tremendous expansion on the military side, beginning with the establishment of an airfield at Rendcombe during the early part of 1916. A number of units began to undertake their flying training at the new station which was under the control of 21 Wing RFC with headquarters nearby. Two non-flying

Pictured in 1983 one of the few remaining buildings on the old airfield at Rendcombe.

(Rennison Collection)

In this photo taken in 1983 cattle graze happily on the site of the old airfield at Rendcombe. Some of the few remaining WW1 buildings are just visible through the morning mist.

(Rennison Collection)

establishments had also been set up by the RFC in the county. The first of these was No.6 School of Aeronautics at Marlborough House in Cheltenham. The school's job was to give basic instruction to cadet pilots. It was a large establishment with a strength of over 1,600 personnel. The Town Hall, a local riding school and some 33 private houses were taken over for accommodation. During the war the school moved to Shorncliffe and its place was taken by No. 9 Observers School of Aeronautics which had a similar task. A second training unit was set up at 10 Elmdale Road, Clifton, No. 6 School of Aeronautics. This unit boasted a staff of over 1,000 and a maximum capacity of 600 cadets who underwent a six to seven-week course. An aircraft repair depot had also been set up in the south of the county during 1917 at Yate, and it became

A 'ground-looped' Avro 504K in front of a canvas Besso-neaux hanger. A common sight at Leighterton and Minchin-hampton during the period 1917–1920.
(Rennison Collection)

A group of young RFC flight cadets under canvas in 1917.
(Rennison Collection)

known as No. 3 (Western) Aircraft Repair Depot. Fighter aircraft and engines were overhauled at the depot which had a staff of 1,800.

The county also became home to No. 1 Wing of the Australian Flying Corps during the latter part of the war. The AFC headquarters had been established at Tetbury in 1917 and two airfields had been picked out at Minchinhampton and Leighterton for flying training. Both airfields opened during February 1918 and an air-firing range was pegged out at Long Newnton. Two Training Squadrons, Nos. 5 and 6, were based at Minchinhampton (No. 1 station), whilst Nos. 7 and 8 Training Squadrons were at Leighterton (No. 2 station), together with an aircraft repair section. Main equipment of the squadrons was the Avro 504 biplane trainer, although a variety of other types was used. Many Australian pilots and observers destined for the Western Front and the Middle East were trained by these units. The

casualty rate during flying training was high, as evidenced by the 23 AFC graves in the small cemetery at Leighterton. Three of these airmen were victims of an incident that occurred on Wednesday, 28th August 1918. Two aircraft from Minchinhampton were carrying out a mock combat exercise over Minchinhampton Common when they collided. One of the aircraft was a single-seater being flown by a trainee pilot, Cadet Lieutenant Jefferys. The other was a twin-seater piloted by Lt. C.W. Scott and crewed by Lt. R.L. Cummings. During the mock fight one aircraft turned directly into the path of the other at about 1,500 feet and collided with its "opponent". Both machines fell to the ground and all three airmen were killed.

The Royal Flying Corps was no stranger to this type of tragedy either. One incident involving an aircraft from Rendcombe was witnessed by a local man in 1918. As a small boy, Ben Legg, who still lives at North Cerney, saw an aircraft pass over the village making louder noises than usual. As the

Airmen surround this Avro trainer in a scene typical of 1918. The proximity of the aircraft to the building looks sus-piciously like the result of an oversight on someones part?
(Rennison Collection)

A 'bent Sopwith' an all too familiar sight in Gloucestershire during the latter part of World War One.
(Rennison Collection)

A Camel passes overhead framed by the early morning sky. A scene redolent of one witnessed many times in the Gloucestershire area during and after World War One.
(Rennison Collection)

Minchinhampton Airfield 13.10.1918
(Ministry of Defence)

aircraft flew over the rectory, pieces began to fall off. Within minutes the machine had crashed some 300 yards away on Scrubditch Farm and burst into flames. The pilot, Sergeant Frederick Ivens, was found dead amongst the wreckage. A wide-eyed Ben ran to the scene with other lads from the village. The incident made a deep impression, enabling details to be recalled with clarity 65 years later.

Leighterton Airfield 17.12.1918
(Ministry of Defence)

Ground crew and pilot pose with their Sopwith Camel, site unknown.
(Rennison Collection)

An Avro 504 trainer is removed tail first from its Bessoneaux hanger.

Following the armistice in November 1918 training activities began to tail off. Strangely, the tempo of construction at the airfields did not slacken due to the continuation of war-time

Typical of the German pilots being encountered over the Western Front by the Gloucestershire trained Aussies, are these pilots all of them aces.

contracts. Work on large, brick-built hangars continued well into 1919. No work was undertaken at Long Newnton, however, and the air-firing range ceased to be used in February of that year. Similarly, after brief spells as emergency landing grounds, all the military airfields had fallen into disuse by 1920—21, as had the Repair Depot at Yate. The Air Acceptance Park at Brockworth was, by 1920 in use only as a storage centre for No. 7 Group of the RAF. However, the Gloucestershire Aircraft Company began renting hangarage on the airfield and the firm's activities became increasingly centred on the site. In 1928 the company purchased the whole 200 acre site for the princely sum of £15,000.

Three years earlier, the old Western Aircraft Repair Depot at Yate had also been taken over by an aircraft company, George Parnall & Co., an event of much greater significance to the local population than many realised at the time.

Aerial view Rendcombe March 1917.
(via 48 Squadron Records)

Remaining buildings at Leighterton pictured in 1983.
(Rennison Collection)

Some of the AFC Headquarters staff based near Tetbury.

Leighterton's Australian War Cemetery.
(Rennison Collection)

Brockworth was the scene of much excitement during September 1929 when Sir Allan Cobham brought his Municipal Aerodrome Campaign to Gloucester. Sir Allan took many youngsters aloft in his De Havilland biplane *Youth of Britain*. He also provided air experience for local dignitaries. The campaign lasted from May to October 1929 and visits were made to 110 towns and cities, and some 40,000 passengers were carried. A quarter of these were children who travelled free, their flights having been financed by Sir Charles Wakefield.

The 1930's were years of great change, some nations preparing for war whilst others buried their heads in the sands of indifference and blind, idealistic pacifism. They were, however, colourful and exciting years in the history of aviation. Flying had begun to catch the public imagination. Fuelled by stories of aerial combat during the war, record-breaking flights, travelling air shows and the larger than life characters that abounded, public interest rose to fever pitch. Gloucestershire was no exception, and during April 1931 Cheltenham Air Week was held at Kaytes Farm alongside the road to Bishop's Cleeve. It was run by the Berkshire Aviation Company, a famous flying circus of the thirties, under the direction of Captain F.J.W. Holmes. Although basic by today's standards, the programme was pretty exciting stuff half a century ago. There was wing-walking, formation flying, inverted flying and what was described as the "Bridal Pair". No description of this latter undertaking survives, unfortunately. A pleasure flight would have cost you 5/- (25p); certainly

An Avro 504 two seater of the Berkshire Aviation Company run by Cpt. F. J. W. Holmes. This Flying Circus gave a show at Kaytes Farm Cheltenham during 1931.
(Rennison Collection)

value for money, as testified to by an intrepid reporter from the 'Gloucestershire Echo' who went aloft. He described his flight over the racecourse and Pittville Park in the most glowing terms.

In 1932 it was again the turn of the famous Sir Alan Cobham. During April he applied to

Cheltenham Corporation for permission to stage one of his National Aviation Day Campaign shows on two vacant fields near the St. Mark's housing estate. There was some disagreement over the possible venue, but a landing ground at Parton Farm, Churchdown was chosen. On 7th May Cobham flew into Brockworth and went to Parton Farm where he was met by the Deputy Mayor of Gloucester and the city's High Sheriff. Cobham examined the site and made a speech, still in his flying overalls, to the small crowd that had gathered. The show came to town on 9th May. Young and old lined up for the chance of a flight in the Imperial Airways airliner *Pretoria*. A large number of women was in evidence, many of them making their first flight. Once again, there was wing-walking, crazy flying and an air race. Another event featured balloons being shot at and burst from an aircraft. The "Bridal Pair" was once more on the bill and some detail is available to throw some light on this rather bizarre piece of entertainment. Apparently, on this occasion the event featured a supposedly newly-wed couple being pursued in their car by an aircraft. The car was "bombed" and set on fire! Not exactly the most advantageous start to married life that one

Entirely New!

SIR ALAN COBHAM'S

NATIONAL AVIATION   DAY CAMPAIGN

AIR DISPLAY

PALLADIUM, OSSETT
Enter Our Novel Parachute Competition
Monday to Friday, July 15th—19th
and WIN A FREE FLIGHT in
Sir Alan Cobham's Air Liner!

Jo King, pilot of the Airspeed Ferry in Cobham's shows poses complete with washing in front of his aircraft 'Youth of Britain II'. Jo lived in Prestbury and Cheltenham for many years after the war and was a great friend of the redoubtable Tom Sopwith. *(Rennison Collection)*

Cobhams Air-Speed Ferry G-ABSI. Many youngsters had their first flight in this aircraft at one of Sir Alan's shows during the thirties.

(Rennison Collection)

The flying displays of C. W. Scott were amongst the last of the 1930's. This team featured a number of Cobhams old aircraft and pilots; notably Jo King and Airspeed Ferry G-ABSI.

could imagine. Another attraction on show was Sir Henry Seagrave's 230mph car, the *Golden Arrow.*

Cobham's shows were always a great success and are remembered with affection by many half a century later. He probably did more to promote aviation during the thirties than any other individual. He also brought a touch of glamour to many lives and places during what was for many a time of economic hardship and even poverty, as the great Depression took hold. It was due in no small measure to his activities that the British public became air-minded. Many young men, who were in a few short years to prove the salvation of this country, had their desire to fly

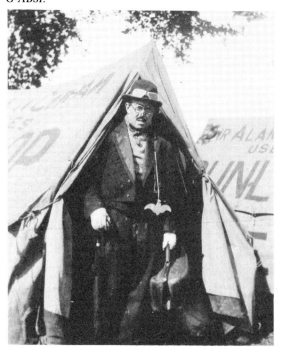

'Mad' Mackay was well known on the air show circuit of the 30's for his stunt act.

(Rennison Collection)

Joan Meakin, woman pilot extraordinary chats between displays during an air show in the 1930's.

(Western Daily Press and Bristol Mirror

fired by Cobham's shows. Similarly, his travels up and down the country led to the identification of many potential airfield sites that were to be put to good use during the Second World War. The band of outstanding airmen and airwomen that he gathered about him consisted of people such as Captain Joe King, one of Cobham's chief pilots and the man who flew the show's famous Airspeed Ferry, Joan Meakin, glider pilot extraordinary, "Mad" Mackay, Geoffrey Tyson, R.J. Ashley, and famous parachutists like Naomi Heron-Maxwell and Ivor Price, who made over 500 jumps at Cobham's shows. When coupled with his record-breaking long-distance flights and his later work in the field of air-to-air refuelling, his air show activities during 1929—35 make his overall contribution to the development of aviation one of inestimable value.

In May 1934 the famous Hawker Aircraft Company made a takeover bid for GAC. It was accepted, and under the new management the Hucclecote factory began a programme of expansion. The factory floor space was to grow to almost one million square feet prior to the outbreak of the war. Although the Gloster name was to survive for many years to come, the factory now began to produce a run of Hawker aircraft: Harts, Audaxes and later Hurricanes.

In March 1935 Adolf Hitler announced to a stunned world that, in defiance of the edicts of the Versailles Treaty, Germany had created its own air arm. The newly-formed Luftwaffe was said to have a strength of nearly 2,000 aircraft and 20,000 personnel, and had been placed under the command of the World War One fighter ace, Herman Goring. That same month, military conscription was reintroduced in Germany. Almost as if in anticipation of this announcement, the British Government had revealed a major expansion scheme for the RAF in July 1934. The strength of the service was to be raised to 75 squadrons. New stations were to be built and aircraft production was to be increased.

The effect on Gloucestershire was to be considerable. The aircraft industry underwent major expansion. New orders came pouring in. Bristols at Filton were contracted to build Hawker aircraft: Furies, Audaxes and also Gloster Gauntlets. At the same time, the factory was being tooled-up for production of the new Blenheim bomber. The number of staff almost doubled in the last six months of the year and the factory premises were modernised and expanded.

During the summer of 1935 the Home Office issued a document to all local authorities, detailing precautionary measures regarded as advisable to protect the civilian population against attacks by hostile aircraft. Further circulars were issued, dealing with such emotive subjects as anti-gas training and decontamination, and training schools began to appear to provide the back-up. In March 1936 German troops reoccupied the Rhineland and later volunteers were sent to fight alongside Franco's fascists in the Spanish Civil War, an ideal testing ground for the latest military equipment. In Britain the RAF Volunteer Reserve came into being, providing a pool of partially-trained airmen, and some 13 civilian flying schools were given approval to carry out the basic training of military personnel. Within the RAF, new Fighter, Bomber, Coastal and Training Commands were created as part of the expansion programme. The war clouds, still unseen by many, were gathering with increasing momentum.

Tangible signs of the RAF's expansion began to appear in the county during 1936 when construction of a new airfield began at South Cerney. Negotiations were also under way in the summer of 1937 for the sale of 100 acres of land for an RAF storage unit at Ripple, near Tewkesbury. In addition, work had started on the new bases at Kemble and Little Rissington.

Construction of this sort was often hazardous and there were frequent casualties. Three workers were killed at Kemble alone during a three-month period in 1937. Earlier in the year a countywide scheme for the organisation of Air Raid Precautions had been drawn up and copies had been sent out to all local authorities in the area. The county was to be divided into seven districts (this was later to be changed). Following this, the first meetings of ARP committees were held during May.

In August 1937 a large summer camp was held for members of the Combined Cadet Force at Hunting Butts Farm near Cheltenham. Thousands of cadets descended on the farm and a veritable forest of tents arose. Many were on hand to see a specially arranged display of aerobatics performed by an RAF Blenheim bomber and an Audax biplane. Many local people watched enthralled as the two silver-painted aircraft cavorted across the sky. By the middle of the month the first contingents of airmen were arriving at South Cerney despite the fact that the station was still nowhere near complete.

As a result of growing public interest in ARP, the Cheltenham ARP Commissioner, Mr. Grimwade, gave a lecture on the subject of protecting the public during air raids in September 1937. This took place in the Town Hall, and a similar lecture was later given to members of the fire service who were attending a conference in the town at that time. By the end of the year, Parliament had approved the Air Raid Precautions Act 1937. Under this act, county and county borough councils were obligated to submit ARP schemes for their areas to the Secretary of State. They also had to provide information likely to be of use in the event of mass evacuations of the public because of air raid threats. Cheltenham and Gloucester joint councils approved an application by the RAF during January 1938 for partial use of Staverton airport as a training base. On the other hand, somewhat short-sightedly, the Traffic Commissioners in Bristol turned down an application made during the month for Bristol Tramway Co. to lay on a service between Cheltenham and the site of the new airfield at Little Rissington. There was some excitement at Bourton on 11th January when an unidentified bomber got into trouble in a snow blizzard and made a forced landing near the main road to Stow. The aircraft came down in a field owned by Mr. D.N.A. Gibbard and was unable to take off again due to the damage it sustained during the landing.

Hind light bombers 'sitting' for the camera prior to World War II. It was an aircraft of this type that crashed at Tewkesbury Road Cheltenham in 1938.

(Rennison Collection)

Snow was the cause of another unexpected descent on the county by an RAF aircraft during February 1938. Once again, fortunately, nobody was injured but the event was a deal more traumatic for those involved than the January incident. During the afternoon of Thursday, 17th February 1938 a formation of five Hawker Hind aircraft of No. 3 Flying Training School was passing near Cheltenham when one of the machines, K5501, became iced up in a snow storm. The Hind began to lose height and was very difficult to control. The pilot, George Thompson, decided that he had better use his parachute whilst he still had sufficient height to do so. At about 1,000 feet he clambered out of the cockpit and jumped over what he thought was open countryside. To his shock he found himself descending over a large town; Cheltenham. The aircraft spiralled down, narrowly missing St. Peter's church and several nearby gas holders before smashing into the roofs of two houses in Tewkesbury Road. It was lunchtime, and a fair number of people were on the street, including

several children returning to school after lunch. As tiles, bricks, beams and pieces of aircraft rained down, K5501 rampaged across the roof-tops like a huge silver moth before finally crashing into the rear of a house just off Hope Street. Mr. Wilmore, the occupant, had a lucky escape. He had just sat down in an armchair when he heard the sounds of the activity going on outside. He went to the front of the house to see what all the commotion was about. Just at that moment the doomed aircraft struck the rear of the house, completely demolishing the scullery in which he had been sitting.

The damage done to No. 80 Tewkesbury Road, the home of the Wakefields, was considerable, as was the damage to the home of their neighbours, The Jefferies. Mrs. Jefferies had been working in the kitchen and on hearing all the noise she had gone to her front door, rather like Mr. Wilmore. She had a similar lucky escape. The kitchen chimney was struck by Thompson's rampaging aircraft and came crashing down into the room below. Mr. Herbert Jefferies had only just left the house to take his son back to school when shouts drew his attention to the runaway aircraft. Father and son watched with incredulity as the aircraft went into a shallow dive and headed straight for their house. Immediately they began to run back towards home and looking up, saw George Thompson's parachute emerge from the clouds overhead. Thompson, in fact came down in the back garden of Major Allardyce at 67 Hatherley Road and was immediately put to bed, suffering from shock.

The Wakefield's house was devastated; gaping holes were left where the roof had collapsed. The bedrooms were full of smashed furniture and the whole house was filled with clouds of plaster, dust and soot. The Jefferies discovered that the tail section of the Hind had come to rest in their back garden although incredibly, the rest of the aircraft seem to be largely intact. George Thompson called on the homes of those involved a few days later and apologised profusely for the damage that had been caused. The most amazing thing about the whole incident is the fact that nobody was killed or injured. The damage to the houses was in many ways somewhat similar to that which might have been sustained in an air raid; a foretaste of things to come.

Regional ARP officers were appointed by the Home Office during February and the first regulations pertinent to the ARP act were issued on 10th March 1938. These regulations were the ARP (General Schemes) Regulations 1938 and ARP (Fire Schemes) Regulations 1938. As a result of their issue the Gloucestershire ARP scheme was scrapped and a new system was set up. This time the county was divided into 15 areas arranged into four divisions, each under the control of a Divisional Officer. During this same month there was yet another death at Kemble when an employee of Kier & Co. fell 30 feet to his death while working on one of the hangars. It was the fourth such fatal accident at the new airfield since the start of the construction work.

Saturday shoppers in Cheltenham's Promenade were given a shock during the morning of 12th March. At about eleven o'clock a light aircraft swooped out of low mist and roared along the Promenade a few feet above the ground, almost hitting the trees. The unknown and obviously disorientated pilot pulled the aircraft up and banked to starboard over Cavendish House. As the engine noise faded in the direction of Prestbury, many shoppers stood peering with disbelief into the mist. The pilot's identity was never discovered and the event has remained something of a mystery to this day.

Two days later, on 14th March the Home Secretary broadcast an appeal for people to come forward as volunteers to join the Civil Defence organisation. He followed this up with a telegram to local authorities, asking them to make arrangements for the enrolment of those who offered their services.

More signs of the RAF's expansion were in evidence in March. Discussions were going on with the Air Ministry concerning housing for a proposed RAF Depot at Quedgeley. Local auctioneers Moore & Sons of Tewkesbury sold 12 acres of land to the Air Ministry for a depot near the LMSR railway bridge over the River Severn. A work force of over a hundred immediately began excavation work for the foundations of the buildings. Construction work on the new airfields claimed another victim during March when John Wixey, an employee of Wilson Lovatt & Son Ltd., fell 40 feet to his death from a hangar roof. This incident occurred at Minchinhampton, where the old first war base was being revamped for the RAF. It was to be renamed RAF Aston Down and was to be much larger than its predecessor.

The Great Western Railway Company also began to get in on the ARP act during April when the company ran a course for officers and heads of sections at Paddington. These courses continued throughout 1938 and many company employees from Gloucestershire attended.

28th May 1938 was earmarked as Empire Air Day and celebrations were planned all over the country. The fledgeling air base at South Cerney, although less than a year old, was opened to the public and an ambitious air display was organised. Aerobatics and parachute jumping were featured, plus a demonstration of how to pick up messages from the ground without landing the collecting aircraft. This involved suspending the message in a streamer attached to the centre of a piece of twine strung between two ten foot high posts. The aircraft came in low and slow and a hook beneath the fuselage plucked the twine from the posts, the streamer at each end preventing it from slipping through the hook. The aircraft then climbed away, the hook being raised and the message pulled aboard. The highlight of the show was an attack by three twin-engined bombers on a mock-up fort. There was also an anti-gas demonstration by ground personnel. The gas chamber was open to the visitors, as were the sick quarters, barracks, engine repair sheds and armoury. On view was the

"Britain First" bomber, later to become known as the Blenheim. The production of this aircraft had been financed by Lord Rothermere of the Daily Mail in an effort to put Britain ahead of the opposition in the field of medium bombers. The Government later took over the finance and ordered the aircraft into production. As part of the wider celebrations an armada of 80 bomber aircraft from various bases flew across the county on 25th May. Once again, an adventurous 'Echo' reporter was aloft, recording the event for posterity.

The Gloster Aircraft Company had been taken over in 1934 by Hawkers and was by 1938 not only producing its own designs but also batches of Hawker aircraft. Well known biplanes like the Hart, Audax and Hartbee were much in evidence. With a constant flow of new orders coming in, the Brockworth factory was continually expanding. Work began on a new, 43 acre site during 1938 and was to continue for nearly two years. Towards the end of the year the company was to start production of 200 Hawker Henleys, and preparations were also under way for the commencement of Hurricane production. The new RAF station at Little Rissington was opened on 26th August 1938. The total cost of the airfield amounted to £503,000, a small part of the £30,000,000 total sanctioned in 1935.

On 2nd September 1938 an inaugural meeting was held to form a local branch of the Civil Air Guard. The meeting took place in the Cotswold Aero Club at Staverton and was attended by the famous Amy Johnson, at that time living at nearby Stoke Orchard. The Civil Air Guard was formed from concerned civil pilots and others who were keen to fly. Their intention was to provide support for the military in a secondary role. It was very much an auxiliary formation with many members providing their own aircraft. Although conditions varied from unit to unit, the uniform usually consisted of denim flying overalls with silver buttons. Pilots also wore wings with the CAG legend in the centre. Often scorned by the "uniformed service", the CAG nonetheless provided valuable training for budding airmen and airwomen, many of whom were later to prove themselves in combat.

A series of mock air attacks was staged in Stroud during September. The RAF cooperated, with the "enemy" bombers being provided by the new base at South Cerney. Trenches were dug in Cashes Green and Stratford Park. In one instance,

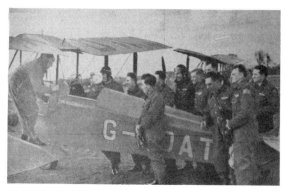

Civil Air Guard pilots gather round a Tiger Moth for a lecture. These volunteers did an invaluable job during the immediate pre-war years fostering interest in military flying.

a hut was set on fire at the Boys' Central School and the ARP services handled the blaze with great aplomb. The demonstration at the Marling School playing fields was witnessed by several thousand people. They were shown how to deal with incendiaries and how to recognise other types of bomb. Gas mask fitting centres were set up and a census was taken by the redoubtable ladies of the W.I. The 1938 version of the CND, an organisation known as the Peace Pledge Union, was much in evidence. Their leaflets informed the public that the demonstrations were all part of a Government plot to turn Britain into a police state and that the ARP wardens were a truncheon-equipped army intended to support a new dictatorship. Captain Martini, the District ARP Officer, announced himself well-pleased with the results of the exercises. One thing he omitted to mention was the acrimony caused by the digging of trenches around the town. This was, perhaps, the only unfortunate aspect of an otherwise highly entertaining month for the inhabitants of Stroud.

Towards the end of the month, a public meeting was held at Brockworth, at which Mr. A.W. Robinson, the Head Warden for Hucclecote, addressed a large gathering on the subject of ARP. At the end of the meeting he called for volunteers, particularly women, to join the Civil Defence Organisation. A standby exercise was also held during the month on instructions from the Home Office. This was, of course, the time of the "Munich Crisis" and the stand-to ordered on 26th September affected not only the Civil Defence but also the Observer Corps. ARP telephones were manned throughout the day and night, as were Observer Posts.

The roots of the Observer Corps can be found in the responsibility levied upon the police force during the First World War to report enemy aircraft movements. This requirement ceased with the end of the hostilities, but the practice was revived during the 1920's when the Corps was formed, its members being classed as Special Constables. Throughout the next decade the organisation was built up by its two commandants, Air Commodore Masterman and Air Commodore Warrington-Morris. By 1938 it consisted of some 30,000 members manning 32 Reporting Centres and over 1,000 Observer Posts, all under the administrative control of the RAF.

Several new booklets on ARP were issued at this time, including ARP in the Home and ARP in County Schools. In Gloucester's Barton Street a seven foot deep air raid shelter was under construction and "house-to-house" fitting of respirators was being undertaken in Stroud. The often irrational love of the British for their animals manifested itself on 29th September when details were drawn up for yet another booklet, to be entitled Air-Raid Precautions for Zoos. On 30th September Neville Chamberlain returned from Munich, declaring that it was to be "Peace in our time", and waving Hitler's guarantee. The "Munich Crisis" was over, but life was destined never to be quite the same again.

In the first month of 1939 the Government requested that local authorities provide details of emergency accommodation in their districts with particular reference to homes suitable for children evacuated from urban areas. At this time the cry from many wardens was for more air-raid shelters. One scheme proposed in the county was an ambitious one for a £12,500 shelter beneath the new hotel in Cheltenham's High Street. It was envisaged that the shelter could be used as an underground garage in peace time. Aircraft Components Ltd. of Arle Court, Cheltenham had developed its own ARP organisation and during January they brought their ARP plan into full effect. The firm had teams of fire-fighters and first-aiders drawn from amongst its 500 employees. A system of fire bells had been installed and weak points were reinforced with steel plates and sand-bags. In practice, it was proved that the entire work force could be evacuated into trenches within five minutes.

Captain Hayes, the County ARP organiser, helped set up an ARP demonstration involving a mock air attack in Alstone Lane, Cheltenham on 23rd January. A Fire Control Post was organised and loudspeakers were installed. Three aircraft from Little Rissington flew overhead in a simulated bombing attack. Two cottages were due to be demolished and were thus used to add realism. A fire was started in the upstairs room of one of them to simulate an incendiary bomb. Other "incendiaries" were littered around and a mock gas attack was staged. A crowd of several hundred watched the proceedings with great interest.

It was announced during the month that Mr. Robert Perkins, M.P. for Stroud, had joined the RAF's Volunteer Reserve as a sergeant pilot. He had learnt to fly in 1929 and had operated his own Hornet Moth aircraft from a strip at Jackbarrow Farm, near Stroud, for a number of years. Perkins was a contemporary of another well-known local airman, Sir Nigel Norman. A senior officer in the Royal Auxiliary Air Force, Sir Nigel also had interests in civil aviation. He was often to be seen piloting his own Moth biplane from the grounds of Marsden Manor near North Cerney. In fact, the Manor's small airstrip was on occasion used by people attending Sir Nigel and Lady Norman's fly-in garden parties. Together with Allan Munz, another airman of some reputation, Sir Nigel set up the famous "model" airport at Heston in Middlesex and formed Airwork Ltd to run it. The airport opened during July 1929 and was to lead the way in the development of civil airports with concrete aprons, floodlights and from 1936, a blind landing system. After distinguished service, Sir Nigel was tragically killed during the war and subsequently buried locally. His sons were also to have an involvement with aviation, the later Britten-Norman Aircraft Co. on the Isle of Wight and other aeronautical undertakings having Norman family involvement.

Robert Perkins had joined the RAFVR unit at Staverton airport where there were immediate vacancies for 80 sergeant pilots and up to 100 observers. The trainee pilots received basic training on Tiger Moth biplanes and then progressed to more advanced types. They were paid an annual retainer of £25.10s.6d, plus 6/6 (32½p) for each of 15 days' annual training. Number 31 Elementary Reserve Flying Training School had begun on a small scale the previous October at Staverton and had clocked up over 1,000 flying hours by January 1939. The unit was quite well equipped, possessing its own floodlighting for use during night flying training.

Somewhat short-sightedly, the Home Office refused a loan to finance the building of the shelter-come garage in Cheltenham's High Street.

It was the official opinion that "Cheltenham was in one of the safest areas in the country". An easy thing to say in February 1939, but certainly not a statement borne out by subsequent events. There was a good deal of flooding throughout the county during February and one unfortunate airman, Ray Chamberlain, was unlucky enough to have to make a forced landing on the floodwaters at Walmore Common near Gloucester. Whether he was related to that other, more prominent gentleman of similar name who had been in the news so recently is not known. The going under foot however, was to prove equally soft for both men.

Proposals were put forward during March for the formation of an Anti-Aircraft Artillery Unit in the county within the Territorial Army as part of the 46th Anti-Aircraft Brigade. It was envisaged that the headquarters would be at Horfield Barracks in Bristol and that batteries of 3.7 in. guns would be sited at Gloucester, Cheltenham and Moreton-in-Marsh. The expansion of the AA defences had been fairly rapid. The two AA Divisions of 1936 were to become seven by mid-1939 and the Anti-Aircraft Corps was to be given Command status. On 14th March Hitler annexed the remainer of Czechoslovakia and just over one week later his troops occupied the Baltic port of Memel. At a meeting held in Gloucester on the last day of the month, the Clerk of the County Council announced that a regional authority was to be set up to coordinate civil defence in wartime. General Sir Hugh Elles was appointed South-West Regional Commissioner the following month.

Even singer-comedian George Formby showed a more sombre side when appearing in uniform in his latest film It's in the Air which was being shown in Gloucestershire cinemas during April 1939 The RAF chose this time to launch a nationwide squadron adoption scheme. A town or city could adopt an operational squadron and, accordingly, Cheltenham took on the Blenheim-equipped 57 Squadron and Gloucester chose 18 Squadron, at that time equipped with Hawker Hind light bombers which were due to be replaced with Blenheims. Both squadrons were stationed at Upper Heyford in nearby Oxfordshire.

The inhabitants of Upper Slaughter were party to a somewhat dramatic incident on 4th April. Three Fairy Battle bombers from Andover were flying in formation over the area when one

A Fairey Battle bomber, one of the obsolescent types with which the RAF began World War Two. It was a Battle that made a forced landing at Upper Slaughter in April 1939.

developed engine trouble. The aircraft made a forced landing in a field, narrowly missing the church tower and a row of cottages during its descent. The three occupants were somewhat shaken but uninjured. The following day a further incident occurred near South Cerney aerodrome during night flying training. Sergeant T.H. Nicholls crashed in his trainer aircraft but was able to step out of the wreckage and walk back to the airfield. The aircraft ploughed through a hedge and a wall, uprooted a tree and came to rest on its nose in Minute Lane only a few feet from a second wall. The wreckage was scattered over a wide area. Fortunately, the pilot only suffered cuts and bruises.

Anti-aircraft defence took a step forward in April 1939 with the formation of the 98th Heavy Anti-Aircraft Regiment, with batteries at Cheltenham and Moreton-in-Marsh. The unit was to be commanded by Lt. Col. F.H. Longueville, DSO., MC, from Forthampton. Major H.T. Moor was to command 300 (Cheltenham) Battery, and Major R.C. Freer was to take charge of 301 (North Cotswold) Battery. With the Italian invasion of Albania on 7th April, the Government

The view across the '100 Acre Field' near the Shurdington Road on the outskirts of Cheltenham. This location was a possible site for a military airfield, which did not materialise although anti-aircraft guns were placed nearby at Hunt Court Farm. (Rennison Collection)

This Nissen Hut is one of the last surviving vestiges of the Anti-aircraft gun site at Hunt Court Farm, adjacent to the Shurdington Road on the edge of Cheltenham.
(Rennison Collection)

issued instructions to local authorities to give civil defence matters priority over other business for the following three months. Air-raid sirens were tested in Cheltenham at 11.34 hours on 27th April. Cars stopped, windows were thrown open and there was much talk of air-raids in shops and on the streets. The wailing of the sirens could be clearly heard on Cleeve Hill. Many felt their first real twinge of apprehension as the banshee wailing died away; somehow, the possibility of war seemed to have come a lot closer. Planning

A 3.7 inch anti-aircraft gun and crew.

permission was granted at the end of the month for Smiths Instruments to build a new factory alongside the road between Cheltenham and Bishop's Cleeve. The permission also covered the use of land surrounding Kayte Farm on the opposite side of the road as an airfield. This was logical enough, given the previous use made of the fields by the Berkshire Aviation Company.

Hitler began to stoke up the Polish situation in May and Britain warned Germany that any interference in Polish affairs could lead to war. On 20th May 1939 some 78 RAF airfields were scheduled to be open to the public for "Empire Air Day". The new station at South Cerney was one of those on the list and threw open its gates from 11.30 in the morning, allowing some 20,000 people in to see the RAF at first hand. The programmed air display was nothing if not prophetic, including a mock attack on the airfield by "enemy aircraft". As part of the "Empire Air Day" celebrations the RAF organised a mass flypast of 72 Fairey Battle bombers over the West of England and South Wales. The aircraft assembled over Abingdon on 18th May and flew along a route: Cirencester (12.06 pm), Newport, Cardiff (12.37 pm), Barry, Bristol (12.52 pm), Bath, Devizes, Reading (13.21 pm), Wallingford and Oxford to disperse over Swindon at approximately 13.45 hours. This airborne armada made a stirring sight and is still recalled today by those who witnessed it as children.

Over the Whitsun weekend the first of Cheltenham's 3.7 in AA guns arrived and was the cause of much interest. There was also a parade in the town during the weekend involving the Royal Gloucestershire Hussars, the British Legion and local ARP personnel. A major ARP exercise was held from midnight on 7th July 1939 to 4 am the next morning. The country was supposedly under attack by the air forces of a mythical enemy, "Blueland". Attempts to simulate air attacks were in many cases frustrated by bad weather which kept the RAF on the ground. However, incidents were staged all over the county. Sirens were sounded, there were mock gas attacks and a blackout was requested. The emergency services were also called out to deal with supposed fractures of gas and water mains. Indeed, the desire for realism was so strong that in some areas the water mains were deliberately tampered with to simulate more closely an actual situation. The public were asked to cooperate but there was no compulsion.

CHIEF WARDEN: LT.-COL. G. DARELL, M.C.
DEPUTY CHIEF WARDEN: BRIG. C. C. FOSS, V.C. C.B. D.S.O.

3 GROUPS

	DURSLEY.	CAM.	WOTTON-UNDER-EDGE.
HEAD WARDENS	BRIG. C. C. FOSS. V.C. C.B. D.S.O.	J. N. TOD, Esq. C.B.E.	BRIG.-GEN. A. E. IRVINE. C.B. C.M.G. D.S.O.
	2 SUB GROUPS.	SECTORS. SENIOR POST WARDENS. POST WARDENS.	SECTORS. SENIOR POST WARDENS. POST WARDENS.

	DURSLEY.	ULEY.
HEAD WARDENS	F. E. FRANCILLON, Esq.	W. MURRAY BROWNE, Esq.
	11 SECTORS. SENIOR POST WARDENS. POST WARDENS.	3 SECTORS. SENIOR POST WARDENS. POST WARDENS.

SECTORS with CODE LETTER prefix for messages.

DURSLEY.	CODE LETTER.	CAM.	CODE LETTER.	WOTTON-UNDER-EDGE.	CODE LETTER.
SECTORS Nos. 1 to 11.	D1 — D11	COALEY	C	SECTORS Nos. 1 to 12.	W1 to W12
ULEY.		ASHMEAD	A	NORTH NIBLEY	NN
No. 1. NORTH	U1	UPPER CAM	UC		
No. 2. SOUTH	U2	LOWER CAM	LC		
NYMPSFIELD	N	WOODFIELD	WD		
		SLIMBRIDGE	SL		
		STINCHCOMBE	S		

(P.T.O.

A further major exercise of this type was held on the night of 8th/9th August. This exercise once again involved a "war" between two imaginery (but fairly obvious) adversaries with the rather unimaginative names of "Eastland" and "Westland", the latter being the friendly and defending power. Realism was once again much in evidence, and participating RAF aircraft carried special markings. The "Westland" forces carried a white cross upon their aircraft. In one incident dedication to duty brought about a little more realism than was envisaged. An ARP warden,

Certificate No. 9 / 93.

County and City of Gloucester.

Air Raid Precautions.

This is to Certify that   MR. A. E. THOMPS.

of   CAM.

has completed a Course of Anti-Gas Training under the auspices of the County and City of Gloucester Air Raid Precautions Central Authority, and has acquired sufficient knowledge of Anti-Gas measures   TO ACT AS A MEMBER OF A PUBLIC A.R.P. SERVICE.

Nature of Course attended   MODIFIED FULL.

Name and qualification of Instructor   MR. R. C. BARNES. 29/L.A.G.C.

Date   12th JANUARY, 1939.

County & City Organiser.

(See over for conditions of award.)

---

speeding down a country lane whilst on duty, was spotted by police and wrongly identified as a wanted man. They set off in pursuit, caught up with the warden and arrested him. The error was, of course, later rectified, much to the embarrassment of the police officer involved. The air war side of the exercise continued for several days and local blackouts and incidents were staged throughout. The cost of the ARP exercises was £150,000, but it was money well spent in the light of future events.

THE FIRE GUARD'S POCKET CHART

including

A TABLE OF WAR GASES

•

PICTURES
DIAGRAMS
TABLES

•

Compiled by
T. M. ROSS

4d.

100 copies, 30s.

5-lb. EXPLOSIVE INCENDIARY
PHOSPHORUS, OIL AND MULTIPLE-EFFECT BOMBS
FIRST AID
TABLE OF WAR GASES
ORGANIZATION
DUTIES
TRAILER PUMPS
STIRRUP PUMP TEAM IN ACTION
METHODS OF ESCAPE
RESCUE
CARE OF STIRRUP PUMP
MISCELLANEOUS NOTES

JORDAN & SONS, LIMITED, 116 Chancery Lane, London, W.C.2

By mid-August work had begun on the construction of a new RAF training camp at Innsworth Lane, near Churchdown. The Air Ministry had purchased 100 acres of land and a contracting firm had begun to erect the first wooden huts, many of which are still standing today, 40 years on. Before the end of the month Germany announced the signing of a non-aggression pact with the Soviet Union. There was, however, no lack of aggressive intent on the part of the German troops concentrated along the Polish border. As the situation worsened, local War Instructions were issued from Gloucester to all local authorities. There were 20 numbered instructions, to be implemented on receipt of the codeword "GLIN" and the appropriate number. They concerned matters like the issue of respirators, the switching-off of street lighting, the call-up of ARP volunteers and the manning of control centres. During the evening of 31st August the first of the "GLIN" telegrams were received at local centres and a number of instructions were implemented. On 1st September 1939, despite repeated warnings from Britain and France, Hitler ordered his troops to invade Poland. This was the so-called "Operation White" and involved 48 divisions, six of them armoured, supported by 1,600 aircraft. The much-vaunted Nazi "War Machine" had begun to roll.

Those first few uncertain days of the hostilities

SOME THINGS YOU SHOULD KNOW IF WAR SHOULD COME

PUBLIC INFORMATION LEAFLET   NO. 1

Read this and keep it carefully. **You may need it.**

Issued from the Lord Privy Seal's Office July, 1939

EVACUATION WHY AND HOW?

PUBLIC INFORMATION LEAFLET   NO. 3

Read this and keep it carefully. **You may need it.**

Issued from the Lord Privy Seal's Office July, 1939

YOUR FOOD IN WAR-TIME

PUBLIC INFORMATION LEAFLET   NO. 4

Read this and keep it carefully. **You may need it.**

Issued from the Lord Privy Seal's Office July, 1939

YOUR GAS MASK
How to keep it and How to Use it
—
MASKING YOUR WINDOWS
—

PUBLIC INFORMATION LEAFLET   NO. 2

Read this and keep it carefully. **You may need it.**

Issued from the Lord Privy Seal's Office July, 1939

Child evacuees arriving in Gloucester (a supposedly safe area!) on September 1939.

Shelters being erected in Kings Square Gloucester in September 1939.

Photo: Citizen

September. Shortly after 11 o'clock on 3rd September, the public was informed that Great Britain was at war with Germany. Most had accepted this as having become inevitable over the last few weeks but it still had a numbing effect. Britain was once again at war with its old adversary, a scant 20 years after the "war to end all wars". There were few with any illusions, and the quiet beauty of the West Country would not remain unscathed for long.

were traumatic for many, and much was to change irrevocably. Tangible signs in Gloucestershire included the arrival of thousands of evacuees, mainly from Birmingham. This went off rather more smoothly than one might have expected. There had in any case, been a gradual evacuation of schoolchildren for some weeks prior to

Chapter 2

Attack From the Air

The German acceptance of the inevitability of conflict with Britain can be clearly discerned from the activities of the Luftwaffe in the months prior to the outbreak of war in September 1939. Throughout the year Dornier and Heinkel high altitude reconnaissance aircraft had been systematically photographing potential targets and areas of military interest. In fact, this type of clandestine activity had been the order of the day since 1938. In some cases the photographs were taken by "passengers" on civil airliners. The famous Battle of Britain airfield at Biggin Hill is a case in point, having been photographed from a German passenger aircraft landing at Croydon. The Parnall aircraft factory at Yate in Gloucestershire was photographed in August 1939, prior to the outbreak of war. Electronic reconnaissance was also carried out during 1939. In one instance the Germans used a Zeppelin air ship to investigate radar installations on the east coast.

It was probably a reconnaissance aircraft that caused some excitement at Filton Sector Headquarters on 10th November 1939. At 11.00 hours two enemy aircraft were reported to be approaching from the direction of Swindon. The plot was later changed to one aircraft. A Hurricane fighter was scrambled to intercept, but was unable to make contact owing to poor visibility. Hurricanes were again sent out from Filton to investigate a possible "raider" on 12th January 1940. The Observer Corps had reported an aircraft to the north of Gloucester at 20,000 ft. The Hurricanes closed in on their would-be target, only to discover that it was a Blenheim bomber.

Despite the abortive nature of both alerts, valuable experience was gained by both RAF and Observer Corps personnel.

The first German bomb had fallen on British soil on 17th October 1939, at Hoy in the Orkneys and, by macabre coincidence, the first death due to enemy bombing in Britain also occurred in the Orkneys, on 16th March 1940. The first bombs to fall on mainland Britain fell near Wick in Scotland on the night of 10th April 1940. The day before, Hitler's forces had attacked Norway and occupied tiny Denmark. Holland and the other Low Countries were to follow in May. Churchill became Prime Minister on 10th May, and four days later the Local Defence Volunteers (later the Home Guard) was formed. Many members of Civil Defence applied to join the new organisation. There were difficulties attached to being in the two organisations simultaneously and in some sectors dual membership was not allowed. Many personnel did, however, continue to lead double lives until 1943, when new regulations made it impossible.

On 24th May Middlesbrough in Yorkshire was raided, and on 18th June bombs fell in fields in the London district of Addington. The "Phoney War" was coming to an end; "total war" was soon to be more than just a newspaper expression. The front line of this conflict was to run through the homes and lives of the ordinary people of Britain. Abbreviations such as "HE" for "High Explosive Bomb", "IB" for "Incendiary Bomb" and "UXB" for "Unexploded Bomb" were to become everyday expressions. The air raid warning system was to become almost a litany

If the
INVADER
comes

WHAT TO DO — AND HOW TO DO IT

THE Germans threaten to invade Great Britain. If they do so they will be driven out by our Navy, our Army and our Air Force. Yet the ordinary men and women of the civilian population will also have their part to play. Hitler's invasions of Poland, Holland and Belgium were greatly helped by the fact that the civilian population was taken by surprise. They did not know what to do when the moment came. *You must not be taken by surprise.* This leaflet tells you what general line you should take. More detailed instructions will be given you when the danger comes nearer. Meanwhile, read these instructions carefully and be prepared to carry them out.

I

When Holland and Belgium were invaded, the civilian population fled from their homes. They crowded on the roads, in cars, in carts, on bicycles and on foot, and so helped the enemy by preventing their own armies from advancing against the invaders. You must not allow that to happen here. Your first rule, therefore, is :—

(1) IF THE GERMANS COME, BY PARACHUTE, AEROPLANE OR SHIP, YOU MUST REMAIN WHERE YOU ARE. THE ORDER IS "STAY PUT ".

If the Commander in Chief decides that the place where you live must be evacuated, he will tell you when and how to leave. Until you receive such orders you must remain where you are. If you run away, you will be exposed to far greater danger because you will be machine-gunned from the air as were civilians in Holland and Belgium, and you will also block the roads by which our own armies will advance to turn the Germans out.

II

There is another method which the Germans adopt in their invasion. They make use of the civilian population in order to create confusion and panic. They spread false rumours and issue false instructions. In order to prevent this, you should obey the second rule, which is as follows :—

(2) DO NOT BELIEVE RUMOURS AND DO NOT SPREAD THEM. WHEN YOU RECEIVE AN ORDER, MAKE QUITE SURE THAT IT IS A TRUE ORDER AND NOT A FAKED ORDER. MOST OF YOU KNOW YOUR POLICEMAN AND YOUR A.R.P. WARDENS BY SIGHT, YOU CAN TRUST THEM. IF YOU KEEP YOUR HEADS, YOU CAN ALSO TELL WHETHER A MILITARY OFFICER IS REALLY BRITISH OR ONLY PRETENDING TO BE SO. IF IN DOUBT ASK THE POLICE-MAN OR THE A.R.P. WARDEN. USE YOUR COMMON-SENSE.

III

The Army, the Air Force and the Local Defence Volunteers cannot be everywhere at once. The ordinary man and woman must be on the watch. If you see anything suspicious, do not rush round telling your neighbours all about it. Go at once to the nearest policeman, police-station, or military officer and tell them exactly what you saw. Train yourself to notice the exact time and place where you saw anything suspicious, and try to give exact information. Try to check your facts. The sort of report which a military or police officer wants from you is something like this :—

" At 5.30 p.m. to-night I saw twenty cyclists come into Little Squashborough from the direction of Great Mudtown. They carried some sort of automatic rifle or gun. I did not see anything like artillery. They were in grey uniforms."

Be calm, quick and exact. The third rule, therefore, is as follows :—

(3) KEEP WATCH. IF YOU SEE ANYTHING SUSPICIOUS, NOTE IT CAREFULLY AND GO AT ONCE TO THE NEAREST POLICE OFFICER OR STATION, OR TO THE NEAREST MILITARY OFFICER. DO NOT RUSH ABOUT SPREADING VAGUE RUMOURS. GO QUICKLY TO THE NEAR-EST AUTHORITY AND GIVE HIM THE FACTS.

IV

Remember that if parachutists come down near your home, they will not be feeling at all brave. They will not know where they are, they will have no food, they will not know where their companions are. They will want you to give them food, means of transport and maps. They will want you to tell them where they have landed, where their comrades are, and where our own soldiers are. The fourth rule, there-fore, is as follows :—

(4) DO NOT GIVE ANY GERMAN ANYTHING. DO NOT TELL HIM ANYTHING. HIDE YOUR FOOD AND YOUR BICYCLES. HIDE YOUR MAPS. SEE THAT THE ENEMY GETS NO PETROL. IF YOU HAVE A CAR OR MOTOR BICYCLE, PUT IT OUT OF ACTION WHEN NOT IN USE. IT IS NOT ENOUGH TO REMOVE THE IGNITION KEY; YOU MUST MAKE IT USELESS TO ANYONE EXCEPT YOURSELF.

IF YOU ARE A GARAGE PROPRIETOR, YOU MUST WORK OUT A PLAN TO PROTECT YOUR STOCK OF PETROL AND YOUR CUSTOMERS' CARS. REMEMBER THAT TRANSPORT AND PETROL WILL BE THE INVADER'S MAIN DIFFICULTIES. MAKE SURE THAT NO INVADER WILL BE ABLE TO GET HOLD OF YOUR CARS, PETROL, MAPS OR BICYCLES.

V

You may be asked by Army and Air Force officers to help in many ways. For instance, the time may come when you will receive orders to block roads or streets in order to prevent the enemy from advancing. Never block a road unless you are told which one you must block. Then you can help by felling trees, wiring them together or blocking the roads with cars. Here, therefore, is the fifth rule :—

(5) BE READY TO HELP THE MILITARY IN ANY WAY. BUT DO NOT BLOCK ROADS UNTIL ORDERED TO DO SO BY THE MILITARY OR L.D.V. AUTHORITIES.

VI

If you are in charge of a factory, store or other works, organise its defence at once. If you are a worker, make sure that you understand the system of defence that has been organised and know what part you have to play in it. Remember always that parachutists and fifth column men are powerless against any organised resistance. They can only succeed if they can create disorganisation. Make certain that no suspicious strangers enter your premises.

You must know in advance who is to take command, who is to be second in command, and how orders are to be transmitted. This chain of command must be built up and you will probably find that ex-officers or N.C.O.'s, who have been in emergencies before, are the best people to undertake such command. The sixth rule is therefore as follows :—

(6) IN FACTORIES AND SHOPS, ALL MANAGERS AND WORKMEN SHOULD ORGANISE SOME SYSTEM NOW BY WHICH A SUDDEN ATTACK CAN BE RESISTED.

VII

The six rules which you have now read give you a general idea of what to do in the event of invasion. More detailed instructions may, when the time comes, be given you by the Military and Police Authorities and by the Local Defence Volunteers; they will NOT be given over the wireless as that might convey information to the enemy. These instruc-tions must be obeyed at once.

Remember always that the best defence of Great Britain is the courage of her men and women. Here is your seventh rule :—

(7) THINK BEFORE YOU ACT. BUT THINK ALWAYS OF YOUR COUNTRY BEFORE YOU THINK OF YOURSELF.

(52194) Wt.

---

that the majority could quote faultlessly:

Warning YELLOW — Possible attack, preliminary caution.

Warning PURPLE — "Lights out", with the exception of certain specified, essential installations. SIREN SOUNDS

Warning RED — Enemy attack imminent SIREN SOUNDS

Warning WHITE — Raiders have passed.

A formation of Heinkel III bombers heading for Britain.
(B. Rijnmont Collection)

The first bombs fell on the county of Gloucestershire during the latter part of June 1940. This was the first incident in a diary of events, both tragic and humorous, embodying countless displays of courage and fortitude. The lengthy catalogue of incidents somehow seems strangely out of place against the largely rural background of Gloucestershire.

1940

Tuesday, 18th June

A single Heinkel bomber attacked the Bristol Aircraft Works at Filton. Two HE bombs were dropped in a field two hundred yards south of the aerodrome close to factory buildings. Nobody was killed but two airmen on a nearby balloon site were injured.

Tuesday, 25th June

Eleven high explosive and 60 incendiary bombs fell at Hallen and a farm-house was damaged. A number of bombs were also dropped close to Hullavington airfield just over the Wiltshire border.

Wednesday, 26th June

At ten minutes past two in the morning Cheltenham had its first alert but no bombs were dropped on the town. However, bombs did fall at Nether Westcote, near Bourton-on-the-Water. Roads, cottages, a farmhouse and the Methodist chapel were damaged. HE bombs were also reported to have come down at Avonmouth shortly after three o'clock in the morning. The airfield at South Cerney came under attack late in the evening when a single Heinkel bomber unloaded a number of HE and incendiary bombs at a quarter to twelve. One bomb was of the delayed action type, weighing 100 kg. Although the "all clear" was sounded at quarter to three on the morning of the 27th, the rogue bomb was not actually exploded until quarter past five. Most of the hardware had come down near the south-east corner of the 'drome and no serious damage was done to the airfield.

Sunday, 30th June

Night flying at South Cerney was again disrupted by a number of alerts. Twenty-two bombs were dropped in a line between Swindon and Down Ampney, parallel to the main Cirencester — Cricklade road. One HE bomb also came down at Marston Meysey.

Wednesday, 3rd July

Four HE bombs fell at Whittocks End. Farm buildings were damaged and a hayrick was set on fire. There were casualties here, too: one pig, five ducks and two rabbits were killed.

Thursday, 4th July

At twenty past three in the afternoon a single enemy aircraft penetrated the balloon barrage at Filton and dropped two HE bombs on a balloon winch site opposite Rodney works. Three people suffered minor injuries and damage was done to the winch lorry and the barrage balloon. The road and railway tracks in the area were also damaged.

Tuesday, 9th July

Two HE bombs fell at Stoke Gifford where railway property was damaged. Four HE bombs came down in open fields at Horton, and three more (all UXBs) came down at Badminton. A further sixteen HE bombs caused damage to roads and houses at Bromsberrow. A water main was burst and telephone connections damaged at Haresfield when four HE bombs fell there.

Friday, 12th July

During the early hours the Luftwaffe mounted an attack on South Wales and it is possible that one of these raiders was responsible for the bombs which fell at Avonmouth and Weston during the night. At the same time as the bombs were falling two barrage balloons were seen to fall to the ground in flames, apparently having been struck by lightning.

Sunday, 14th July

There was scattered cloud cover over most of mainland Britain, and the Luftwaffe was reasonably quiet. A small number of bombs fell on Avonmouth during the late evening.

Monday, 15th July

A small group of Ju.88 bombers attacked the airfield at Yeovil in Dorset home of the Westland Aircraft Co. Twelve bombs were dropped, damaging a flight shed and the airfield's grass surface.

Tuesday, 16th July

There was a good deal of fog in evidence throughout the country, weather not conducive to air operations. However, a number of enemy aircraft were noted passing close to the Filton Sector Control Centre.

Saturday, 20th July

There was no enemy air activity over the county of Gloucestershire during the day, but the enemy was active on minelaying operations over the Bristol Channel.

Thursday, 25th July

At two o'clock in the afternoon the airfield at South Cerney was attacked with four HE bombs. No major damage was done, although some crops in nearby fields were scorched. Two enemy aircraft were involved in this raid and at about the same time a third aircraft was seen flying low over Cheltenham. For many, this was their first sight of the enemy. It was possibly the latter aircraft that was brought down at Oakridge Lynch at twenty-five minutes past two, probably as the result of a combination of fighter attack and a collision. The circumstances surrounding this incident are still somewhat obscure and are the subject of debate even today.

From the information available it would seem that the enemy aircraft may have been rammed by or collided with Hurricane P3271 of the Kemble Defence Flight, which was being flown by Pilot Officer A.C. Bird, a volunteer from No.4 Ferry Pilot Pool. However, it also appears to have been attacked by the Spitfire of Flight Lieutenant P.P. Hanks of No. 5 OTU from Aston Down, although his claim that he shot the raider down was never confirmed. The German pilot recalls that one of the gunners, Uffz. Theiner, shouted out a warning of fighter attack and seconds later the aircraft staggered, as if struck by a giant hand. There had been some sort of impact in the area of the rear fuselage and tail. The aircraft became extremely difficult to control and the crew abandoned it. Whatever the cause, the enemy raider crashed in flames at Oakridge near Stroud. Unfortunately, Pilot Officer Bird's Hurricane also came down shortly afterwards and he died in the crash. The aircraft had appeared to go into a spin, possibly as a result of Bird losing control owing to damage sustained in the collision. Sadly, the circumstances of his death led to some difficulties in identifying him. The only personal documentation found in the wreckage was an unsigned driving licence.

Pilot Officer Charles Alex Bird was killed in action on 25th July 1940 aged 23. He was born in Kirkstall Leeds, his father had been an Observer in the RFC during World War I (awarded the M.C. and mentioned in despatches three times). Following in his fathers footsteps he paid for private flying lessons and joined the RAF in October 1938.
(via Severnside Aviation Society)

Four Luftwaffe crewmen were seen to take to their parachutes as their stricken aircraft descended. A regular "manhunt" was launched with the aid of the Home Guard, and in a short space of time three of the enemy airmen were captured. These three were Uffz. Dorner, who was wounded, Uffz. Hugelschafer, and Gefr. Treue. The body of a fourth, Uffz. Theiner was found in Oldhill Woods; his parachute apparently had failed to open.

One of the German airmen had been confronted by 19-year-old Mavis Young as he descended into the grounds of Major Le Baily's country house. Mavis gave her apprehensive young captive a drink as they waited for the authorities to arrive and he gallantly kissed her hand in appreciation. Captain Guise, Platoon Commander of the local Home Guard, and Captain Weston, headmaster of the local school, were quickly on the scene and took the young airman into their custody. One of the other crew members landed in a corn-field and was promptly surrounded by a group of Land Army personnel, armed with pitchforks and scythes. This confrontation, perhaps fortunately, was a brief one as a car-load of local policemen arrived and quickly took over. The other surviving crew member narrowly missed hitting Captain Weston's house as he descended and came down on the lawn outside. The Captain's 14 year-old daughter ran up and, thinking the airman to be one of her own countrymen, asked if he was all right. To her consternation, he replied in a foreign tongue. She immediately ran off to get her father. This young airman was also given a drink before being taken away, and for this consideration he thanked Captain Weston in broken English.

The wreckage was an instant attraction for young and old alike. The locals came from miles around to see the "fallen eagle". Among them was an excited young Margaret Breakspear, from Stroud, overawed by finding the war almost in her back garden. Many other youngsters gathered to stare wide-eyed at their first German bomber. Almost without exception, they, like Margaret, still recall the incident vividly.

A number of maps were recovered from the wrecked aircraft and were forwarded to 41 Group Headquarters.

The controversy over the Bird and Hanks involvement will, no doubt, continue. One fact is undeniable however: Ju.88 9K+GN was brought down at Oakridge. In all fairness, it should perhaps be said that Pilot Officer Bird at least does not

The wreckage of the Ju88A of 5/KG-51 (9K + GN) brought down on the 25.07.1940 at Oakridge, Stroud, Glos.
(Severnside Aviation Society)

seem to have received the recognition he deserves for his part in bringing down this aircraft. The confusion surrounding the incident will probably ensure that nobody will ever be able to claim complete credit for the victory.

Friday, 26th July

During the night a cold front arrived, bringing with it cloud and widespread rain. Despite the unfavourable conditions individual enemy raiders still operated, mainly on mine-laying sorties around the coasts of southern Britain. It was one such raider that was attacked by the Hurricane fighter of Pilot Officer Cock of 87 Squadron over East Portishead Point. The enemy aircraft, a Heinkel 111 of KG 4, crashed at Longfield Farm, Smeathorpe, near Honiton in Devon, at five minutes to one in the morning after explosions on board the aircraft.

Saturday, 27th July

There was heavy enemy activity over the

A drawing of Pilot Officer Bird's combat with the Ju88 of KG-51 on the 25th July 1940.
By Barry Walding of the Severnside Aviation Society

'EDELWEISS' IN THE COTSWOLDS
Pilot Officer Charles Alec Bird, of No. 4 Ferry Pilots pool, Kemble, engaging a Junkers Ju88A of 5/Kampfgeschwader 51—'Edelweiss' above Oakridge, Gloucestershire, 25th July 1940.

county during the night, part of a series of widespread attacks mounted against the South West. Bombs fell at the following locations: Arlingham (three HE), Aust (two HE and one IB), Blaize Bailey (one IB), Frampton Cotterel (one IB), Golden Valley, Bitton (two HE and one IB), Hewels Field (two HE), Ingst, Alveston (two HE), Newnham (seven HE), Staple Hill (eight HE), Tidenham (two HE), Tutshill (six HE), Box Edge Farm, Westerleigh (four HE and one IB).

Some considerable damage was done to houses at Staple Hill. Whilst there were no human casualties, a number of animals were killed: at Newnham one piglet, three rabbits and three sheep; elsewhere a lamb was killed and a duck wounded . . .

Sunday, 28th July

A quiet day with only two air raid warnings. Two HE bombs fell in adjoining fields between Woodbridge and Compton Abdale. One of the bombs made a crater 25 feet in diameter and seven feet in depth. The heat from the explosion was sufficient to scorch the bark from trees in the vicinity.

Monday, 29th July

During the small hours an enemy raider, possibly with Little Rissington airfield as his target, released a number of bombs which fell over Lower Slaughter and south-westwards towards Compton Cassey. They fell in open country and there were no casualties. Some 14 HE bombs are recorded, of which three were UXBs.

Wednesday, 31st July

A number of raids were carried out against South Wales during the early hours. One incendiary bomb fell at Westerleigh, probably a premature release by one of the raiders heading for the Bristol Channel and the industrial areas around Cardiff. In addition, minor damage was done to two cottages at Moorend when two HE bombs were dropped.

Saturday, 3rd August

A day of widespread activity, this was also the date of Cirencester's first alert. At quarter to one in the morning two HE bombs fell at Togghill Wick and slight damage was caused to farm buildings, though fortunately, there were no casualties. During the evening there was further activity. At quarter past ten two HE bombs were

dropped at Falfield and caused damage to telephone cables. At the same time, a further six HE bombs came down at Waterly Bottom. Some 30 minutes later, 18 HE bombs fell near Calcot farm amongst cornfields. The resultant craters were on average nine feet wide but only three feet deep. This lack of penetration was probably due to the fact that the August sun had baked the ground to a concrete hardness. The RAF airfield at Babdown Farm was the probable target as the enemy aircraft dropped flares over the area in an apparent effort to locate the base.

Luftwaffe records show that a Heinkel bomber of KG.55 failed to return from a sortie over the Bristol area on this date, apparently having been brought down by anti-aircraft fire over the English coast. The crew of Ofw. Geisler, Uffz. Ohmann, Uffz. Wever, Uffz. Theiem and Uffz. Westphal were reported as either missing or dead.

A Heinkel III pictured from another aircraft as it releases its bombs.

Sunday, 11th August

Sporadic attacks were launched against Portland and Weymouth during the day and later against Liverpool. There was also some minelaying in the Bristol Channel. Bristol itself came under attack at 11.30 in the evening, and damage was caused to railway engines, trucks and the signal box at St. Phillips. An air-raid shelter at Shirehampton was damaged and 15 people were trapped inside for some time. Fortunately, only two were later found to have suffered injury. A "Whistling Bomb" fell on an electricity sub-station at Clifton. Elsewhere, 12 HE bombs came down at Cinderford at eleven o'clock and five HE fell on farmland between Wanswell and Halmore in the Berkeley area nine minutes later. A cow and a horse were injured and there was minor damage to telephone wires. However, no human casualties were reported.

Monday, 12th August

German records show that a Heinkel He.111 of KG.27 was shot down by a night fighter at 20 minutes past midnight after attacking Bristol docks. The enemy aircraft, coded 1G+AC, came down at Sturminster Marshal near Wimborne, Dorset. The crew, Mjr. Schlichting, Mjr. Brehmer, Obfw. Logneng, Obfw. Bendrich and Obfw. Frey, took to their parachutes but were later captured. A second Heinkel, belonging to KG.55, crashed at Rambervilliers in France upon its return from a sortie in the Bristol area. Both the bomber's engines had been severely damaged by an attacking fighter. The aircraft was a write-off, and three of the crew members were injured. The previous evening's attacks had been avenged, albeit in small measure.

Tuesday, 13th August

Southampton came under attack and there were a number of light raids throughout Wales and the West country. Between twenty to four and ten to four in the morning five HE bombs rained down in the Arlingham-Newnham area but only slight damage was caused to telephone lines.

Wednesday, 14th August

Some ten HE bombs fell at Mangotsfield at 27 minutes past midnight and damage was done to railway buildings.

Widespread attacks were launched against airfields and railways during the day. The RAF station at Kemble was on the target list and came under attack by two enemy aircraft. Four oil bombs and 18 HE were dropped on the station. Nine Whitley bombers were damaged and the Pioneer Corps were called in to deal with the bomb craters. Hullavington in neighbouring Wiltshire was also hit but was less fortunate. Heinkel bombers dropped 16 bombs and in the ensuing carnage three airmen were killed and a further ten injured. A petrol bowser exploded and a hangar was damaged, together with several aircraft.

Three enemy raiders also attempted to strike at Filton airfield shortly after five in the afternoon but were beaten off by heavy anti-aircraft fire. Two of these aircraft were thought to have been shot down by fighters some time later. A large number of bombs fell in the Chedworth — Coln St. Dennis area. Damage was done to roads and telephone lines. A bungalow was damaged in the Chipping Sodbury district when eight HE bombs

came down, and two people were later treated for shock. Newmans Industries at Yate was also hit by a number of HE and petrol bombs which damaged the machine shop, electricity plant and other equipment. Four people were injured, two seriously. Neighbouring Swindon also suffered an attack during the afternoon when 20 bombs were dropped on the town. The radio operator of one bomber baled out when his aircraft went out of control after being attacked in the Cheltenham area. Uffz. Friedl Dorner of KG.100 came down near Balcombe, Dorset and was taken prisoner. The pilot of the Heinkel bomber that Dorner so precipitately abandoned managed to regain control and got the aircraft back to its French base, minus one radio operator.

Thursday, 15th August

Southern Britain was sitting beneath a canopy of high pressure air and the weather was fine and clear. The Luftwaffe made considerable efforts to attack both eastern and southern England, and also made a sortie against the Short Brothers aircraft factory in Northern Ireland. Bristol was to suffer its first heavy raid late during the evening. The first attack officially ended at 23.17 hours and was followed by a second raid some four hours later. No incidents of major consequence are recorded as a result of the first attack; the real damage was to be done during the early hours of Friday morning.

Friday, 16th August

Following the previous evening's attack on Bristol a second wave of bombers struck at the city during the small hours. By the time the attack was over at 03.32 over 50 HE bombs had fallen, a number of them on the Filton aircraft factory. No.3 shed at Rodney works was damaged and the

A Heinkel bomber being refuelled in France before taking off for a raid.

canteen windows were shattered. At least ten bombs fell directly into the sea off Avonmouth and a further 17 HE fell at Hallen further north. More HE bombs came down close to a cemetery in the Knowle district of the city. In the aftermath, casualties amounted to one child killed and another injured, plus 19 adults injured. Three houses were completely demolished and ten partly so, whilst another 142 were damaged. Bombs also came down elsewhere in the county: three HE at Northleach, killing a horse, a pony and a rabbit, and wounding another horse. Four hundred incendiary bombs and 34 HE showered down upon Poulton where four houses and a water main were damaged. At Ablington 21 HE bombs were dropped and some damage was caused to roads in the area.

Typical of the smaller incendiary devices is this 1kg bomb dropped on Bristol.

Saturday, 17th August

There were two distinct phases of activity on this date, the first taking place during the early hours of Saturday morning, commencing seconds after midnight when four HE bombs fell at Thornbury, fortunately causing neither casualties nor damage. Some fifteen minutes later three HE bombs were dropped in the St. George division of Bristol and an hour after this a further three fell in fields at Patchway. At 02.40 a single HE bomb caused damage to the aerials of a wireless station at Portishead. At about three o'clock 13 HE bombs fell at Emersons Green and Westerleigh in the Mangotsfield, damage being caused to electric cables and water mains. Other HE bombs fell at Clevedon, at Tickenham near Yatton, where damage was caused to GWR property, and at Weston-in-Gordano.

The second phase began at 22.45 when a number of HE bombs came down close to the St. George division in Bristol, causing damage to six houses. Nine minutes later two HE bombs fell at Chavenage to the north-east; however, no damage was reported. From 23.02 through to two o'clock the following morning nearly 40 bombs were dropped, mainly in the Bristol area, as follows:—

23.02 hours	—four HE at Westerleigh
23.14 hours	—one HE at Warmley
23.15 to 02.00 (on the 18th)	—34 HE at Almondsbury, Patchway, Little Stoke, Charlton, East Hallam, Stoke Gifford and Pilning.

Two houses were completely destroyed and a number of others damaged. Fortunately, there were no casualties.

Sunday, 18th August

As noted above, a number of HE bombs were already falling on the Bristol area as the new day began until approximately two o'clock. A number of HE were also reported in the St. Briavels — Woolaston area but they were not to be immediately lethal, turning out to be UXBs. During the evening a dramatic incident occurred in the east of the county above the grass airfield at Windrush. Night flying training was in progress and a line of lights had been laid out along the landing strip. Drawn like a moth to a candle, a marauding Heinkel bomber of KG.27 arrived overhead. After dropping several HE bombs the intruder turned its attention to a lone Anson trainer which was making a night approach. This aircraft, Anson L9164 belonged to No. 6 Flying Training School and was being flown by Sgt. Bruce Hancock, who had almost completed the course. The unit had been warned of enemy activity in the area but the warning was not taken too seriously. Bruce himself wanted to complete this last part of his training and get an early posting to an operational squadron.

The Heinkel attacked the Anson from above and behind, peppering it with machine gun fire. According to witnesses, Hancock doused the lights of his aircraft and banked to port, causing the Heinkel to overshoot. Suddenly, with apparent destructive intent, the Anson pulled up and smashed into the enemy aircraft. Was it perhaps the last vengeful act of a mortally wounded Bruce Hancock, or simply the erratic movements of a crippled aircraft, or, more probably, a calculated sacrifice demanding courage of the highest order? Bruce Hancock had previously told his brother-in-law that if faced with attack whilst flying an unarmed aircraft he would attempt to ram his attacker. What really happened that night will perhaps never be known with certainty. The Heinkel crashed in flames at

Unteroffizier Herbert Rave aged 22 years from Hamburg Altora poses with Heinkel He111P W. NR1408, IG+?T of the 5th Staffel, Kampfgeschwarder 27, the aircraft in which he was killed at Aldsworth, Glos. on 18.08.1940. (Severnside Aviation Society Collection via Frau Else Krombach)

Blackpits Farm, Aldsworth, near Northleach. The crew, Obfw. Dreher, Uffz. Schmidt, Uffz. Rave and Uffz. Cohrs, all died instantly. The body of Sgt. Hancock was only found after some time, quite a distance from the wreckage of the Anson. Once again, this is an incident where it would seem that the RAF pilot involved has never received due credit. Hancock was not serving with

Extract from the Chronicle and Graphic showing wreckage of the Heinkel brought down by Sgt. Hancock at Aldsworth on the 18th August 1940.

(via Norman Preece/Paul Aston)

HEINKEL WRECKAGE

A close-up of the tail of the Heinkel 111 bomber which was brought down by an Avro-Anson trainer on Sunday night.

a combat unit but with a flying training unit; thus it is that he can never be counted as ''one of the few'' for he was not on the strength of a unit officially involved in the Battle of Britain.

Monday, 19th August

A cloudy but dry day, during which there were scattered attacks against a number of objectives, including Portsmouth and Southampton. Eight RAF airfields, including Bibury, also came under attack. Half-a-dozen Spitfires had just arrived at the grass strip from Pembrey in time for lunch, the intention being that these aircraft would carry out night patrols from Bibury. Almost on cue a lone Ju.88 bomber of KG.51 arrived over the airfield at quarter-past two in the afternoon. Apparently, the raider's intended target was Little Rissington and it is possible that he got the two airfields mixed up. Perhaps he simply could not resist the sight of six Spitfires lined up impotently on the ground. Whatever his reasons, the enemy pilot dived towards the ground and made a low pass over the airfield, dropping four HE bombs. One airman was killed and several of the Spitfires were damaged, one being a write-off. Stung into action, the Spitfire pilots ran to their aircraft and two of them took off in hot pursuit. One of the pilots, Flt. Lt. Wade, finally caught up with the enemy aircraft over the Solent and, after a brief combat, shot it down into the sea. The crew of the Ju.88, coded 9K+FR (Werk. No.7069), consisted of Fw. Haak, Fw. Muser, Fw. Schachtner and Uffz. Bachauerau, all of whom were killed.

There was more action during the late evening when, shortly after eleven o'clock, nine HE bombs fell at Hawling. One of the bombs was of a delayed action type and did not explode until quarter to one the following morning. The only casualty of the attack was a dead sheep. As midnight approached another HE bomb fell near Andoversford railway station but no damage was done.

Tuesday, 20th August

In the early morning at around half-past three a large number of HE bombs were dropped in the localities of Coates, Ready Token, Eastington and Fosse Hill Farm, plus a further two close to the Cirencester — Tetbury road. No casualties are recorded and it was only at Eastington that damage was reported. Electricity and telephone cables were severed and damage was done to a number of houses.

HEINKEL BOMBER DESTROYED BY ANSON TRAINER

The wreckage of the German Heinkel 111 brought down on Sunday night in a clover field near a small town in the South-West, after being rammed by an unarmed Anson training 'plane.

1. Looking over the bits and pieces of the big German Heinkel bomber. The Heinkel's crew of five were killed.
2. Examining a part of the wing of the Heinkel a quarter of a mile away from the bulk of the wreckage.
3. More Heinkel scrap.
4. While our photographer was taking pictures of the Heinkel a delayed-action bomb dropped by the Heinkel exploded in a field in the distance. Our photographer turned his camera on the column of smoke which shot into the air.
5. One of the Heinkel's engines which landed 50 yards from the burning fuselage.

Extract from the Chronicle and Graphic August 24, 1940 showing wreckage of the Heinkel brought down by Sgt. Hancock at Aldsworth on the 18th August 1940.   *(via Norman Preece/Paul Aston)*

35

GERMAN AIRMEN BURIED IN SOUTH-WEST CEMETERY

Five German airmen who lost their lives last week, when a 26-years-old sergeant-pilot rammed their Heinkel bomber as it was attacking him, were given a military funeral in a little South-western hill town. The British airman sacrificed his own life in carrying out his gallant action. About 200 people gathered in the peaceful country cemetery, and a contingent of R.A.F. men from a South-west aerodrome acted as bearers and formed a firing party. The service was conducted by a R.A.F. chaplain, assisted by a local curate.

1.—The five coffins arrived on a trailer attached to a R.A.F. lorry. 2.—The cortege arriving at the cemetery. 3.—The R.A.F. chaplain (left) and curate leading procession past the guard of honour. 4.—Lowering the coffins into the long grave. Each one was numbered. 5.—The firing party's last volley.

Extract from the Cronicle and Graphic August 31, 1940 showing the funeral of the German airman at Northleach.
(via Norman Preece/Paul Aston)

Wednesday, 21st August

A cloudy day with some rain showers that seem to have curtailed the enemy activity, although there were hit-and-run raids on a number of coastal towns. Gloucestershire was mainly quiet but some Bristol residents did come under attack from the air. Two barrage balloons came down unbidden and caused damage to several houses.

Thursday, 22nd August

A quiet day, but the respite was to be brief. By ten o'clock in the evening a formation of 23 Heinkels had begun to attack the Bristol Aircraft factory at Filton. Some 418 bombs were dropped, of which 250 were incendiaries. BAC's number four factory was damaged, together with the test bed installation. The surrounding areas of Almondsbury, Patchway, Stoke Gifford and Aust also fared badly. The Memorial Hall at Almondsbury was half destroyed, a cottage was burnt out, a fuel depot was hit and three roads, including the A38, were blocked. Twenty HE bombs fell in a field near the railway station. Gas and water mains were damaged at Patchway, while at Stoke Gifford seven houses were wrecked and two more were seriously damaged at Little Stoke. The raid continued on into the early hours of Friday morning, ending at approximately three o'clock.

Friday, 23rd August

Upon their return to base many of the Luftwaffe crews involved in the Bristol raid reported being badly blinded by searchlights whilst over the target. One of the Heinkels reported attacking a Bristol railway station, although the crew were unable to assess the extent of the damage. A second raider reported attacking anti-aircraft gun positions near Bristol with ten HE bombs at quarter to three in the morning.

After a brief breathing space during the daylight hours the county was once again the focus of the enemy's attention during the evening, albeit on a much smaller scale. Some 200 incendiaries came down in the area of Bedminster Down and a number of fires were started. Other areas also collected their share of high explosives. Twenty-two HE bombs fell around Chipping Camden, five HE bombs (all UXBs) came down at Moreton-in-Marsh and another five were reported at Hallen. In nearby Wiltshire 13 HE bombs fell near Shrivenham road in Swindon, causing slight damage.

Saturday, 24th August

It was a fine, clear day in the south of the country and thus there was a high level of enemy activity, mainly concentrated in the south-east: Portsmouth, Ramsgate and Rochester as well as London were hit. There was scattered bombing in the southern part of Gloucestershire and its southern border areas. HE bombs, including a number of UXBs, came down at Hallen, Frampton-on-Severn and Avonmouth where several houses were damaged. In addition, HE bombs also fell around Chipping Campden. One person was wounded and a sheep was killed. HE and incendiary bombs also fell in open countryside near Dursley, Wotton-under-Edge and Nailsworth, where the bombs narrowly missed a large herd of cattle, and Chipping Sodbury.

During the late evening Bath also came under attack; several houses and a garage were damaged. The Auxiliary Fire Service in the city found things to be somewhat hotter than usual when their station was set alight by incendiary bombs. Altogether, over 50 fire bombs were dropped and things were further complicated by a number of UXBs. However, the local services were able to bring the situation under control fairly quickly.

Sunday, 25th August

Local fish were given a severe headache at just on five o'clock in the morning when half-a-dozen HE bombs fell into the Severn some 30 yards or so from the Severn Tunnel. The weather in the morning was clear and bright but by late afternoon it had begun to cloud over.

The industrial Midlands was to bear the brunt of the evening's raids but rural Gloucestershire would nevertheless get its fair share of attention. Fortunately, a large number of the bombs dropped turned out to be duds. UXBs were reported at Hester's Way, Cheltenham, close to the railway station at Gotherington, and at Hampton Court Farm, Patchway, near Bristol. A regular assortment of ordnance fell at Littledean during the evening, including the usual incendiary and HE bombs plus some of the particularly unpleasant oil bombs. Several of the latter also fell at Newnham, with incendiaries coming down at Elton nearby. Seven HE bombs fell at Ablington at ten o'clock; they were probably intended for the airfield at Bibury.

Monday, 26th August

A few minutes after midnight the post office at

Minsterworth had a near miss, when a single HE bomb was dropped close by. A number of UXBs also came down at the Reddings, near Cheltenham, the likely target having been Staverton airfield.

Tuesday, 27th August

A clear day with some light rain in places. The Bristol — Avonmouth area was, once again, on the enemy target list for that evening. The National Smelting works and the Shelmex factory came under attack with HE and fire bombs. Railway goods wagons containing carboys of acid were set on fire at Hallam and a clutch of HE and incendiary bombs fell at Barrow Gurney.

Wednesday, 28th August

Probably influenced by the fine weather, the Luftwaffe made its first attempt to launch a major massed attack against a British city. Liverpool was the target and 150 aircraft from Luflotte 3 were dispatched to carry out the raid. The concentration of bombing was poor and the raiders left a trail of destruction across the North-west. Nearer home the Gloster Aircraft Company's factory at Brockworth was the objective of a number of Heinkels from KG.100. The concentration and accuracy of the bombing was, once again, poor and the hardware fell over a wide area around the factory between eleven-thirty and midnight. Bombs were reported at Churchdown, Leigh and Norton. Some slight damage was caused to telephone wires and water mains near Staverton, and a barrage balloon post near the airfield received a direct hit and three airmen were killed. Further south, bombs also fell

Heinkels in formation.

38

during the evening at Badminton, Berkeley, Olveston, Tormarton, Woolaston and Wickwar. At Almondsbury ten HE bombs and one oil bomb were dropped on Cattybrook Farm. Quarry Hill Farm also suffered damage when a string of eight HE fell on farm buildings. Cranham Mill, Painswick, was shaken somewhat when a bomb fell nearby. A large incendiary bomb that had fallen 500 yards from the post office at Harescombe was not found until three days later. The casualty list for the day showed a dead owl at Tetbury and a dead rabbit at Cirencester.

Thursday, 29th August

Bombs were still falling a few minutes after midnight and a number of houses were damaged in the Brockworth area. One HE bomb also came down at Tewkesbury, damaging water mains.

During the last two hours of the day there were a number of scattered incidents. Shortly after ten o'clock incendiary bombs fell at Chavenage Green and caused grass fires. At about the same time two HE bombs fell at Gotherington. Shortly after half-past ten a number of HE bombs exploded north-west of Wotton-under-Edge in an area around Kitesnest Farm, Howley Farm and Cannons Court Farm, rendering the Charfield to Nibley road impassable for some time. At quarter-past eleven more incendiaries fell at Kempley, near Newent, and five minutes after seven more came down at Alderton. A further 12 plus two HE bombs rained down on Grange Court some minutes later. Bream on the far side of the Severn was hit by an HE bomb and damage was caused to electricity cables, and at Almondsbury, near Thornbury, a horse was killed by an oil bomb during the night.

Friday, 30th August

Af half-past midnight several HE bombs fell near Longhope and around Grayhill and Blaisdon. Also during the early hours HE bombs were dropped near the Shipton Moyne — Easton Grey road.

By late evening more hardware had fallen at Cadbury Camp, Tickenham, near Bristol, Minsterworth, Oventon and Westbury-on-Severn. Thirty incendiaries fell at Almondsbury and damaged the brickworks. Further north, a single HE bomb fell close to the railway station at Churchdown. Weston-super-Mare also came under attack and a number of buildings were damaged. Once again, Liverpool received a dose of the "Blitz" medicine and many inhabitants of Gloucestershire listened with trepidation to the details of the attacks. What was happening there could happen elsewhere!

Saturday, 31st August

Another typically fair summer's day. Large parts of the city of Liverpool lay smouldering in the sunlight whilst its citizens counted the cost, wondering if nightfall would bring with it further attacks.

Their fears were justified. The enemy did indeed return under cover of darkness. A number of HE bombs also fell within Gloucestershire's boundaries, mainly in the north-east, around Blockley, Batsford and Bourton-on-the-Hill. A single HE bomb fell at Tirley and two more at St. Briavels in the west.

Sunday, 1st September

It had been a long night but by dawn it became possible to assess the pattern of the bombing. HE and incendiary bombs were reported at Naunton, Oxenton (plus one petrol bomb), Blockley, Batsford, Stockend, Churchdown and Minsterworth.

After a brief daytime respite more attacks were launched against the Bristol area during the evening. The Shirehampton Co-op store was badly damaged, as were buildings of the GWR, and two people were killed. A number of houses were hit in the Clifton division of Bristol. A petrol bomb caused a fire in business premises in the St. George division and two people perished. Buildings were also damaged in the Bedminster division. Around midnight a UXB fell in Temple Street and the main railway line was damaged at Pilning junction by HE bombs.

Monday, 2nd September

The attacks of the previous evening continued throughout the hours of darkness, a darkness more intense than usual in some areas, for, only a few minutes after midnight most of west Gloucestershire was plunged into blackness as exploding bombs damaged power cables. A number of UXBs came to earth at Rudgeway, Nobley and Hambrook near the main road. Eight rather more volatile HE bombs crashed down at Moorend near Hambrook, damaging houses. More damage was caused at Pilning junction north of Bristol and rail traffic ceased for a while. HE bombs were also reported at Westerleigh,

Winterbourne, and Yate. Weston-super-Mare and Portishead were also attacked. The attacks on Bristol killed five people and injured four. Fourteen houses were rendered uninhabitable and 37 were badly damaged, with another 335 suffering slight damage.

A resumption of the destruction was heralded late in the evening, when, shortly after ten o'clock, flares were dropped over Yate, Selsey, Kemble and Brockworth. Less than an hour later, HE bombs were falling at Frampton Cotterel. The A432 road was closed two miles west of Chipping Sodbury when a UXB was discovered and two further UXBs were reported at Rudgeway.

Tuesday, 3rd September

The catalogue of destruction continued into the early hours, with HE bombs falling at Buckland, Dorn, Batsford and Hazel Lane. Pieces from an enemy aircraft were discovered in the Bristol area during the morning. It would appear that one of the raiders had struck a balloon cable during the attack.

The evening was to bring a further attack on Bristol. The first bombs fell at about half-past ten in the area of Olveston and Portishead where four people were killed and five injured. Minutes later, at Clevedon, bombs hit a bungalow in Wellington Terrace. Four people were hurt and the house was gutted. Only two minutes after this, two HE bombs fell in High Street, Worle, near Weston-super-Mare, killing three people and injuring a fourth. Houses were damaged, as were water and gas mains.

More action followed in the north of the county during the evening. Two oil bombs fell near a searchlight position in Prestbury, just to the north

A typical night scene over Bristol during the terror raids of 1940-41. The sky is a kaleidoscope of tracer and searchlights.

The Miles Arms at Avonmouth in September 1940.

o'clock. It came down at Kenilworth Avenue and crashed into the house of Mr. G. Norman Bruton. Fortunately, it did not explode and was later dealt with by Bomb Disposal. By the end of the day HE bombs had also fallen at Bagstone near Rangeworthy and near the Cross Hands pub at Pilning, wrecking two houses and slightly injuring one person.

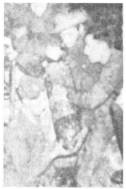

Gloucester's first bomb was a UXB that went through the roof of Mr. G. Norman Brutons house in Kenilworth Avenue in September 1940.

(Citizen)

of Cheltenham. Other HE bombs came down at Wickwar almost on the stroke of midnight and at about the same time HE and incendiary bombs caused damage to water mains at Avonmouth. Earlier in the evening a single HE bomb had fallen at Hallen and a UXB was later reported from the same location.

Wednesday, 4th September

As enemy raiders headed for home during the early morning, the picture of the night's activity gradually became clearer. Further HE bombs were reported coming down at Tirley and Notgrove. UXBs were reported from Tibberton and Barrington Leyes Farm. At Severn Beach eleven HE (including two UXBs) fell close to the GWR track and damaged the sea wall. Four unexplained canisters parachuted down at Marshfield on the Wiltshire border. The morning news broadcasts brought some consolation for those who had been on the receiving end of the enemy's wrath: RAF Bomber Command had struck at Berlin during the night.

At about nine o'clock in the evening another series of widespread attacks began. Once again, Bristol came in for the lion's share. Approximately forty HE bombs and large numbers of incendiaries were dropped in the Knowle, Clifton and St. George districts. Seven of the HE turned out to be UXBs but damage was caused to the GWR's Bristol East Depot. Four people were killed and eleven injured. Sixty-seven houses were destroyed, 23 badly damaged and over 600 slightly damaged. The Bristol Aircraft factory was damaged and the airfield at Filton was looking slightly the worse for wear with five bomb craters within its perimeter. Gloucester had its first HE bomb at eleven

Thursday, 5th September

The previous evening's attacks continued into Thursday morning. By the time that the last bombs had fallen and the "all clear" had sounded, the list of locations attacked was a long one. Bombs had come down at Quedgeley, where damage was caused to telephone and electric cables, Whitminster, Coln St. Aldwyn, east of Cirencester, where HE and petrol bombs damaged houses, Northam, near Almondsbury, and at Painswick.

The Royal Engineers were to almost cause more damage at Painswick than the enemy when exploding a delayed action bomb some days later. After one controlled explosion the ceilings of two nearby houses collapsed and windows in four others were shattered. Bombs were also reported at Chedworth Bottom, Stinchcombe, Windrush, Northwood, Barnwood, and in the areas around Bibury, Pucklechurch, Cherrington, Taynton and Coney Hill. The earlier attacks had also spread southwards and one of the worst incidents occurred at Banwell, five miles south-east of Weston-super-Mare. A dozen HE bombs were dropped and destroyed the post office and three houses. Five people were killed, including two policemen. Gas mains were fractured and telephone wires were damaged. All roads into the village were blocked by debris. The Central Electricity Board also reported damage to overhead power lines between Portishead and Bridgwater.

As daylight began to wane enemy plots began to appear on the maps at Filton Control Centre and alerts were sounded. Two HE bombs were dropped at Elton, damaging farm buildings and killing livestock. Incendiary bombs fell at Blaisdon before midnight. As reports of incidents were compiled it became obvious that this was one of the worst twenty-four-hour periods on record. The following locations had suffered the attentions of the enemy:

Almondsbury	10 HE, 2 petrol bombs
Alveston	1 petrol bomb
Badminton	10 HE
Barnwood	1 HE, 1 petrol bomb
Chedworth	3 HE, 1 petrol bomb. 10 cattle killed and 3 injured.
Cherrington	8 HE
Coney Hill	1 HE
Easter Compton	8 HE, 1 UXB
Frampton Cotterell	15 HE. Damage to Cross Hands Inn, road blocked. Damage to houses and telephone lines. Chickens killed.
Harry Stoke	4 HE
Hatherop Hill	4 HE, 1 petrol bomb
Hawkesbury	12 HE, 1 petrol bomb
Hortham	9 HE, 1 petrol bomb
Hucclecote	1 HE
Northwood	22 HE
Oaklands	2 HE
Painswick	1 HE, 1 UXB, 1 petrol bomb
Pilning	10 HE. 2 petrol bombs. 2 houses destroyed, many others damaged.
Pucklechurch	3 HE. Damage to one house.
Quedgeley	7 HE. 7 pigs killed, 1 horse injured, 3 houses destroyed, one barn and one car burnt. Damage to other houses and to gas and electric systems.
Rissington	1 HE
Severn Bridge	7 HE
Sparks Hill	6 HE
Stinchcombe	1 HE
Taynton	1 HE
Whitminster	20 HE
Windrush	1 HE

Friday, 6th September

By dawn, the enemy raiders had sown a harvest of destruction in and around the northern suburbs of Bristol. Seventeen HE and two oil bombs had fallen on Upper Kempton Farm and Oaklands Hill Farm near Almondsbury. The Winterbourne — Northwood area had been hit by 22 HE bombs and one oil bomb. Six HE bombs had fallen on Home Farm in the area of West Littleton and Marshfield and a single oil bomb had been dropped on West Farm. Poplar Farm near Pilning had also been hit with four HE and three oil bombs. Further afield, Ampney St. Peter had received one HE bomb as had Drybrook and Awre. At Elton four HE bombs had killed two pigs and a horse, as well as causing damage to buildings.

A comparatively quiet evening was interrupted by the explosion of a single bomb near Cinderford at quarter-past ten. The adjacent road was damaged but there were no human casualties.

Saturday, 7th September

In spite of clear weather across the British Isles, the enemy did not appear over Gloucestershire. It seems probable that the Luftwaffe was gathering its strength, for Goring had decided to concentrate his attacks on London and was to launch hundreds of bombers against the capital that night.

Sunday, 8th September

Two incidents occurred during the early hours. At ten minutes past one some 30 HE bombs were dropped at Redmarley. A man and a woman were injured and farm buildings were damaged. Some time later at twenty-past two eight HE bombs fell at Blockley, one turning out to be a UXB. As a result, the road to Bourton-on-the-Hill was closed for some time.

Tuesday, 10th September

Following an all too brief two-day lull, enemy raiders once again appeared over the county during the early hours. A number of HE bombs fell at Downend causing damage to electricity and telephone cables.

Late in the evening two HE bombs fell near the police station in Mangotsfield. Damage was caused to a large glass-house, the Lamb Inn and various other buildings. There was a good deal of concern throughout the county at this time because of a shortage of steel helmets for civil defence personnel. This shortage was almost certainly attributable to a lack of steel rather than a lack of finance, for the helmets of the day cost only 14/- (70p).

Wednesday, 11th September

The sporadic attacks that had begun the previous evening continued throughout the night. At Northwick, near Aust, a clutch of HE bombs killed two cows and injured two more, plus a colt and a horse. A number of HE also fell into the Severn near Aust. At Elmore a cottage was damaged by HE bombs and at Churcham 17 HE bombs fell only 60 yards from the main railway line. A single HE also exploded on Barrow Hill near Hasfield. Sixty five incendiary bombs were unloaded on Sodbury Common but failed to cause any fires. The worst incident of the night occurred at Frenchay, Bristol, where 23 HE bombs were dropped, causing considerable damage. A Ministry of Health sanatorium and a market-garden centre were hit, and telephone and electricity services were disrupted. An odd incident occurred near Pucklechurch when a load of mysterious red powder was apparently dumped from an enemy aircraft. At least one person is known to have suffered burns caused by the powder. Samples were sent to the Home Office for analysis.

The evening brought more bombardment, although not all of it was attributable to the enemy. In the St. George division of Bristol two unexploded anti-aircraft shells came crashing back to earth. One smashed through the roof of a shelter and a number of people inside were injured. Earlier in the evening a load of 20 incendiaries fell on Chipping Sodbury and at twenty-five minutes to midnight two HE bombs were dropped at Birdlip.

Thursday, 12th September

Daylight brought with it cloud and rain and consequently enemy air activity was restricted. At some point during the night three HE bombs fell at Winterbourne, just to the north of Bristol.

Friday, 13th September

Despite the date, things remained quiet, at least as far as Gloucestershire was concerned.

Sunday, 15th September

The lull was broken when a number of HE bombs fell around Hawling. Other HE bombs were dropped on the road between Stow-on-the-

Wold and Andoversford. In addition, incendiaries fell at Hallen on the edge of Bristol, where a hedge was set on fire. A UXB was also discovered on a coal dump at Avonmouth.

Monday, 16th September

Shortly after eleven o'clock in the morning the Control Centre at Filton began to track an enemy raider, "Raid 146". The aircraft came up the Bristol Channel to a point north of Avonmouth and then turned and passed over Hepton Farm and flew on towards No.24 Balloon Site. With malicious intent the raider dived down to 50 feet and strafed the site with machine-gun fire. The balloon was damaged but did not catch fire. Fortunately, there were no human casualties.

There was a good deal of cloud and rain during the day but it was not to deter the enemy from mounting attacks later in the evening. At Inglesham ten HE bombs were dropped one hour before midnight but, fortunately, they caused little damage. At about the same time a suspected UXB was reported from Rendcombe.

Tuesday, 17th September

The Bristol area was on the receiving end yet again during the night. HE bombs fell in the sea and on the beach near Portishead. Four HE also came down between the wireless station and the sea wall. Once again, the balloon barrage inadvertently contributed to the general confusion. Balloon hawsers damaged overhead power lines at Gloucester and Chipping Sodbury, bringing about an extremely effective blackout!

At ten minutes to midnight a number of HE bombs were dropped on the St. George division of Bristol; many of them, however, were UXBs. Some 480 people had to be evacuated and damage was caused to private property and to a slaughterhouse.

Thursday, 19th September

The Aust — Beachley ferry came under attack just before half-past seven in the evening. The ferry was in use at the time and although HE bombs fell on both sides of the river no casualties were reported. At five minutes to nine Lechlade was rocked by the explosions of ten HE bombs. Once again, no casualties or notable damage were recorded.

It was on this date also that more information became available on the mysterious red powder that had been dropped just over a week earlier. It

A KG53 Heinkel returns from mission. The pilot is handing over a canister of film to a despatch rider.   *(Central Press)*

was similar to a substance that had been dropped over Yorkshire in the earlier part of the month. It was a sodium compound capable of causing serious skin infections. Various explanations are possible but this would seem to be an early attempt at chemical warfare against a civilian population.

At least one of the raiders dispatched to the Bristol — Filton area that evening got a little more than he had bargained for. Heinkel G1 + GL (Werk No. 2146) was hit by anti-airctaft fire and later crashed at Thorley Wash, Spellbrook, near Bishops Stortford in Hertfordshire, at twenty minutes to midnight. Three of the crew, Uffz. Pohl, Uffz. Goliath and Fw. Alpers, were killed and the fourth member, Uffz. Gert, was captured after baling out.

Saturday, 21st September

It was a fine day and during the afternoon the Luftwaffe carried out a number of high-level reconnaissance sorties. One of these high-flying snoopers was intercepted at 25,000 feet over Liverpool and shot down. A similar sortie was obviously in progress when the Filton Control Centre registered "Raid 46" at 20,000 feet over the city. Two Spitfires from Middle Wallop airfield were sent after the high altitude Ju.88 but were unable to get to grips with it. Possibly aware that he was being pursued, the German pilot made a long, high-speed dive to the south-west. The aircraft was last plotted at 500 feet over the Bristol Channel, heading south at a great rate of knots. It is highly probable that this "recce" flight was the lead-in to the large raid on the Bristol Aircraft

Works that was to follow a few days later.

News filtered through to GAC employees at Brockworth that a single enemy raider had made a daring low-level attack on one of their sister Hawker factories at Brooklands during the day. As the story spread many wondered just how long it would be before the enemy took a greater interest in their factory.

Monday, 23rd September

The fact that the war had reached the furthest corners of Gloucestershire was underlined by the decision of the County Emergency Committee to approve the building of public air raid shelters in Cinderford.

Wednesday, 25th September

Once again, it was a typically fine, late September day, with much to recommend it. If the citizens of Bristol had any idea, however, of savouring the sunshine and the day, their thoughts were to be crudely dashed before noon. At approximately twenty minutes to twelve more than 60 Heinkel bombers of KG.55 with fighter escorts approached the city from the south. Within minutes they had released 90 tons of high explosive plus oil bombs, in all a total of 300 bombs, over the northern suburbs of the city. Forty-one houses were destroyed, another 100 were left unrepairable and a further 756 suffered damage of some sort. The main A38 road was closed to traffic; Patchway — Filton rail junction was blocked. Three warden's posts were put out of action and considerable damage was done to telephone and electrical cables and to water and gas mains.

The Filton aircraft works was hit by over 160 bombs. Direct hits on six air-raid shelters caused carnage amongst those sheltering within. Even with hindsight it is difficult properly to assess the casualty figures; however, it is thought that 72 people were killed and 166 were injured. Of the latter, 19 were later to die of their injuries. Rubble-strewn roads and unexploded bombs hampered the rescue and fire services. A number of personnel were injured and several ambulances damaged by the detonation of delayed action bombs. At least eight newly-produced aircraft were destroyed and more than 20 others damaged. Needless to say, the destruction was not confined to Filton alone. At Westbury-on-Trim four houses were destroyed and 50 others damaged. There were also human losses: one person was killed and 20 were injured. At Winterbourne five HE bombs caused damage to a house and farm buildings. Four UXBs were reported from Nailsea and another at Wraxall. Three HE fell at Stoke Gifford around midday, destroying three houses and damaging 26. Two cows were killed in the explosions and 13 more injured. The all-clear sounded at sixteen minutes past twelve, signifying the end to a holocaust of amazing rapidity. What must have seemed to many to be the longest lunch break of their lives had, in fact, lasted little more than thirty minutes.

Retribution was to be swift, if not quite on a comparable scale. After some initial difficulties, due to a misjudgement regarding the potential target of the enemy formation, fighters from 152, 238, 601 and 609 Squadrons were able to get to grips with the raiders. Three Heinkels were shot

A KG55 Heinkel, which crash landed in France after being shot up by fighters (Bundesarchiv)

'The vanquished tyrant', this young Nazi airman was captured in Kent but the scene is typical enough to jog the memories of many people in Gloucestershire.

down and a third, badly damaged by fighters, barely made it back to France before crashing. One of the defending Bf.110 fighters was also shot down. Two other fighters crash-landed in France and a fourth ditched in the Channel on the way back to base. In addition, the anti-aircraft defences brought down a Heinkel which crashed at Racecourse Farm, Failand, near Portbury, after a shell exploded just beneath it. There were a number of UXBs in wreckage which had to be defused later. The Luftwaffe losses over Southern England were as follows:

1) Heinkel He.111 G1 + BH (Werk No. 6305):
   Shot down by fighters at Studland, Swanage, Dorset, at 1200 hours.
   Crew: Hptm. Kothke — POW
         Fw. Jurges — POW
         Gefr. Weissbach — POW
         Uffz. Altrichter — wounded and later died.
         Flg. Muller — POW

2) Heinkel He.111 G1 + EP (Werk No.1525):
   Shot down by fighters at Woolverton, Somerset, at 1200 hours.
   Crew: Hptm. Brandt — POW
         Ofw. Wittkampf — killed
         Offw. Kirchoff — killed
         Uffz. Mertz — killed
         Gefr. Beck — killed

3) Heinkel He.111 G1 + LR (Werk No.2803):
   Attacked by fighters and damaged. Engines on fire, aircraft abandoned over Branksome Park, Poole, Dorset, at 1208 hours.
   Crew: Oblt. Brocker — killed
         Oblt. Scholz — killed
         Uffz. Weidner — killed
         Uffz. Hanft — killed
         Uffz. Schraps — wounded, POW, rescued from Poole harbour.

4) Heinkel He.111 G1 + DN (Werk No.2126):
   Shot down by anti-aircraft fire, Racecourse Farm, Failand, Somerset, at 1150 hours.
   Crew: Oblt. Weigel — POW
         Ofw. Narres — POW
         Fw. Engel — wounded, POW
         Fw. Gerdsmeier — POW
         Gefr. Geib — POW

5) Messerschmitt Bf.110 3U + GS (Werk No.3591):
   Shot down by fighters at Wellbottom, Boyton, Wiltshire, at 1200 hours.
   Crew: Gefr. Schumacher — killed
         Fw. Schere — wounded, POW

MeIIO's ready for take-off (Bundesarchiv)

Thursday, 26th September

Although there was a major raid on Supermarine's Woolston works at Southampton, Gloucestershire remained relatively unscathed. However, a number of delayed action bombs left over from the Wednesday raid on Bristol detonated during the day. As a result, communications links between Filton Control Centre and the Observer Corps Centre in Plymouth were cut.

Friday, 27th September

Yet another fine autumn day that was to be disrupted by the Luftwaffe. An enemy reconnaissance aircraft, a Ju.88, caused the first alert of the day when it passed close to Bristol. It was to pay dearly for the disturbance. Shortly after half-past nine in the morning it was attacked and shot down at Porlock in Somerset. At twenty-three minutes past eleven the sirens began to wail in the Bristol area. The numbness still in evidence following Wednesday's attack evaporated rapidly. Many had seen the carnage caused by the previous raid at first hand and one thought was uppermost in everyone's mind: survival. The workers at the Filton factory hurriedly made for the shelters. Some, however, preferred to leave the factory environs altogether. Even shelters did not seem as

Ju88's of KG51 gather like ravens as they prepare to take off on a raid.
(Bundesarchiv)

invulnerable as they had 48 hours earlier. The apprehension was almost tangible. Was this to be a repeat of Wednesday lunchtime?

On this occasion the enemy formation consisted of 90 plus fighters and fighter bombers and they certainly seemed to be heading towards the city. This time, however, they were to be "seen off" in no uncertain fashion. The Hurricanes of 504 squadrons scrambled from Filton itself and fought the enemy over the northern suburbs of the city. Other fighters from 56, 152, 238 and 609 squadrons became embroiled with the enemy aircraft as they hurried home in disarray across Dorset. Altogether, seven enemy aircraft were brought down over land and two others crashed off the Dorset coast. One of these Messerschmitt Bf.110 fighters was shot down at Fishponds, Bristol, by a Hurricane of 504 Squadron. After

The actual aircraft Bf110C-4 (U8 + FK) which came down at Fishponds Bristol on the 27.09.1940.
(Severnside Aviation Society Collection)

being hit, Bf.110 U8 + FK (Werk No.2162) dived to rooftop height, trailing smoke. Suddenly it exploded and disintegrated, the pieces showering down over a large area. Large chunks of aircraft structure and a cascade of fuel splattered down in the grounds of the Stapleton Institute (now Manor Park Hospital). Both crew members, Ofw. Tepelt and Uffz. Brosig, were killed.

The waterfilled crater and wreckage that mark the last resting place of the 'Fishponds 110' (U8+ FK)
(Severnside Aviation Society Collection)

A police constable removes part of the main wing spar of Messerschmitt 110 U8+FK which was shot down at Stapleton Institution (now Manor Park Hospital) Fishponds Bristol on the 27th September 1940. (Bristol Evening Post)

A number of bombs fell in the Patchway district of the city and the B4057 road was blocked. Four people were killed and one injured. These casualties occurred by the Charlton road junction, one man being killed in his car and two children and an adult being killed nearby in a pony and trap. Apparently, the enemy aircraft had been briefed to attack the Parnall Aircraft Factory at Yate to the east of Bristol. This did not become known until much later and the popular view was that the RAF had saved Bristol from another pasting. No matter what its destination, the raid was a failure from the Luftwaffe's point of view. An unacceptable number of aircraft and crews had been lost for very little return and the propaganda victory, as well as the physical one, belonged to the RAF. The Yate factory had escaped damage, but as history was to prove, this was only delaying the inevitable.

Monday, 30th September

On a fairly bright but cloudy afternoon the Luftwaffe launched an attacking force of 40 bombers against the Westland Aircraft Factory at Yeovil in Somerset. The Heinkels of KG.55 were unable to locate their target because of cloud and focussed their attention on nearby Sherborne. They came under repeated attacks from 10 Group Spitfires and Hurricanes, and were severely mauled.

Tuesday, 1st October

Although Gloucestershire appeared to be having a quiet period, trouble was never far away. At four in the morning two oil bombs fell in fields on the outskirts of Swindon in neighbouring Wiltshire.

Thursday, 3rd October

The spell of calm came to an end at half-past one in the morning when an oil bomb and an HE bomb fell at Milbury Heath.

Monday, 7th October

A cloudy day with widespread showers. During the afternoon a force of Ju.88 bombers with fighter escorts forced their way through a screen of RAF fighters and again attacked the Westland factory at Yeovil which, fortunately, was not seriously damaged. The cost of the attack in human terms, however, was horrific: over 100 casualties. A direct hit on one of the factory shelters was responsible for many deaths. The enemy lost nine aircraft during the raid.

Thursday, 10th October

Yet another lull was ended by the explosions of two HE bombs that came down in the Hatherop — Eastleach area at twenty to eleven in the evening. The enemy was much more active elsewhere, attacking Liverpool, Manchester and London during the night.

Saturday, 12th October

There was widespread fog during the day which began to clear towards evening. The Luftwaffe were quick to take advantage of the improving visibility. At twenty-six minutes to ten in the evening a large number of incendiaries were dropped just to the south of Pilning, setting tons of hay on fire and creating a fiery beacon. The sight made many of the locals wince since it was bound to attract more unsavoury company. Sure enough, only half-an-hour later nine HE bombs were dropped on Station Road, Pilning, damaging a number of cottages.

Further afield to the north-east of Cheltenham, an oil bomb was dropped at Greet at quarter to ten. A few minutes later two HE bombs and 60 incendiaries were unloaded over Foxcote to the south. At half-past eleven two HE bombs were dropped in fields at Dowdeswell.

Tuesday, 15th October

A bright, moonlit night, of which the enemy took full advantage. A massive raid was launched against London. It resulted in over 400 deaths and twice that number of injuries. In spite of the raider's preoccupation with the capital, Gloucestershire was not entirely to escape their attention. Shortly after half-past seven in the evening a large attack on Bristol began to develop. HE and incendiary bombs were dropped on the Central, Clevedon, Clifton, Shirehampton and St. George districts. The destruction spread northwards like the ripples of disturbed water. In the Pilning area bombs fell on both sides of the GWR track at Cattybrook. Hanham, Newton, Whitfield and Little Haresfield were also bombed, with a variety of ordnance. Cheltenham also found itself beneath the hammer. Shortly after eight o'clock in the evening two HE bombs were dropped on the LMSR goods yard near Arle Road bridge. A GWR guard, Mr. Jack Davis was injured and two men, Mr. H.R. Ash and Mr. Harry Staite, were concussed.

Wednesday, 16th October

Perhaps because Cheltenham had seemed an easy target the previous evening, the enemy returned to the area around tea-time. A lone raider machine-gunned the streets at Brockworth and some nurseries at Churchdown. Some houses were damaged and a number had to be evacuated. Four HE bombs were dropped, one of which turned out to be a UXB, as did the single oil bomb that was dropped. German radio broadcasts hailed the attack as a great success, stating that the raider had made numerous hits on "sheds at an airfield near Cheltenham"!

Friday, 18th October

Eleven HE bombs and one incendiary were reported to have been dropped at Bibury at half-past eight in the evening. Fifteen minutes later three HE bombs fell at Manor Farm, Turkdean, to the north.

Saturday, 19th October

At Hammonds Court, Northwoods, near Winterbourne, nine HE bombs were reported as having fallen at nine-thirty in the evening.

Sunday, 20th October

The citizens of Little Sodbury had their Sunday morning rudely disturbed at six o'clock when two HE bombs and one oil bomb fell at Maisemead. No casualties or damage were reported, however. A further two HE bombs also came down at Almondsbury.

Shortly after eleven in the evening the enemy raided nearby Swindon. Two HE bombs and one oil bomb were dropped in the centre of the town. Eight people were killed and eleven injured. Five houses were also demolished.

Monday, 21st October

A single intruder attacked the Gloster Aircraft Factory at Brockworth — Hucclecote during the lunch-hour. Three HE bombs were dropped and came down harmlessly in fields near the factory. However, an oil bomb came down with devastating accuracy on the roof of No.7 Machine Shop. Although damage to the factory was not extensive a considerable number of people were killed and injured. Shortly after this incident, at quarter to two in the afternoon, a lone Ju.88, possibly the perpetrator of the Brockworth attack, machine-gunned a convoy at Tilshead in Wiltshire.

Two HE bombs and an oil bomb were reported from Mickleton during the evening hours and a single HE bomb fell between the North and South Piers at Sharpness Docks. That same evening a stranger-than-fiction event occurred at Painswick. An unexploded anti-aircraft shell came crashing down through the roof of a house in the village. It smashed a dressing-table and a gas stove and scattered a bag of onions all over the house before coming to rest in a passageway. At first it was thought to be an unexploded bomb and the local inhabitants were duly evacuated. After daylight on the morning of the 22nd, one of the village policemen borrowed a spade and dug the shell out of the ground, having told nobody of his intentions. He then carried the offending shell into the police station and placed it on the guardroom table, much to everyone's consternation. He doubtless received some advice from the occupants of the station as to what to do with such an item another time! Unfortunately, the details of any such exchanges have not been recorded for posterity.

Tuesday, 22nd October

Fog and rain covered most of the country during the day but it had begun to clear by early evening. From about twenty-past eight attacks began to develop across the southern part of Gloucestershire. By ten minutes to twelve HE and incendiary bombs had fallen at Barnsley, Berkeley, Beverstone, Brentry in Bristol, Drybrook, Hallen, Rodmarton and Sharpness Docks. In addition, five HE, together with three incendiaries, came down at Great Witcombe, damaging a house. A single incendiary also fell on Leckhampton. An initial report of HE bombs at Sharpness Bridge was later cancelled. Coventry, Liverpool and London also came under attack.

Thursday, 24th October

During the early afternoon the Filton Control Centre began to plot "Raid 29". This enemy aircraft approached the southern fringes of the city and dropped eight HE bombs at Yatton, damaging about 100 yards of rail track. The Hewish signal box was also put out of action for some time. One of the bombs was a UXB and two others fell in open fields.

Friday, 25th October

At half-past ten in the evening three HE bombs and up to 100 incendiaries fell near the Puesdown Inn on the Cheltenham to Oxford road. One bomb, a delayed action type, fell right in the middle of the main road and, as a result, traffic had to be diverted. Earlier in the evening, four HE bombs had fallen between Ashton Keynes and Cerney Wick. Two more fell at Codrington and a further two at Hinton.

Saturday, 26th October

Three HE bombs were reported from Rodley at twenty-past six in the morning.

Sunday, 27th October

A quiet day but things began to warm up, quite literally, in the evening at Forest Green. A number of incendiaries fell at quarter to ten. At least one penetrated the galvanised roofing of Harry Grist's Flockmill and both machinery and flock were damaged by fire. Other incendiaries were widely scattered in surrounding gardens. HE bombs were also reported at Witcombe where two calves were injured and property was damaged. Incendiaries dropped at the same time caused fires in Witcombe woods. Other incendiaries also came down at Newent, Prestbury and Cooper's Hill Farm, near Brockworth. A UXB was also discovered in a field at Westcote.

Monday, 28th October

At quarter to two in the morning enemy raiders were active in the north-west part of Gloucestershire. A number of HE bombs fell around Rudford, Tibberton, Kents Green and nearby Normans Farm. At almost the same time 100 incendiaries were dropped in the Newent area.

The daylight hours were cloudy but the weather began to clear up later in the day. Needless to say, enemy aircraft were active over the county during the evening. HE bombs were dropped at Apperley, Chedworth, Compton Abdale, Stowell Park near Northleach, and Sherborne, damage being caused in several instances to electricity and telephone cables, whilst at Apperley gas and water mains were cut and a road was blocked. Seventy incendiaries came down at Forthampton at ten minutes to ten, causing damage to some buildings.

Tuesday, 29th October

Four HE bombs were reported to have fallen at Marsden at an unknown time. A delayed action bomb exploded at Berkeley at eight in the morning, not far from the Berkeley Hunt kennels.

Friday, 1st November

At half-past eight in the evening three HE bombs came down near Snowshill. No damage or casualties were reported.

Tuesday, 5th November

The Luftwaffe, although uninvited, decided to contribute to an otherwise lack-lustre Guy Fawkes Night by providing a few bangs of their own. A trail of HE and incendiary bombs was laid in the north-west of the county in a line from Sandhurst — Ashleworth — Hartpury — Upleadon — Pauntley shortly after ten o'clock in the evening. They also provided the fireworks in the south-east of Gloucestershire, although with somewhat more deadly effect. Several HE bombs fell in fields to the north of Lechlade police station and three horses were killed. Other bombs were dropped just west of Great Barrington near to Windrush. Presumably, the nearby airfield was the target.

Wednesday, 6th November

During the late evening HE bombs fell at

Northleach, North Cerney, Miserden and Ampney Crucis. Roads were blocked at Cerney and a horse was killed at Northleach.

Thursday, 7th November

A few minutes after two o'clock in the morning HE bombs were dropped at Chedworth and Daglingworth. The main A417 Cirencester to Gloucester road and Perrots Brook road at Daglingworth were closed because of UXBs.

Saturday, 9th November

Shortly after eleven-thirty in the morning a probable pair of raiders attacked Beachley Camp and Woolaston on the west banks of the Severn. At Beachley a number of HE bombs were dropped, some of which turned out to be UXBs. The raiders then strafed the area. One person was killed, one seriously injured and two others slightly injured. The casualties were due to a combination of machine-gun bullets and bomb splinters. Further north at Woolaston HE bombs fell on the GWR track but two of them turned out to be UXBs. One of the latter was reported to have been removed by workmen.

Sunday, 10th November

A delayed action bomb detonated during the evening at Hartpury, following a wait of 123 hours.

Wednesday, 13th November

At twenty-past four in the afternoon more than a dozen HE bombs fell at Upton St. Leonards. There were no casualties but several local roads were closed for a time.

Thursday, 14th November

This was the date of the famous Coventry "Blitz" or operation "Mondlicht Sonate", as it was known to the Luftwaffe. Over 500 people were killed and more than 800 seriously injured. Despite the fact that 81 raids in all were made on provincial towns, things remained relatively quiet in Gloucestershire. This is surprising, when one considers that many of the raiders flew across the county on their way north. In fact, one of their main navigational turning points was in the area of Moreton-in-Marsh.

Quiet it may have been, but the villagers of Dowdeswell to the east of Cheltenham received a shock during the evening. At five minutes past nine two HE bombs were dropped. No damage was caused but several cottages had to be evacuated. Three-quarters of an hour later three HE bombs fell near Northleach.

Friday, 15th November

At half-past midnight two HE bombs fell near Sudeley to the north of Cheltenham. Two other HE bombs were dropped near Blockley during the evening. By the end of the day reports had also come in of bombs at Eastleach and Daglingworth.

Saturday, 16th November

A large clutch of HE bombs, including several UXBs, fell at Upper Oddington, north-east of Stow-on-the-Wold at twenty to five in the morning.

Sunday, 17th November

At quarter-past seven in the evening two HE bombs descended on Cerney Wick. Twenty-two houses were damaged, along with the church reading room.

Monday, 18th November

A new phenomenon, the parachute mine, made its presence felt in the small hours of the morning. These large cylindrical bombs came in various sizes, the biggest ones having a length of over six feet and a weight of more than 2,000 pounds. They were normally dropped suspended beneath a grey-green parachute. Two mines were dropped, one at Latteridge and the other at Frampton Cotterell. Fortunately, both failed to explode. Some attacks were reported from the southern suburbs of Bristol, with HE and incendiary bombs dropped in the Bedminster Down, Bishopsworth areas just after four o'cock. The worst incident occurred at Lulsgate Bottom where a relief landing ground had opened three months previously. Buildings were demolished and two people were killed. A number of other people were injured in a nearby inn. A single bomb also fell at Stroat, north-east of Chepstow, during the early morning.

Tuesday, 19th November

Two oil bombs fell at Tytherington, near Thornbury, at twenty to one in the morning. Between three o'clock and a few minutes after four, HE bombs fell at North Cerney, Taynton and Kemble, where one horse was killed and a second injured, together with four cattle.

During the evening a large-scale attack was made on Birmingham. Once again, many of the raiders crossed Gloucestershire on their way north. No doubt they were responsible, at least in part, for the bombs that fell on the Cotswold area that night. HE bombs were reported from Andoversford, Worcester Lodge near Blockley, Brockhampton, Foxcote Manor near Andoversford, Hackett Wood, Hangman's Stone just west of Northleach, Hardwicke, Hawling, Northleach, Prestbury and Snowshill. At Gotherington a cottage received a direct hit and the occupant, Miss Elizabeth Kearsey, was killed. The local Rector, who was also the Head Special Constable in the district, was the first on the scene and made a brave effort to penetrate the inferno to save Miss Kearsey. In fact, the bomb fell in front of the cottage but, being thatched, it burned rapidly. Two evacuee children, Joy Bartholomew aged twelve and Danny Wyatt aged ten, were injured by flying glass. They were in another nearby cottage owned by Mr. William Jones.

Things were decidedly hot in Cheltenham too: some 18 delayed action bombs had been scattered across the town. They had come down at Pilley Crescent, Southfield Farm, Church Road in Leckhampton, Shurdington Road close to the railway bridge, Burrows sports field at Moorend Road and Hall Road allotments. Numerous people were evacuated and many spent a makeshift night in the Old Pate's Grammar School buildings at St. Margaret's Road. One of the bombs that came to earth in Pilley Crescent smashed through a house and buried itself under the kitchen. Hillesley to the south of Wotton-under-Edge was hit by a single HE bomb and a shower of over 100 incendiaries came down at Kilkenny.

Thursday, 21st November

A relatively quiet day, with one HE bomb being reported at Hatherop and another at Hallen near Bristol.

Friday, 22nd November

A small number of incidents occurred during the late evening. Two HE bombs fell at Dymock to the north-west of Newent just after nine-thirty. Half-an-hour later, a single HE was dropped at Notgrove station. An oil bomb was reported from Hazleton and a lone incendiary fell at Laverton. HE bombs were also dropped on Brimpsfield, Chedworth and Sudeley.

Further south, a truant barrage balloon rampaged across Devon, causing havoc with

electricity supplies as its cable trawled a way through overhead power lines.

Saturday, 23rd November

At ten minutes past one in the morning 14 HE bombs came down in the Tarleton — Kemble area. Fortunately, five of them proved to be UXBs.

Sunday, 24th November

This is the date that marks the start of an intense and violent "Blitz" on Bristol which was to continue spasmodically for months. In an orgy of fire and destruction the Luftwaffe attempted to burn the heart out of the city. Although it in no way served to redress the balance, an event occurred earlier in the day which is still etched in the memories of many of those who witnessed it. One small element of the Luftwaffe was to get its "come-uppance" that Sunday afternoon.

At about three o'clock the inhabitants of Ampney St. Peter were treated to a very close look at an enemy intruder. A Ju.88 came flashing over the village at roof top height, closely pursued by at least two Hurricane fighters. The Hurricanes

A Ju88 bomber at low level over the countryside. A scene reminiscent of that on the 24th November, when a Ju88 was chased at rooftop height across Gloucestershire by Hurricane fighters.

(B. Rijnhout Collection)

belonged to the recently-formed 308 (Polish) Squadron based at Baginton which was not as yet considered operational! Two Poles, together with an RAF Wing Commander, had taken off from their base to the south of Coventry at quarter-past two for a short training patrol. One of the fighters flown by P/O Grodzinski had to break off and return to base because of problems with oxygen. The German crew must have wondered what they had got themselves into as they fled at low level, weaving from side to side in an attempt to break

A pair of Hurricanes turning in. A similar sight must have featured large in the view of the Ju88 brought down at Coates Manor by Hurricanes of 308 (Polish) Squadron.

Sgt. Mieczylaw Parafinski Photographed in France during 1939. Parafinski the victor at Coates in November 1940, when a Ju88 was shot down was already a holder of the Polish Cross of Valour. He had seen action in both Poland and France before his arrival in Britain he was to die later in an aircrash, while flying a Hurricane in 1941.
(Severnside Aviation Society Collection)

ONE FOR POLAND IN THE GLOUCESTERSHIRE SKIES
Sergeant Mieczyslaw Parafinski of No. 308 Polish Fighter Squadron, Bagington, Coventry, downs a Junkers Ju88A-5 of 123(F) Aufklarungsgruppe, at Coates Manor, Cirencester, 24th November 1940

An illustration of the Coates Manor incident drawn by Barry Walding of the Severnside Aviation Society.

away from the tenacious Hurricanes. They had been briefed for an attack on Coventry but now their only desire was to escape from their pursuers. Non-operational they might have been, but the Poles of 308 Squadron were determined to strike a blow against this tangible symbol of the tyranny that had so recently wiped their country from the map of Europe. The chase continued at very low level across the village of Ampney Crucis with live bullets and spent cases spattering across the roof tops. The intruder and the pursuers sped westwards over the fields towards Cirencester like a fox with the hounds close behind. The inhabitants of Cirencester had a grandstand view as Sergeant Parafinski, the leading fighter pilot, closed in on his quarry and opened fire again. His attack was closely followed by that of Wing Commander Oliver, the pilot of the second fighter. The scene is well remembered by Ralph Wilkins, then a schoolboy:

"Being an energetic youngster, I couldn't get out of Sunday School quick enough. It was a beautiful, bright afternoon and I jostled my way along the side alley impatiently, for I could see my parents waiting in our little Austin Seven.

Just as I dashed out into Sperringate Lane I was stopped in my tracks by a rat . . . tat . . . rat . . . tat . . .tat noise somewhere behind me and above the spires of Watermoor Church. All the waiting mums and dads seemed to be looking above the high school chimney and then further beyond the four ash trees in the school playground. Although we were at war, the conflict had had little effect on Cirencester and nobody seemed particularly worried, even when the siren at the town's police station emitted a rather belated up-and-down wail, which even I of tender years knew was the 'alert' and not the 'all clear'. My first reaction was one of disappointment because no-one dived for his gas mask: I did so want to wear that 'Mickey Mouse' model!

Suddenly a cheer went up from the parents and their offspring as a Hurricane was clearly visible circling a German bomber — a real German plane over Cirencester in broad daylight! There was the atmosphere of the bull ring, the Hurricane being the relentless matador. Another rat . . . tat . . . tat . . .; only a short burst this time, but there was a spontaneous cheer in unison. Pieces seemed to fly off the German plane and the Hurricane strutted around just like the rampant cockerel that we had at home. Smoke was billowing out from the apparently doomed foe, and it was going down.

'Quick, into the car', said my father, and almost at the same time we could hear the distant clanging of a fire-engine bell from the direction of the Council Depot at Querns Hill. Off we sped in the Chesterton direction in an endeavour to catch up with the speeding fire-engine and we in turn were pursued by running pedestrians and frantically pedalling cyclists.

The Hurricane suddenly dived low from the Victoria Road direction and did a cocky Victory Roll and then swooped off straight into the clear, blue sky to seek further prey.

We managed to pursue the Auxiliary Fire Service tender by following the water splashes along the Tetbury road until we could suddenly see a spiral of black, oily smoke in the Coates direction. We were eventually stopped in full flight by the police and RAF personnel just as we were about to enter Coates village. The wreckage of the downed aircraft was in close proximity to a large country house in fields to the right. The German crosses were clearly visible . . The might of the Luftwaffe lay burning in a Gloucestershire field.

We waited patiently until the Auxiliary Fire Service had extinguished the fire and then drove proudly down Tetbury Hill past the Querns towards home.

Even now I can remember this incident quite vividly, despite my then tender years, and I recollect that I was firmly convinced that this one incident ensured that we were going to beat Hitler and win the war."

The elation displayed in the Hurricane's Victory Roll was not misplaced. Ju.88 4U+HL (Werk No.451) had come to earth in a cascade of flame and wreckage in the grounds of Coates Manor. The crew of four, Lt. Hollstein, Fw. Schwingshakl, Gefr. Gran and Uffz. Koch, all perished in the crash. The aircraft had broken up on impact to an incredible extent. The heat from the fire was so intense that several of the manor windows were cracked and scorched.

The devastating attack on Bristol began shortly after half-past six in the evening, announced by the intimidating moans of the sirens. The sky became bright with flares dropped from "pathfinder" aircraft. Bursting into life, they hung over the city, harbingers of the horror to come. The "pathfinders", first to arrive over the city, were Heinkel aircraft of KG.100. They dropped over 5,000 incendiary bombs and a number of small HE bombs. Most of these seem to have come down on Knowle and Totterdown. A four-hour nightmare of incredible ferocity had begun. Successive waves of bombers were to drop nearly 1,000 HE bombs on the city, causing widespread

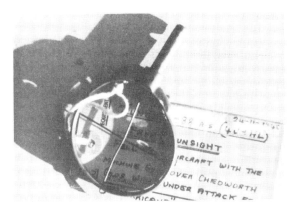

The gun sight from one of the machine guns of the ill-fated Coates Manor Ju88. The gun itself fell from the aircraft near Chedworth and was handed in to Chedworth Police Station (to P. C. Hughes) some time later.

(Rennison Collection)

damage and casualties in the following districts and locations:—

Bedminster Division

Bennet Bros. — Counterslip — Luckwell School — Robinson's Oil Cake Mill — Wills Factory (water main burst) — gas-holder, Marksbury Rd. — houses in Catherine Mead St. (seriously damaged) — Temple Meads station GWR (damage to tracks and to platforms 3, 4, 5, 6 and 9; train services also disrupted) — electricity sub-station, Mill Lane — Bedminster meter test room (destroyed) — Feeder Rd. power station (structural damage) — LMSR shed, Avon St., St. Phillips (damaged; also fire in coal yard). In addition, the Windmill Hill School shelter was hit, causing 50 casualties. Others were also injured in the Herbert Street shelter.

St. George Division

Speedwell School — ICI works, Nethan Rd. — Cotton Mills, Maze St — Avon Tannery — electricity sub-station, Vetnor Rd (destroyed) — plus general damage to water mains, houses shops and sewers. An Anderson shelter received a direct hit, killing five people and injuring a warden.

Central Division

Anderson's Rubber Factory — Hornby's dairy — Ford and Canning's building, shops in Stokes Croft, Broadmead, Wine St and Castle St.

Knowle Division

John Hall paint works — Co-op clothing factory — Holy Nativity Church (demolished) — plus damage to railway track at Sandy Park and Bath Road which was itself blocked.

Clifton Division

Triangle Cinema — Princess Theatre — Museum and Art Gallery — University Buildings — Canynge Hall — Lennards Buildings — Chesterfield nursing home — Clifton Down station coal yard — damage to shops and houses in Norland Road, Queens Road and College Green. Clifton Parish Church, St. Anselm's and Tyndall Baptist Church were all hit.

As the flames rampaged through the city an orange glow illuminated the night sky which could be seen for miles around. The sirens wailed the "all clear" shortly after midnight. The raid was over, but the fight to save the city continued throughout the night. Fire appliances and Rescue Teams were brought in from surrounding districts to assist as the city writhed in agony.

The ripples of destruction had spread outwards from the city during those fateful evening hours. Hanham, Soundwell and Warmley were hit with HE bombs. At Soundwell the bombs came down on the West Gloucestershire Company's reservoir and adjacent buildings, killing two people. At nearby Kingswood a fire started on the premises of Aero Engines Ltd. Four casualties occurred here, including a fireman who fell from a ladder. A boot factory was also set on fire and gutted. Gas mains were damaged and two casualties were reported. In the north HE bombs and incendiaries fell at Stoke Gifford, Haywards Farm, Alveston, Staple Hill, Syston Common and Bitton. Pilning also reported the fall of HE bombs as did Dyrham just north of Cold Ashton. At Whitchurch airfield south of the city an Ensign transport aircraft and a Douglas DC3 were destroyed by HE bombs.

Queens Road Clifton Bristol, built around the turn of the century these buildings were destroyed in seconds by Luftwaffe bombs.

Monday, 25th November

As dawn broke, Bristol counted the cost of the night's raid beneath a pall of smoke: some 200 people were dead, including eight auxiliary firemen, 22 wardens, two messengers and two ambulance drivers. Nearly 700 people had suffered varying degrees of injury and some 10,000 houses had been damaged or destroyed. German propaganda boasted that Bristol had been wiped out. "Sore wounded", perhaps, thought most of the locals, but "wiped out" was going too far. The arrogance of the bulletins only served to harden the resolve of the majority. Perhaps the spirit of the public during the raid is best displayed in the attitude of Frederick Wilshire, an unusual combination of barrister and musician. He held regular services at Colston Hall in Bristol and one had just commenced as the sirens announced the imminent attack. Frederick was undaunted, knowing that if he allowed the congregation of 2,000 to leave they would be walking straight into danger, for they had no time to get into the shelters, and he said, "We shall carry on." Carry on they did; all 2,000 remained, sang and prayed throughout the raid without the slightest sign of panic. There can be little doubt that Frederick Wilshire saved many lives on that dark and dangerous night.

The city had lost much of its architectural fabric. Many old and much-loved buildings had been smashed into rubble or turned into smouldering heaps under the onslaught of the enemy bombers. Buildings such as the "Dutch House", Upper Arcade and St. Peter's Hospital were no more. The spirit of the city, however, survived and would sustain it through ordeals yet to come.

A 'reclining bus' surrounded by devastation at Easton Bristol during 1940-41.

The Shirehampton area came under attack during the evening when incendiary and HE bombs were dropped between quarter to nine and nine-thirty. Fires were started at the National Smelting Company's plant and part of a canning factory was damaged. A school and houses were damaged and a searchlight post was set on fire. Once again, the "pathfinders" of KG.100 had led the way over the target.

Thursday, 28th November

A large raid was launched against Liverpool during the evening and thus enemy aircraft were once more in evidence, heading north across the county. A few minutes after eight o'clock two HE bombs were dropped at Tiddenham north-east of Chepstow, causing damage to a farmhouse. One HE and one incendiary fell at Haresfield Beacon and another single incendiary fell at France Lynch. Yet another incendiary came down at Staunton, near Newent, some time later.

Friday, 29th November

At three minutes past midnight a parachute mine was dropped over Olveston Common. The explosion damaged 25 houses in the area and the cap of the bomb was found half a mile from the crater. Two bombs also fell just outside Coates, uplifting a beech tree and throwing it across a road.

Monday, 2nd December

Shortly after six o'clock in the evening Bristol's sirens wailed forth another warning and within minutes flares began to appear overhead. Once more, KG.100 led the raiders to their target. The ten Heinkels from this unit unloaded over 8,000 incendiaries and nearly 50 HE bombs on the city. As the crews turned for home they could already

Dutch House Corner, Wine Street, Bristol after the raid on the night of the 23-24th November 1940.

see at least one large red fire developing. The raid involved well over 100 enemy aircraft and continued until eleven o'clock. The bombing was not as intense as that of the previous big raid and the fire and emergency services were able to cope without outside help. However, public utilities and the railways were badly hit. Bomb damage in districts was as follows:—

Clifton Division
Clifton Down station (debris on tracks) — Durdham Down cleansing station — Children's hospital — regional ARP headquarters. Churches were very much in the firing line, with hits of the Bishop's Palace, St. Peter's church hall, Sea Mills Methodist church, and All Saints church. The Bishop School was also hit. One warden was killed and two others injured.

St. George Division
Carlton Park School — All Saints church — widespread fires in the Redfield, Stapleton and Fishponds areas and many houses were damaged. About 30 casualties were reported.

Knowle Division
Railway station (booking hall and waiting-room destroyed) — Wells Road blocked.

Central Division
St. Paul's Church — scout HQ — unemployed welfare centre — Balowing St (building collapsed) — Gloucester Road blocked — large number of fires and widespread damage to public utilities.

Bedminster Division
Temple Meads station (damage to two branch lines).

Again, the destruction spread outwards from the city centre. At Henbury a number of HE bombs fell on the Avonmouth — Filton railway line near a tunnel. A passenger train then complicated the situation by running into one of the craters and blocking the line. Over a hundred incendiaries and oil bombs came down in open country near Dews Hill Woods and on rail sidings at Westerleigh, east of Winterbourne. A number of rail trucks in the siding were set on fire. A dozen HE bombs fell at Cadbury Heath, killing three cattle. At Charton a single HE bomb made a direct hit on a private air raid shelter, killing the occupants, two men and a woman. A cascade of incendiaries fell between Old and Little Sodbury and more fell on GWR sidings at Stoke Gifford.

An HE bomb was dropped close to West Street bridge between Bitton station and Oldland Common Halt. A gas main was fractured at Staple Hill, causing a fire. In addition, two UXBs were reported at Cattybrook and at Patchway. Four HE bombs fell on the foreshore at Tiddenham, near Chepstow, and two more fell in playing fields close to Beachley army camp. Preece Moor Farm at Longhope was hit by two HE bombs at just on nine-thirty. A few hours earlier bombs had been reported from Pucklechurch (Green Farm), Marshfield, East Compton and Pilning. At least three HE bombs fell into the river at Severn Beach and two others came down up river at Aust wharf.

Friday, 6th December
Just before twenty to eight in the evening parachute flares began to cast their glow over the city of Bristol again. The inhabitants needed no further indications. The Luftwaffe was back and the raid was likely to be a large one. At least one of the "pathfinders" had got it wrong, however, for a number of flares appeared over Stinchcombe Hill, way to the north. As the incendiaries and high explosive rained down, numerous fires broke out in the centre of the city. Within a short time they formed a series of fiery markers for the incoming raiders. Railway and electricity services were to be badly hit. The Bristol General Hospital was to receive a direct hit but, mercifully, there were to be no casualties. Damage was perhaps not as widespread as in the 24th November raid, but it was nevertheless quite serious.

Bombs fell at the following locations:—
Central Division
Welsh Back and Queen Charlotte Street (fires) — council house — Assize Courts — GPO —

Devastation in Victoria St. Bristol in 1940, although the Centuries old famous leaning tower has survived the on-slaught unmoved.

Corn Street — Clare Street — LMSR train hit at St. Phillips — Eventide Homes, Jamaica Street (13 people trapped). Many other minor incidents.

Bedminster Division
Bristol General Hospital — Temple Meads (two rail coaches hit; many casualties, including 20 dead) — Temple Back electricity station.

Knowle Division
Wells Road (houses hit) — gas mains damaged (supply cut) — A37 blocked — widespread casualties.

St. George Division
Power station — Corporation Baths, Eastville Park — five people trapped in shelter.

Clifton Division
St. Michael's Church (set on fire).

As on previous occasions, there was a "creep back" from the main target and the destruction began to spread outwards from the city. HE and incendiaries were dropped at Yate in and around a housing estate not far from a chemical works. A rectory and a hotel were set on fire, two houses were destroyed and one person was killed. A stick of bombs fell alongside the railway track near the Parnall aircraft works. The resultant explosions rocked the factory and blew out all the windows. Within hours, however, production was back to normal. HE bombs were also reported from Pucklechurch, Hardwicke, Warmley, Notgrove and Willsbridge, where a house was damaged. At eight-thirty the Ambassador cinema and its shelter in Kingswood were hit and many were killed. HE bombs, including some UXBs, were reported from Wick and Yate Rocks, north of Chipping Sodbury. Two bombs caused over £100 of damage to greenhouses and windows at Selsley Common. A further two HE bombs came to earth at Downton and Dyrham. 150 incendiaries fell on Winterbourne, damaging houses. Another 200, plus HE bombs, were reported from Hanham. A lone HE bomb came down near Upton Cheyney during the night.

A number of UXBs which had fallen on Prince Street in Bristol were to cause trouble for some days. One of them detonated and damaged the quay wall and a nearby bridge. Similarly, the Henbury to Avonmouth railway line which had been damaged was not to be back in full working order for another seven days.

Saturday, 7th December
The inhabitants of Charlton Kings, a village on the outskirts of Cheltenham, were given a shock during the late morning. At eleven o'clock a single HE bomb exploded. It had possibly been dropped in a previous attack and lain dormant, for there was no enemy air activity apparent at the time. Happening as it did right on Cheltenham's doorstep, it could almost have been construed as a harbinger of things to come.

Wednesday, 11th December
The war came to Cheltenham with a vengeance during the early evening. At twenty-past seven flares were dropped over the town. Within ten minutes clusters of incendiaries began to rain down. By quarter-past eight HE bombs were also falling. The first wave of raiders found their target easily. The Sunningend works was very quickly hit and set on fire. Despite the efforts of the fire service who were on the scene extremely quickly the factory began to burn fiercely, creating a beacon for the bombers approaching the town. Birmingham was also on the target list for the night and it is quite possible that a number of raiders may have mistaken an "illuminated" Cheltenham for its northerly neighbour. The anti-aircraft guns barked and roared their reply to the intruders and the clatter of shrapnel across the roof tops mingled with the explosions of the bombs, providing a nightmarish background music to the whole frightening scenario. In all, the raiders dropped over 100 HE and oil bombs and several hundred incendiaries.

A large bomb came down by the embankment at one end of Stoneville Street, demolishing half the houses in the area. Ten people were killed, including several children. A second bomb blew

The Luftwaffe's calling card a bomb crater in Kipling Road Cheltenham after the raid in December 1940.

'The bomb that arrived by the front door!' A House in Parabola Road Cheltenham devastated after the raid in December 1940.

(Echo)

up one of the town's gas-holders. Parkwood Mansions in Shurdington Road received a direct hit and five people were killed. The bridge over the GWR line at Pilley was hit and destroyed. There was bomb damage elsewhere: in Kipling Road, Parabola Road, Christchurch Road, Merriville Road and Lansdown Road. Several houses suffered damage in Kipling Road, their fronts collapsing into the street. The bomb impacted about mid-way between Shelley Road and Spencer Road, causing a large crater. A family sheltering beneath the stairs of their house in Old Bath Road amazingly escaped unscathed when their home was hit by a bomb. There was also damage at the Police Headquarters, St. Mary's cemetery and chapel and St. Phillip's & St. James' Church. A number of UXB's were reported, one notable one being just at the rear of the Conservative Club. The Black and White bus station and headquarters were hit and severely damaged. Bristol No. 79 coach was blown over a wall by the explosion and a man was killed. In Suffolk Street an elderly woman was found dead under wreckage. Some 600 people were rendered homeless, many having to take up temporary accommodation in local schools. In the aftermath of the raid a spirit of defiance was much in evidence and Union Jacks were hung up on some of the bombed houses. Railway links out of the town were disrupted and the Kingham and Honeybourne lines were badly damaged. Water mains were put out of action, including the large trunk main from the new town reservoir.

About an hour after the commencement of the Cheltenham attack, enemy bombers also appeared over Bristol. Although the bombing was not as intensive as in previous raids a moderate amount of damage was caused. In the Central Division a goods shed was damaged and windows were shattered at Lawrence Hill railway station. In the Knowle Division gas and water mains were damaged in Woodside Road. A number of incendiaries fell in the Clifton Division, but they were quickly dealt with. Houses in the St. George division were damaged by HE and oil bombs. Elsewhere, a small gas-holder was set on fire and local residents were evacuated. Three Anderson shelters nearby received direct hits but, fortunately, they were unoccupied because of the evacuation. Four people were trapped at Bath Buildings on Cheltenham Road. Three were later rescued alive but the fourth was discovered to be dead.

Incidents were reported throughout the county during the evening. Combinations of incendiaries and HE bombs came down at Witcombe Woods, Crickley Hill, Woodmancote, Upton St. Leonards, Rodley, Brockworth and the area around Newent.

Thursday, 12th December

The previous evening's catalogue of incidents continued into the early hours of the morning. HE bombs were dropped at Cowcombe Woods, near Chalford, Tibberton, Fairford, Taynton, Forthampton and Lemington. Further incidents came to light during the day, with bombs being reported from Hill Farm, Chipping Campden, Cirencester, Wiggold Farm, Weston-sub-Edge, Elkstone, Leckhampton, Prestbury, Toddington, Cleeve Hill and Charlton Hill.

Sunday, 15th December

Two HE bombs and some 200 incendiaries fell near to Leighterton at twenty-five minutes past eight in the evening. It was reported that the bombs were dropped on a decoy made up of lighted flares.

Thursday, 19th December

Although this was a quiet period for Gloucestershire, nearby Swindon was attacked during the evening. Eight HE bombs were dropped, four of them quite close to the GWR works. A number of houses were demolished and damage was caused to gas and water mains. Nine people were injured in the raid.

Saturday, 21st December

Weston-super-Mare, just over the border in Somerset, was attacked with two HE bombs at twenty past eight in the evening. Houses and water mains were damaged and the Langford road was blocked. Some time later, the Filton Control Centre reported flares in the Whitchurch area but no bombing followed.

Sunday, 22nd December

At about half-past six in the evening the crew of a stray Heinkel He.111 of KG.100 decided to attack a target that they later reported as Bristol. In fact, their incendiaries came down at Yate, Iron Acton and Patchway, north of Filton. This aircraft was probably Heinkel 6N+DL (Werk No. 2641) and there are conflicting reports that suggest that it was either hit by flak over Portland or damaged by a fighter whilst returning to base. Whatever the reason, the damaged aircraft made a forced landing near Cherbourg, injuring all four members of the crew. The pilot Fw. Gerg Deininger, must have given silent thanks for his narrow escape. However, during a future attack on Bristol his luck was not to serve him so well.

Later in the evening at twenty-past eight a number of incendiaries came down on the northern boundary of Filton airfield. At about the same time a single HE bomb was dropped at Dowdeswell, near Cheltenham. Two HE also fell at Berkeley, damaging a farmhouse.

Monday, 23rd December

At twenty-past eight in the evening four HE bombs and 40 incendiaries came down at Frampton-on-Severn. Such was the ferocity of the explosions that vibrations were felt as far away as Dursley. There were no fatalities but a cyclist travelling along the main road close to the point of impact was thrown from his bicycle, and suffered concussion. At Rodborough an anti-aircraft shell misfired, causing injury to one person and shattering the windows of nearby houses.

1941

Thursday, 2nd January

In true January style, snow fell during the night in parts of the county. At quarter-to-seven in the morning two HE bombs were dropped on Gloucester. Seven people were killed and a further

Bomb damage in Napier Street Gloucester in 1941.   (Citizen)

twelve were injured. Twenty houses were demolished and a garage and some shops were damaged. One of the fires caused by the bombing was put out by a first-aid team with nothing more than the famous stirrup pump. A parachute mine came down at nine-thirty in the evening at Corse to the south of Staunton. One person was killed and two others injured. There is a distinct possibility that this mine was dropped by a straggler heading for Cardiff where a major raid had begun to develop during the evening.

Friday, 3rd January

The wintry weather continued, twelve degrees of frost being recorded at Tilsdown. Undeterred, the Luftwaffe made its presence felt very early in the day when two HE bombs were dropped near Aust at twenty-past three.

Bristol was once again the target for KG.100 during the evening and at twenty-past seven the pathfinders arrived overhead and began to unload the first of more than 10,000 incendiaries. Within 20 minutes the nine aircraft were on their way home. From their cockpits the crews could see more than half-a-dozen fires already burning fiercely. Well over 100 aircraft are thought to have participated in the raid. The bulk of the damage was caused to residential areas in the central part of the city. However, 8,000 tons of valuable grain was also destroyed during the attack.

Bombs fell at the following locations:—
Clifton Division

Chamber of Commerce — Guildhall — Royal

Exchange Buildings — Grand Hotel — Docks (sheds and buildings damaged) — Queen's Square — Baldwin Street — General Hospital (evacuated).

Bedminster Division

Temple Meads station (booking hall, telegraph offices and clock tower damaged by fire) — numerous other buildings also damaged by fire.

Gas and water mains were damaged in many areas and water carts had to be procured from the military authorities. A number of HE and incendiary bombs were also reported in the Clevedon district.

Saturday, 4th January

Six Heinkels of KG.100 were back on the scene just after seven o'clock in the evening, dropping nearly 7,000 incendiaries. This time the target was Avonmouth and its dock area. Most of the fires caused by the incendiaries were extinguished by ten o'clock and the damage was minimal. Fifteen HE bombs fell at Clevedon, damaging houses, and four people were injured. Several HE were dropped around Battery Point near Portishead and incendiary bombs were reported at Tickenham, Nailsea, Portbury and Clapton-in-Gordano where two hayricks were set on fire. Weston-super-Mare was attacked later in the evening with HE and incendiary bombs and a number of houses were damaged or destroyed.

Further afield, two delayed action bombs were dropped at Alderton, near Winchcombe, both of which exploded the following day.

Sunday, 5th January

Once again, it was an extremely cold, wintry night. Spasmodic incidents occurred across the county during the early morning. At two o'clock two HE bombs were reported from Cow Hill, north-west of Thornbury, and an hour later two more were reported from Barrow Twining, north-west of Kemble. A single HE bomb fell at Harford Bridge, to the north of Northleach, at twenty minutes to seven. An incendiary was dropped on Oldland Common but it was dealt with by local civilians. During the night five HE bombs fell at Uphill, Weston-super-Mare. Nine HE bombs were also reported at Winford, where cattle were killed and property damaged.

Thursday, 9th January

The wintry weather continued and travel became inadvisable in some areas. However, the white snow shroud was to provide little protection from the ministrations of the Luftwaffe. Shortly after nine in the evening incendiaries began to fall in the centre of Bristol and flares began to burst overhead. More flares also appeared westwards towards Avonmouth. By half-past eleven HE bombs and incendiaries had fallen in the Bedminster Division, injuring six people. Others had come down on the docks at Pill and at Portishead, setting fire to a mill. Several water mains in the Avonmouth area were also damaged by bombs. A single bomb fell at Arlingham, damaging an electricity station. Further north, an incendiary came down in Cheltenham at five minutes to eleven. Incendiaries were also discovered at Maisemore and extinguished by wardens, and three HE bombs fell at Sandhurst just before midnight.

Saturday, 11th January

At five minutes to eight in the evening a large bomb was dropped between two farms 500 yards to the east of Tormarton. The resultant crater was nearly 30 feet deep and vibrations from the explosion were felt as far away as Chipping Sodbury.

Thursday, 16th January

A further snowfall on Wednesday added another layer of wintry discomfort to the arctic-like scenery. It was a bright, moonlit evening, with much of the light being reflected back off the snow, giving the whole scene a strange, daytime feel. Even the least clairvoyant could be seen scanning the night sky: it was certainly a bombers' moon.

Shortly after half-past seven flares began to appear over Bristol, closely followed by incendiaries on the ground. Nineteen lead Heinkels, once again drawn from KG.100, showed the way to the target by dropping more than 20,000 incendiaries. Waves of bombers followed them in and an eleven-hour reign of terror began for Bristol and Avonmouth. The initial "fire-attack" on Avonmouth was singularly unsuccessful, most of the fires caused by incendiaries were rapidly brought under control. The early attacks on Bristol itself, however, were much more effective. After the initial flare drop over the Stapleton Road area and the inner city, HE bombs began to fall in the Central and Clifton divisions. The Feeder Road Electricity Generating

Station was hit and power to a number of factories was cut. Power failures were also reported from St. George and Keynsham. Telephone lines were damaged and an emergency system had to be brought into use in some areas. The power loss affected the upper and lower bridges in Cumberland Basin, the latter bridge having to be operated by hand. The Clifton Theological College and several houses in the area were damaged. The previously gutted Bishops Palace was also hit with bombs. Houses were damaged in Long Ashton, and Pill church was set on fire.

At half-past nine Ham Green Hospital was set on fire by incendiaries. The hospital staff showed great courage and resourcefulness throughout the attack. Many doctors, nurses and ancillary staff fought the fires themselves, often with the help of patients.

As on previous occasions, a number of the enemy aircraft released their bombs to the north of Bristol. Reports came during the night of HE bombs at Frampton Cotterell, Frenchay, Little Stoke Park, Hallen, Stoke Gifford, Westerleigh and Winterbourne. However, enemy activity was not confined to the Bristol area alone. Incendiaries were reported from Cheltenham and the northern part of Gloucester, whilst an HE bomb fell at Maisemore. Further to the south, both Exeter and Bath came in for some attention. Six people were killed and 15 injured in Bath when a number of HE and incendiary bombs fell in the Weston district.

Friday, 17th January

At Aston Blank, south-west of Bourton-on-the-Water, eight HE and several incendiary bombs were dropped at twelve minutes past midnight, damaging the railway track. At one in the morning a further dozen HE bombs fell at Gipsy Lane, Minchinhampton, causing a crater 30 feet in diameter and 20 feet deep. Some damage was caused to a bungalow and farm buildings.

A second wave of attacks on the Bristol area commenced just after two o'clock in the morning in continuing bright moonlight. More incendiaries began to fall on Avonmouth and this time the fires could not be contained. Both the police and fire stations were hit and set ablaze and a number of casualties resulted. A timber store on the dockside was also set alight and the SS *Coracero* moored nearby became embroiled in the fire. Her First Officer was killed and a number of the crew were injured. Several other buildings in the dock area

were also set on fire. Within minutes more raiders were overhead, dropping HE bombs on the fires below. These attacks continued for three hours. The Home Office Regional Store was gutted and a serious fire broke out amongst fuel storage tanks belonging to the Anglo-American Oil Company, although this was later brought under control. The Gas Mask Factory in St. Andrew's Road was hit along with the local church, and numerous UXBs were reported. A number of private houses in Portview Road and Creswicke Road also suffered damage and some 20 families were evacuated.

At twenty to three the Ham Green Hospital in Bristol once again came under attack. Incendiary bombs set fire to one wing and patients were evacuated. As a result of these attacks at least six people were killed and more than 70 injured. In order to deal with the fires, teams had to be brought in from Wiltshire, Somerset and Devon and other parts of Gloucestershire. At least one enemy bomber involved in the attack was reported missing, a Heinkel He.111 of KG.100 6N+CL (Werk No.5441).

Saturday, 18th January

A number of incidents occurred during the early morning prior to one o'clock. HE bombs were reported from Chedworth, Hartpury and Northleach. Some two hours or so later three HE bombs were dropped between North Nibley and Wotton, damaging houses. Leftover UXBs from the Bristol attack continued to be reported and categorized during the day.

Monday, 20th January

The enemy was quiet, probably because of the persistent wintry weather. However, the residue of the previous week's air attacks was still at hand. During the day a UXB was discovered at a quarry in West Town Road in Avonmouth, beneath a burnt-out lorry. It was almost certainly one of the bombs dropped on the night of the 16th/17th January.

Wednesday, 29th January

Despite the continued bad weather, the enemy ventured forth during the evening. Flares were dropped over the Cheltenham — Gloucester area. A shower of incendiaries fell on Leckhampton and Hatherley Road in Cheltenham at around half-past six. Several HE bombs followed, two falling in Greenway Lane, Charlton Kings. Others came down around the Reddings, one of which impacted in a carrot patch, scattering the vegetables far and wide. A number of these bombs failed to explode even after passing below houses. Further UXBs were also reported from the Cheltenham area and other bombs fell in the Birdlip district near the Cirencester Road. Barrage balloons also seemed to be in vogue as targets, three being shot down in flames.

Thursday, 6th February

A meeting was held at Shire Hall, Gloucester to discuss firewatching and methods of dealing with incendiaries and it was attended by representatives of most of the local authorities in the county.

Saturday, 8th February

Seven enemy aircraft were active over the Bristol Channel during the hours of darkness, laying mines athwart the shipping lanes.

Sunday, 9th February

The Luftwaffe despatched at least five aircraft for a further mine-laying operation over the Bristol Channel.

Sunday, 16th February

Incendiary bombs were reported to have fallen at Berry Hill, north of Coleford, at two in the morning.

Wednesday, 19th February

Despite much low cloud and fog, the enemy launched the first of three consecutive night raids against Cardiff. There were a number of alerts throughout the county as the raiders made their way north-west. No bombing took place in Gloucestershire, however. Plymouth, further to the south, was not so fortunate, and some 15 HE bombs fell on the city.

Thursday, 20th February

Between half-past seven and half-past nine in the evening 40 plus enemy aircraft passed Plymouth, heading north. Cardiff or Bristol began to look like possible targets. A concentrated attack did not materialise, however, and bombs were scattered indiscriminately across Devon.

Saturday, 22nd February

The day was wet, windy and quiet until shortly before two o'clock in the afternoon when a red warning was brought into force in Dorset. A lone Heinkel had been spotted heading north at low

level. Within minutes the enemy aircraft had crossed the coast and turned up the Bristol Channel. The aircraft was a Heinkel He.111H3 from KG.27, which was based in northern France, and it was obviously heading for the Avonmouth area with evil intent. As the raider came within range the guns of the 76th Heavy AA Regiment batteries at Portbury and Markham opened fire. Their aim was spot on. One shell struck the enemy machine in the port engine with the tail and fuselage also being damaged. To try and facilitate his escape the pilot jettisoned the bomb load, abandoning all thoughts of attacking a worthwhile target.

As it had crossed the South Pier at Avonmouth the aircraft had begun to strafe the docks, causing several servicemen and civilians to throw themselves to the ground. Suddenly the aircraft appeared to strike one of the barrage balloon cables and a loud scraping sound was heard. The pilot of the aircraft, Lt. Rusche, ordered his crew to bale out as the damaged bomber began to lose height. Only seconds after two hunched figures had come tumbling out, the doomed aircraft dived

The wreckage of Lt. Rusche's Heinkel bomber shot down by anti-aircraft fire at Portbury on February 22nd 1941.
(Rennison Collection)

straight into the mud flats off Portbury Wharf. It exploded and began to burn fiercely, in spite of its watery surroundings. The bodies of some of the crew members were recovered from the wreckage. Rusche was one of the two that had jumped for their lives. He had landed safely on some railway tracks and had been quickly arrested by an engine driver armed with a shovel. Two other members of the crew, Fw. Hanke and Uffz. De Wall, are buried at Bristol's Greenbank cemetery. The wreckage was strewn along the water's edge. Several of the machine-guns were recovered but the Daimler-Benz engines had been driven deep into the mud. The bomber's markings were hardly visible due to the fragmentation of the airframe but a badge depicting an eagle clutching a swastika was found on the fuselage.

Wednesday, 26th February

Under cover of thick cloud a force of bombers, led by 15 Heinkels of KG.100, headed for Cardiff during the evening. This attack began at about half-past eight and ended at nine. At ten past eight flares began to burst into life over Bristol. Incendiaries and HE bombs followed, falling mainly in the Clifton and Central divisions. Several fires broke out and the Co-op in Castle Street and a flour store in Broadmead were damaged. The HQ of the 6th Gloucesters in Clifton was damaged, as were a number of shops in the St. Michael's Hill district. One person was killed and eight injured in these attacks. It is possible that some, if not all, of the bombing was carried out by aircraft that were originally intending to cross the Bristol Channel and attack Cardiff.

Firemen struggling to contain a blaze in Broadmead Bristol during 1941.

Thursday, 27th February

As so often before, the Luftwaffe contrived to cause more than a little lunchtime indigestion for the inhabitants of Gloucestershire. Harassing raids by single aircraft were carried out on a wide scale over the county and the surrounding countryside. South Cerney airfield was machine-gunned, as was Hullavington to the south. The aircraft that attacked South Cerney also machine-gunned the house of Mrs. Lister at Poulton, presumably out of pure malice. A lone Heinkel carried out the attack on Hullavington, damaging two aircraft. Upper Heyford airfield in

Oxfordshire was bombed, as was Houndstowe Camp near Yeovil in Somerset. The district around Chippenham was also indiscriminately strafed by another raider.

Without doubt the worst incident of this deadly "lunchtime matinee" occurred at Yate, to the east of Bristol, where the Parnall Aircraft Company came under attack. The factory was jointly owned by Frazer Nash and Parnall and it had long been on the Luftwaffe target list. It was a major manufacturer of power gun turrets for bomber aircraft. A lone raider, obviously well-briefed, appeared to pick up the Gloucester to Bristol railway track somewhere north of Charfield and proceeded to follow it south at very low altitude. The low-flying bomber was spotted as it passed

The parnall factory in happier pre-war days. In the centre of the second row of buildings can be seen the roofs of two World War One hangers, which had become incorporated in the factory premises.

(via K. Wixey)

over Charfield village, the Nazi markings clearly visible on its wings and tail. Within minutes it arrived over Parnall's and eye-witnesses recount that it lowered its undercarriage as it approached. Possibly this was intended to fool the local defences into thinking that it was a friendly aircraft or an enemy aircraft about to surrender. However, any illusions harboured by those manning the guns were soon dispelled as the bomber banked over the factory and released six bombs. The belated wail of the sirens mingled with the sound of the first explosions.

There were several thousand workers in the factory and they had had almost no warning and thus had no chance of getting to the shelters. One bomb crashed through the roof and bounced across the factory floor. A group of mesmerised workmen watched in frozen terror as the bomb

A contemporary advert for the pre-war Parnall Aircraft Company.

Typical of Parnall's output are these two power operated gun turrets of the Frazer-Nash type.   *(via K. Wixey)*

The 'guts' of a four gun Frazer-Nash power operated tail turret.   *(via K. Wixey)*

slithered across the floor towards them before coming to rest at their feet without exploding. The drawing office block was smashed and gutted and many of the clerical staff found themselves trapped as they crouched beneath their desks with rubble crashing down on top of them. For several minutes after the raider had fled unscathed into the overcast sky chaos reigned and was suddenly made worse by the explosion of a delayed action bomb, which caused yet more damage and casualties. The carnage which had been wrought by one raider in a few short seconds was unbelievable: 52 people had been killed and another 150 injured. There were at least ten unidentifiable victims among the dead. A rescue party was sent from Bristol to assist with the recovery work. The following morning an additional UXB was discovered propped up on its tail in the corner of the factory, looking for all the world as if someone had left it there during the clearing-up process.

Left:
Interior pictures of Parnall's factory at Yate. Showing (top) turrets under construction and (bottom) fighter wing leading edges.

(via K. Wixey)

The devastation caused by the lone raider that stuck at Parnall's factory in February 1941 is all too plain here.
(via K. Wixy)

The interior of Parnall's factory at Yate after the February 1941 attack.
(via K. Wixey)

The 'blasted' main entrance to the Parnall factory after the attack in February 1941.
(via K. Wixey)

Cyril Barton VC who worked at Parnall's factory before joining the RAFVR.

It had taken some time but the Luftwaffe had finally made use of photographs taken of Yate the month before hostilities had begun. In such a close-knit community the sense of loss was overwhelming. The true casualty figures were not publicised for fear that they would have a detrimental effect on civilian morale. Memorials were later to be unveiled to the dead in Yate churchyard and near the company offices. One of Parnall's former workers was to die in more auspicious circumstances during March 1944. His

name was Cyril Joe Barton and by 1944 he was a Pilot Officer in the RAF, serving with No.578 Squadron. On the night of 30th March his Halifax bomber was bound for Nuremberg when it was attacked by an enemy night fighter. This fighter was later joined by a second and Barton's aircraft was severely mauled in the ensuing conflict. Despite the damage, Barton pressed on to the target and dropped his bombs. On the return flight the aircraft continually lost height as it struggled along on three engines and with holed petrol

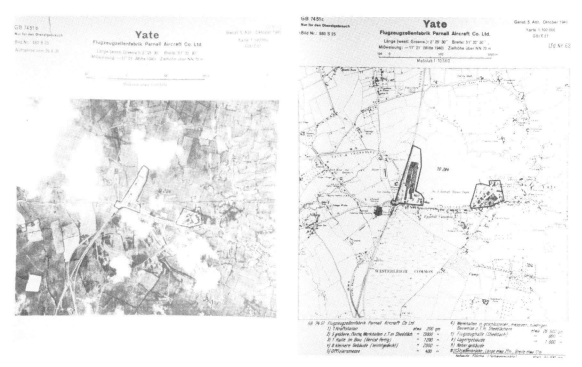

Above are a German target map and photograph (taken October 1940)   *(via K. Wixey)*

Flugzeugzellenfabrik Parnall Aircraft Co. Ltd., Yate (74 51)

Das Werk ist Haupthersteller von „Doppel- und Vierling-MG-Türmen", die u. a. als Heckstände in englische Kampfflugzeuge eingebaut werden. Parnall ist außer der Firma Nash & Thompson, London-Tolworth (78 15, lfd. Nr. 63), der einzige Hersteller dieser Türme, jedoch von wesentlich größerer Leistungsfähigkeit.

Eine Zerstörung des Werkes würde die Kampfflugzeugausbringung stark beeinträchtigen.

Das Werk liegt an der Bahnlinie Bristol—Wickwar, etwa 2 km nördlich der Doppelkreuzung von Westerleigh. An dem Werk zweigt eine Bahnlinie im Bogen nach NW (Thornbury) ab. Unmittelbar am Werk liegt der Flugplatz Yate (10 284).

PARNALL AIRCRAFT FACTORY YATE (7451)

THIS FACTORY IS THE MAIN PRODUCER OF "2 x 4MG TURRETS" WHICH ARE FITTED IN ENGLISH FIGHTER PLANES.

PARNALL IS A SUBSIDIARY OF NASH & THOMPSON LONDON & TOLWORTH (78 15 REF NR. 63) & IS THE ONLY PRODUCER OF THESE TURRETS & ARE ABLE TO PRODUCE IN STILL LARGER QUANTITIES.

TO DESTROY THIS FACTORY WOULD RESTRICT PRODUCTION OF FIGHTER PLANES.

THE FACTORY IS BUILT ALONG THE RAILWAY LINE BRISTOL-WICKWAR APPROX 2 KILOM NORTH OF DOUBLE JUNCTION OF WESTERLEIGH.

ADJOINING THE FACTORY THE RAILWAY LINE BRANCHES OFF TO N.W. (THORNBURY).

ASSEMBLY (SHOPS) AT FACTORY NEAR YATE AIRFIELD (10 284).

TRANSLATION OF GERMAN TEXT.

The Luftwaffe brief on the target together with translation. (Fighter planes is perhaps a poor translation, combat aircraft might be better). Certainly Parnall were producing for bomber aircraft in the main.   *(via K. Wixey)*

tanks. After crossing the coast Barton realised that if the crew did not bale out immediately the aircraft would be too low and it would be impossible for them to jump. He ordered the crew to abandon the aircraft while he maintained it in level flight. By this time the aircraft only had one engine working and Barton gallantly attempted to keep the aircraft aloft and tried to avoid some houses in his path. The aircraft eventually crashed nearby in the colliery yard at Ryhope, Durham. Cyril Barton died in the crash and was later awarded a posthumous Victoria Cross for his conduct that night.

Saturday, 1st March

The brief quiet spell in the county came to an end just after eight in the evening when a number of HE bombs and incendiaries fell in fields near Fairford. Other bombs were reported from Falfield where the Bristol — Gloucester road was blocked. At half-past eight four HE bombs fell between Tytherington and Thornbury near the LMSR branch line. Some cottages were damaged and one person was injured. Seven HE bombs also fell at Wick within the same time frame and over 100 incendiaries fell nearby at Cold Ashton.

Sunday, 2nd March

One HE bomb and several incendiaries were reported from Bibury during the early evening. A single HE bomb also fell in the Knowle division of Bristol some time later.

Monday, 3rd March

There was an evening attack on Cardiff and for a change it seemed that none of the stragglers would unload on Gloucestershire. However, the day was to end with a bang, when seven HE bombs fell at Flax Bourton a few minutes before midnight. They came down in fields between the Jubilee Inn and Cambridge Batch, causing damage to telephone wires.

Tuesday, 4th March

At half-past midnight 20 incendiaries were dropped in fields near Brockworth. Local ARP personnel quickly dealt with the resultant fires.

Cardiff was raided once again during the evening. Nearer home incendiary bombs were reported from Sidcot and Oakridge Hill. Fire bombs were also reported somewhat further south at Banwell, five miles east of Weston-super-Mare.

Thursday, 6th March

At ten minutes past seven in the evening seven HE bombs fell in the Clifton division of Bristol, demolishing 15 houses and damaging a gas main. One person was killed and a further 15 injured. Over 30 people had to be evacuated, an undertaking not to be recommended in the wintry weather. At about the same time an enemy raider strafed the hangars at Filton airfield. An unknown type of enemy aircraft was also reported to have struck cables in the Bristol area although it did not crash as a result.

Further south in Dorset, Frampton, Winterborne Abbas and Maiden Newton were all subjected to machine-gun attacks during the evening. At Maiden Newton, north-west of Dorchester, a train was strafed and though there were no casualties the guards van received some extra ventilation, courtesy of the Luftwaffe.

Friday, 7th March

Another cold day with a good deal of low cloud, and the Luftwaffe was not slow to take advantage of this. In an apparent attempt to follow up the success of the 27th a single enemy raider attacked the Parnall factory at Yate. It was just after two in the afternoon when the raider burst out of the low cloud over the already devastated factory. He machine-gunned the plant and dropped a number of HE bombs.

Following the previous raid, plans had been made to disperse the work force and the machinery, but the operation was still some way from completion. Three people were killed and a further 20 injured. As a result of this additional damage production came to a complete standstill and the total dispersal of the factory was ordered. Much of the equipment was moved to Boulton Mills in Dursley and convoys of lorries were to be in evidence over the next few days as they carried machinery, spare parts and so on to the new location. The bombing also caused some damage to railway signals and telephone wires near to the factory.

Sunday, 9th March

An enemy aircraft was reported circling the Gloucester area and was later said to have returned to base via the Isle of Wight. There was also a report of damage later in the evening from Wotton-under-Edge, where slates had been ripped off the roofs of several council houses. The damage appeared to have been caused by the cable of an escaped balloon.

Monday, 10th March

There was a heavy fall of snow during the night and the day was extremely cold. There was a report of an enemy aircraft south of Weston-super-Mare during the evening but no activity ensued within the Gloucestershire borders.

Tuesday, 11th March

The cold weather persisted throughout the day, although the Luftwaffe did its best to warm things up during the evening. At thirty-four minutes past nine several HE bombs were dropped in the Chacely — Tirley area; a school and a number of houses were damaged. At about ten o'clock around 100 incendiary bombs fell at South Cerney and Condicote. At the latter location two HE bombs were also dropped. Greenhouses were damaged and several scrub fires were started. An anti-aircraft shell caused damage to telephone wires at Broad Oak shortly after eleven o'clock. To the east, Abingdon airfield in Oxfordshire was put out of action for some time during the evening after being hit by 16 HE bombs.

Wednesday, 12th March

During the early hours of the morning it was reported that 20 plus HE bombs had fallen along the eastern bank of the Gloucester — Sharpness canal near to Moreton Valence. It is possible that these bombs were dropped by an errant He.111 of KG.100 that claimed to have attacked Bristol from 3,800 feet just before ten o'clock the previous evening.

At Kingston Deverill near Warminster in Wiltshire a Ju.88 was brought down at quarter to ten in the evening. Two of the crew members were found dead and a third was captured.

Thursday, 13th March

Bristol, Shirehampton and Avonmouth came under attack with HE bombs and incendiaries during the evening. At Brentry 18 houses were seriously damaged and 30 others suffered to a lesser extent. Five people were injured in the attack. A number of incendiaries fell in the dock area of Avonmouth but they were soon dealt with.

Friday, 14th March

For the most part it was a quiet day but a flurry of activity occurred towards evening. At Rodley, south-west of Westbury-on-Severn, a single HE bomb came to earth right on ten o'clock. Other HE bombs were reported around Windrush airfield in the eastern part of Gloucestershire. Reports also came in of an HE bomb at Arlingham, eight miles from Gloucester, and of a further six bombs at Barnwood, again in the Gloucester area.

The evening also brought a welcome boost to morale when a number of people saw an enemy raider brought down at Horseshoe Farm, Milbury Heath, Falfield. Flying Officer Keith Geddes of 604 Squadron was guided onto a Heinkel bomber of KG.55 as it was heading north. He closed in and attacked the enemy aircraft in the area of Codrington to the south of Yate and the noise of his cannon and machine-gun fire could be clearly head on the ground. Shortly afterwards there was a bright flash, once again clearly discerned from the ground against the backdrop of the night sky. Heinkel He.111P G1 + IP (Werk No.3096) broke up in the air after the explosion and came down in fragments. Wreckage was strewn over a large area. Several machine-guns and UXBs were found scattered around the bulk of the wreckage that had come down at Horseshoe Farm. The crew were all

Sergeant Bernard Gannon (left) an A. I. Operator of 604 Squadron Middle Wallop who together with his pilot P/O Keith Geddes brought down a Heinkel at Falfield during the late evening of March 14th 1941.
(Severnside Aviation Society Collection)

killed and were later buried at Bristol's Greenbank cemetery. They were: Oblt. Hensche, the pilot, Fw. Harter, the observer, Fw. Kruger, the radio operator, and Fw. Smolonski, the flight engineer.

Saturday, 15th March

Alerts were very much the thing as the new day dawned although the real excitement was just over the border in Wiltshire. At twenty-five minutes past midnight Lyneham and nearby Christian Malford were strafed. Four HE bombs were also dropped, the obvious target being the airfield at Lyneham. The attack was a waste of effort, however, because the damage caused was minimal.

Sunday, 16th March

During the evening the Luftwaffe began a two-phase attack on Bristol. The first phase was led by aircraft of KG.26, and the second by KG.100. German propaganda was later to claim a devastating attack on the dock area. However, the bulk of the bombs fell in the mainly residential districts in the centre of the city, between Stapleton Road and Clifton Down. Over 8,000 houses were damaged and 416 were completely destroyed. Casualties were heavy: 229 men, women and children killed and a further 422 suffered injury.

One of the main tragedies occurred when a bomb scored a direct hit on the crypt of St. Barnabas Church where 300 people were sheltering. The Wotton AFS team, called in to assist, were involved in extracting the bodies from the wreckage. This one team alone recovered the bodies of 27 people. It had been a night of unparalleled terror in the centre of the city and the wave of destruction had once again spread outwards. HE and incendiary bombs were dropped at Winterbourne, Oldland Common, Warmley, Severn Beach, Cold Aston and Kingswood, where two people were killed and six injured. A number of fires were started by incendiaries in the aero-engine factory at the latter location but they were quickly put out. Four HE and some incendiary bombs came down in fields at Pilning.

Monday, 17th March

The attacks on Bristol continued into the early hours; in fact, alerts were still in force as late as half-past three in the morning as enemy aircraft were still very much in evidence.

Wednesday, 19th March

At approximately half-past two in the morning Filton Centre began to track "Raid 335". The enemy aircraft circled the Gloucester area for almost an hour and three-quarters. It is possible that the raider was attempting to find the GAC factory at Brockworth/Hucclecote as a number of bombs were dropped in the Brockworth area at around quarter to five. The raider then set off towards Cardiff and was later plotted returning home via Weston and Swanage.

At a few minutes before midnight half-a-dozen HE bombs were dropped near Aldsworth. It is likely that the intended target was Windrush airfield nearby.

Friday, 21st March

A single enemy aircraft circled Bristol during the

day but no bombing took place. Throughout the week a stream of lorries had been on the move in the southern part of the county between Yate and Dursley. The heavily-laden convoys were carrying machinery from the ill-starred Parnall factory to its new home at Boulton Mills in Dursley.

Wednesday, 26th March

Enemy aircraft were active in the south-west during the daylight hours. Abbots Bickington in Devon was strafed by a low-flying aircraft at half-past one in the afternoon. Wilton in nearby Wiltshire also came in for a machine-gun attack at lunchtime. The single raider not only strafed the town but also unloaded two HE bombs on the railway line towards Dinton. Fortunately, the bombs failed to explode but a number of vehicles and railway rolling stock were damaged by bullets. The Westland factory at Yeovil was also attacked by a single Dornier Do.17 during the lunch period. One person was killed and several others were injured. Inside the Gloucestershire borders another lone raider dived out of low cloud and strafed aircraft on the ground at Babdown Farm airfield.

Gloucester itself came under attack during the day when four HE bombs fell in the vicinity of the GWR and LMSR railway station. Six people were killed and 28 injured. A number of houses were demolished and there was minor damage to railway rolling stock and a signal box. The enemy raider was cursed roundly in a foreign tongue by one particular group of railway passengers. Trapped on board one of the trains that came under attack were Polish airmen from 307 Polish Nightfighter Squadron. The unit was in the process of transferring to Exeter where it would provide a nightfighter defence for the South-West. the rage and impotence felt by the Poles as they sat through the raid was made worse by the fact that two of the bombs dropped, fell quite close to their train. Such events only hardened the resolve of the Poles and the debt would be repaid many times over during the months that followed. The all-black Defiant and later Beaufighter aircraft used by 307 squadron were to account for more than their fair share of raiders.

Saturday, 29th March

Shortly before nine o'clock in the evening eleven Heinkels of KG.100 approached Bristol — Avonmouth, followed by a wave of bombers. The "Fire Raisers" got to work quickly, so much so that the last aircraft had simply to bomb the rapidly spreading fires below. One of the Heinkels dropped its bombs with great accuracy on the storage tanks of the Anglo-American Oil Company. The attack was carried out visually from a height of 3,700 metres and three of the tanks were set alight. The resultant conflagration raged out of control into Sunday. At Shirehampton six people were killed and six more injured when bombs struck the police station and a Salvation Army hall. As always, the bombing spread but without a great deal of effect. At Kingswood ten HE bombs came down in open fields, killing and injuring a number of cattle. Other HE and incendiary bombs were dropped at Iron Acton, Alveston, Pilning, Hallen, Chavenage and North Cerney.

Tuesday, 3rd April

Air Raid Warning Yellow was implemented in the Bristol area at thirty-four minutes past eight in the evening and was followed by a red warning 19 minutes later. At twenty-five minutes past nine clusters of yellow flares began to appear over the city. Once again, the illuminations were provided by KG.100, ten of the unit's Heinkels leading in over 70 bombers. At around half-past nine the electricity failed in the Knowle division and St. George's. Minutes later bombs began to fall at Lawrence Weston Farm. The Canning Factory at Avonmouth was hit and a fire started. Shortly afterwards the National Smelting Company was also hit. Incendiaries caused a fire in a wheat store at the Royal Edward Docks and a burning gas main at Coombe Lane, Westbury-on-Trym, flared into the night sky, beckoning to the raiders with a fiery finger. Damage was caused to residential areas and roads in the Henleaze, Southmead, Bishopston, Westbury, Clevedon and Patchway districts. Other bombs were reported from Anderton, Wilk near Downend, Cinderford, Cold Aston, Littleton-on-Severn, Yate and Woolaston. Two bombs were also reported from Moreton-in-Marsh at twenty five past ten. They fell two hundred yards apart on the north west side of the airfield and brought down nearby telephone wires.

Friday, 4th April

By the time that the all-clear had sounded in Bristol approximately 1,000 houses had been damaged, 22 people were dead and 56 injured. In the Clevedon district alone 48 HE bombs had fallen. Bomb disposal squads were to be kept busy for some time dealing with a large number of UXBs strewn across the city.

A number of raiders were shot down, including one that fell to the guns of a Beaufighter of 604 Squadron, flown by Flying Officer Crew and Sergeant Guthrie. Heinkel He.111H (Werk No.3595) of KG.26 was about to relase its bombs over Bristol when Flying Officer Crew attacked. Crew aimed his first burst with deadly accuracy and the bullets smashed through the perspex nose of the Heinkel into the cockpit area, killing one of the crew members. Other bullets struck the starboard engine, setting it on fire. The enemy aircraft dived away and an attempt was made to jettison the bombload. It would seem, however, that a number of the incendiaries in the bomb bay had been ignited by machine-gun bullets and within seconds the stricken Heinkel was rocked by explosions. The starboard wing became a mass of flame and as the aircraft plunged earthwards the crew took to their parachutes. The flaming aircraft came down at Hewish in Somerset and two of the crew members came down safely, whilst a third was killed when his parachute failed to open. The fourth airman, Gefr. Mathias von Kaldenkerken, who had been killed in the initial attack, was found in the wreckage and was later buried at Weston-super-Mare.

German gunners peer out through the cockpit canopy ever alert to the possibility of fighter attack.

(Bundesarchiv)

Shortly after nine o'clock in the evening incendiaries began to fall in the Shirehampton area and Avonmouth docks. A few minutes later, yellow-white flares were also released over Avonmouth as target markers. By midnight HE bombs had again fallen on the National Smelting Works, damaging offices and adjacent roads. The railway line near Royal Edward Dock was also damaged. Providence intervened at twenty to twelve when an incendiary bomb fell on some

Shell-Mex tanks but failed to start a fire. Bombs were scattered far and wide across the county during the evening. There were reports of HE bombs from Elkstone, Littleton-on-Severn, Guiting Power, Hawkesbury Upton, Severn Beach and Batch, near Warmley. Two HE bombs were also dropped near the Speech House Hotel between Cinderford and Coleford, injuring two people. A single incendiary was reported from Awkley. Quite a few of the bombs intended for Bristol and Avonmouth were dropped on a Starfish Decoy site near Lulsgate Bottom to the south of Bristol. These decoys were elaborately laid out patterns of pyrotechnics that would be ignited to attract enemy bombers. From the air the burning incendiaries resembled an urban street pattern.

Monday, 7th April

After a brief lull the enemy returned during the evening. Bristol came under attack from about 20 bombers. The sirens began to wail just after nine o'clock and by half-past ten HE bombs had fallen at a number of locations. The bombing was mainly concentrated in the Kingsweston, Horfield, Henbury and Stoke Bishop areas. One of the bombs created a large crater in Filton Avenue and fractured a 16 in water main, causing leaking water to flood the area. A single HE bomb fell by Old Inn Cottage in Kingsweston Road and overhead cables were damaged. Other HE bombs were reported in the Shirehampton and Clifton districts. The casualty list shows no fatalities in the city but nine people were injured.

The rest of the county did not remain unscathed, however; two HE bombs fell at Frampton-on-Severn. Houses were damaged at Coaley Junction, south-west of Stroud, when a single bomb was dropped. Five HE bombs also damaged cottages at Whitecroft. Incendiary bombs were also reported from Absom and in the wooded area around Staunton. As estimated three hundred plus incendiaries were dropped in the latter instance, setting fire to some six acres of woodland and the roof of a local barn. Several bombs were dropped at Shepherds Patch near Slimbridge by an enemy aircraft, apparently being pursued by a nightfighter.

Tuesday, 8th April

Bombs were still falling on Gloucestershire just after midnight, three HE coming down at Elkstone. During the night four more HE bombs

were reported from Cirencester and a single bomb fell to the south-east of Warmley, killing and injuring a number of cattle.

Wednesday, 9th April

Seven HE bombs descended on Woodmancote at half-past one in the morning, damaging a house. A single bomb also fell at Swindon Village, near Cheltenham and three others were reported from the Brockworth area.

At twenty-five past one in the afternoon a UXB left over from the night of the 7th exploded in Bristol. Fortunately, no real damage was done. At around eleven o'clock in the evening a number of incendiaries fell on Wick Rissington and at about the same time Avonmouth also received a visitation from the Luftwaffe. At least one Heinkel of KG.100 was in the first wave of raiders, dropping its bombs from 3,800 metres. The crew claimed to have destroyed a barrage balloon and reported two medium-sized fires in the target area. During the subsequent attacks the Avonmouth cinema was destroyed and a shelter was hit. As the attack progressed the bombing spread into Bristol proper: Union Street, Newfoundland Street and Broadmead were all hit. Pragnall's Paintworks was set on fire as was Watkins' furniture shop. Five peope were killed and eleven injured in these attacks.

Thursday, 10th April

The previous evening's marauders were still much in evidence as the new day began. Between half-past twelve and quarter to one in the morning clutches of HE bombs fell at Tunley and Iron Acton, whilst a singleton fell in a field at Edgeworth. The Tunley Farm bombs also caused damage to the adjoining King's House Farm. The lip of one of the bomb craters at King's House Farm was only inches from the farmhouse wall. The farmer, sleeping after an evening spent imbibing home-brewed beer, did not hear the explosion. Incredibly, he was awakened by the sound of china falling from the mantlepiece in the aftermath. A barn was damaged at Tunley Farm and one of the bombs enlarged a nearby pond. The only casualties in the incident were some chickens.

All was quiet until five minutes to seven in the evening when a delayed action bomb exploded at Whitecroft. It was probably a leftover from the raid on the 7th. At half-past ten several HE bombs were dropped at Hampnett, near to the

Northleach landing ground. At Salperton at about the same time a hayrick and a house were set on fire by incendiaries. Something like 1,000 incendiaries fell at Northleach at half-past eleven. They were scattered over an area of almost a mile.

Friday, 11th April

Scattered bombing continued into the early morning of Good Friday. HE and incendiary bombs were reported from Mangotsfield, Coombe Hill, Wick, Mickleton and the Severn Bridge where the only casualty was an injured sheep. Two oil bombs fell on open ground near Churchdown and burnt themselves out. Buckland, Purton and Bagstone also came under attack. Two bombs fell at Oldborough Farm, Moreton-in-Marsh, at three o'clock in the morning; fortunately, one of them failed to explode.

At quarter to ten in the evening the sirens growled into life and howled their message of warning across Bristol yet again. It was a bright, moonlit night and 150 plus enemy aircraft were heading for the city with evil intent. Within half an hour incendiary bombs were clattering across the rooftops. The attack appeared to be carried out in two distinct phases, the first ending around midnight. Portishead was also attacked by a smaller group of raiders. The first bombs released over Bristol came down in the Central division and Purton Road areas. Incendiaries were everywhere and fires broke out almost immediately in the Cotham Park area. The fire bombs were widely scattered, having come down on Bath Buildings, Counterslip Tramway Power Station, St. Paul's Church, Horfield Rectory, the Royal Infirmary, Odeon Cinema and Colston Works, plus numerous other locations by the end of the day. HE bombs followed the incendiaries and many houses were damaged or demolished. The power station on the docks at Portishead had a lucky escape when two HE bombs ended up on a coal dump next door. It was later reported that one of the raiders had been shot down by a 307 Squadron nightfighter between Shaftesbury and Yeovil, a fitting revenge for those members of the squadron which had been trapped on the train in Gloucester on 26th March.

Saturday, 12th April

By the time the all-clear sounded at fifty-two minutes past three in the morning the city had suffered badly. Major fires had broken out at Colston Girls' School and the Cheltenham Road Library. The bulk of the second phase bombing, which had started just after midnight, had been concentrated in the city centre, Bedminster, Knowle, Hotwells and Filton areas. Many private homes and business premises had been damaged, mainly by fire. Even after the flames had been brought under control a pall of smoke still hung over the city and beneath it the citizens began to count the cost: 180 dead and another 382 injured. The anti-aircraft defences had worked flat out throughout the attacks, expending over six and a half thousand shells. Some bombing was reported from further afield: three HE bombs had been dropped on Keynsham and two others had fallen at Wick, damaging houses and a church.

Sunday, 13th April

At ten minutes to three in the morning a UXB that had come down the previous day at Charlton Tunnel near Filton, exploded.

Monday, 14th April

Some 25 HE bombs were dropped on Fairford at quarter past two in the morning. Slight damage was caused to a road and some nearby buildings.

Tuesday, 15th April

In the late evening several HE bombs came down in the Blakeney area. An incendiary bomb also came down just to the north-west at Brains Green and one person was slightly injured. More incendiaries and an oil bomb were reported from Farmington.

During the evening Filton Centre began to track an enemy intruder which was designated "Raid 75". This aircraft was later reported as shot down by a Beaufighter of 604 Squadron from Middle Wallop in Hampshire. A number of people in the Coleford area recall hearing gunfire and seeing what was obviously an enemy aircraft being pursued by a nightfighter. The raider was seen to have an engine on fire and appeared to be a "goner". Strangely, there are no reports of a crashed enemy aircraft in local ARP records and the mystery was to be further compounded the following morning.

Wednesday, 16th April

Enemy aircraft were still in the area until half-past four in the morning. A number of incendiaries were dropped during the night near Avonmouth and there was a curious sequel to the "Raid 75" incident of the previous evening.

Mr. Adams, of Clements End near Coleford, who with his wife had heard the unmistakable sounds of aerial combat overhead on Tuesday evening, went out in the morning to his lorry parked nearby and got rather a shock. Lying underneath it was a somewhat apprehensive German airman who had obviously spent a rather uncomfortable night out in the open. Mr. Adams told the airman to come out and, with typical British aplomb, he took the German home and gave him a cup of tea and something to eat. Afterwards the enemy airman was conveyed in Mr. Adams' lorry to Coleford police station and handed over to the authorities. Apparently, three airmen had come down in the woods near Clements End and all of them eventually found themselves under lock and key in Coleford police station. The three were Gefr. August Heffner, Ob.Gefr. Heinrich Schmidt and Uffz. Szatlinski.

Legend has it that one of the locals, who had spent his life in the Forest, was somewhat mystified when he found a strange mass of material and cords hanging in a tree. He took it to a friend's house to see if he knew what it was; he himself had never seen a parachute before in his life.

It would seem that fate dealt somewhat cruelly with the three airmen. Apparently after giving the order to jump, the pilot had managed to get the Heinkel back under control. Presumably the flames extinguished themselves. The aircraft was able to limp back to base in France. It is highly probable that this aircraft from KG.55, was the one attacked by famed night fighter ace John Cunningham in the area of Monmouthshire. He had three combats on the night of the 15/16th and the incident in question is described in the

The remains of shot-down enemy aircraft were collected in huge scrap yards. The materials could be put to good use.

book 'Night Fighter' by C.F. Rawnsley and Robert Wright.

Friday, 18th April
At half-past three in the morning several HE bombs were dropped at Woolaston, some four miles south-west of Lydney.

Saturday, 19th April
Two HE bombs fell at Tidenham, near Chepstow, at four o'clock in the morning. Fortunately, no damage was caused.

Tuesday, 22nd April
Although Gloucestershire was quiet, news filtered through of a heavy attack on Plymouth during the night of 21st/22nd. This was the first of five devastating attacks on the city which were to cause the deaths of 750 people and render a further 30,000 homeless.

Wednesday, 23rd April
Castle Road, Clevedon, was struck by a parachute mine just after midnight. Three people were injured and another was trapped for some time beneath rubble. Further south at Weston-in-Gordano a number of HE bombs fell at twenty minutes past twelve in the morning. No damage or casualties were reported.

Saturday, 26th April
Shortly after half-past ten and again at eleven o'clock in the evening incendiary bombs were dropped at Brockworth. Two houses and a garage were damaged and a fireman was subsequently injured.

Tuesday, 29th April
Two HE bombs fell in open fields at St. Anne's, Bristol, at twenty-five minutes to ten in the evening.

Thursday, 1st May
At twenty-four minutes past eleven in the evening several HE bombs fell at Tickenham junction on the Failand to Nailsea road in the Clevedon area.

Friday, 2nd May
During the night many people in the Dursley area had heard bursts of cannon and machine-gun fire overhead and had seen tracer flashing across the sky. It later transpired that a Beaufighter had

been in hot pursuit of an enemy raider. Whether the combat ended in victory for the nightfighter or not, there is no record of an enemy aircraft coming down in Gloucestershire. A large number of empty cannon shell cases were picked up in the Nympsfield area in the morning.

Saturday, 3rd May

HE bombs were reported from Olveston and Breakoldown during the late evening. Some slight damage was caused to a house and electricity cables. The Bristol area also came under attack just after half-past eleven when incendiary bombs were dropped at Knowle, Hanham, Hallen and further afield at Pucklechurch. Filton station had a near miss when two HE bombs fell in fields nearby. Telephone wires were damaged and several houses were reported on fire on the Patchway estate.

Sunday, 4th May

Five HE bombs, one oil bomb and a number of incendiaries fell in Highnam Woods at quarter to twelve in the evening. Incendiary bombs were also dropped at Doynton and Wick to the east of Bristol.

Monday, 5th May

Two UXBs were reported from Hawcross, north-east of Newent, during the early hours and a further two were reported from Upleadon, two miles east of Newent during the evening.

Tuesday, 6th May

Incendiaries and HE bombs were reported in the Northleach — Windrush area during the early morning.

Wednesday, 7th May

During the early morning a number of incendiaries were reported to have been dropped on the dispersals at Moreton-in-Marsh airfield.

Thursday, 8th May

Five Heinkels of KG.100 made an unscheduled visit to Bristol during the early morning, arriving overhead at half-past one. Due to bad weather they had turned away from their primary target which was Liverpool. The aircraft bombed the city from between 3,500 and 5,000 metres with the usual assortment of HE and incendiary bombs. Most of the hardware was reported to have fallen in the south-western part of the city and the crews observed a number of fires as they left the target

area. Some time earlier two HE bombs had been dropped to the east of Hicks Common, near Winterbourne. The resultant crater was 30 to 40 feet deep and 20 feet across. At quarter-past two in the morning an HE bomb fell in a field at Frampton Cotterell, shattering the windows of a nearby bungalow. Incendiaries were also reported near Moreton-in-Marsh airfield.

Saturday, 10th May

At ten minutes past one in the morning four HE bombs were dropped at Brockworth and five minutes later eleven more fell at Pirley. No major damage was caused in either incident.

Sunday, 11th May

A single HE bomb was reported from Naunton early in the morning.

Monday, 12th May

Eight HE bombs and one oil bomb fell at West Littleton, south-east of Chipping Sodbury, during the early morning. A cottage suffered slight damage and telephone cables were brought down. A large number of bombs also came down around Marshfield, causing little damage. Further bombs were reported from the Bristol area near Portishead railway tunnel at ten minutes to two in the morning. Two others came down at Shirehampton, damaging power cables. Three HE bombs also fell in fields at Easton-in-Gordano, south of Bristol.

Saturday, 17th May

A single HE bomb was dropped near Postlip paper mill, not far from Winchcombe, at half-past two in the morning.

Sunday, 25th May

During the early morning two HE bombs fell at Wotton. One fell close to the Masonic Hall, much to the consternation of two soldiers within. Many nearby houses had their windows shattered and several roofs were damaged. The second bomb fell on a farmhouse at Hillesley, causing considerable damage.

Friday, 30th May

At half-past midnight four HE bombs fell amongst cattle in open fields near Winford, Bristol. A number of the beasts were killed and injured.

Saturday, 31st May

The Clifton and Shirehampton districts of Bristol were attacked during the early hours. The AFS substation at Shirehampton was hit. Two people were killed and twelve others injured. Two nearby houses were also damaged. Ten minutes afterwards a house at Hotwells, Clifton, received a direct hit. Three people were trapped and many houses in the locality were damaged. The main Westbury road was closed because of a UXB. At the same time, further south bombs were falling on Weston-super-Mare. Several HE bombs came down on the Promenade. Windows were broken and a gas main was split apart and burst into flames.

Sunday, 1st June

Manchester was to be the main target of the evening for the Luftwaffe so Gloucestershire gained a brief respite. ARP and Civil Defence personnel were made to feel the pinch during the day. It was announced that clothing and footwear were to be rationed on a points system: 16 points for a raincoat, four points for a petticoat and two points for a pair of stockings, among other things. Each individual was to be allotted a total of 66 points a year for this purpose.

Monday, 2nd June

Approximately 500 incendiaries were dropped in open country between Standish village church and Little Haresfield at twenty minutes past one in the morning. Some slight damage was caused to the roofs of houses in the vicinity. A few minutes later three HE bombs were dropped on Mickleton just north of Chipping Campden and several houses were damaged. Some time later, just after ten past three, 200 incendiaries came down in fields at Abson, south-east of Pucklechurch.

Thursday, 5th June

Nine HE bombs were dropped on the Upper Clevedon — Bristol road at Tyntesfield at twenty-five minutes past two in the morning. Some houses were damaged and telephone wires were brought down.

Saturday, 7th June

No bombs fell on Gloucestershire but a good deal of heavy rain did. In many areas of the county it was to be the last rain for more than five weeks.

Thursday, 12th June

Many enemy aircraft were active over the south and east of the country during the early hours. Most of Gloucestershire escaped unscathed; Bristol, however, did not. At four in the morning a parachute mine fell on Victoria Park, Bedminster, damaging hundreds of houses and the mains services. At least 15 people were killed and over 60 injured. Bedminster signal box was damaged and Willway Street, Almorah Street and St. John's Lane were blocked.

Sunday, 15th June

The inhabitants of Painswick had a rude awakening during the early morning when bombs began to rain down on the village. Poultry Court, the home of Mr. Lewis, a house in Friday Street and another in Tibbiwell Lane all received direct hits. Four houses were destroyed, seven were badly damaged and 35 were damaged to some degree. Two people, both evacuees, were killed and ten others were injured. Electricity and telegraph cables were damaged which only added to the confusion.

Eight Heinkels of KG.100 reported attacking Filton between one o'clock and twenty to two in the morning. Their aim was less than accurate since no bombs were reported to have fallen on the airfield itself. However, 15 HE bombs were reported to have been dropped at Olveston, killing one man and damaging property. The Tockington to Pilning road was blocked and telephone wires were brought down. Eight HE bombs fell just to the east of the GWR line near Stoke Gifford at one in the morning. Three more fell at Frenchay, damaging 50 houses and injuring one person. Almondsbury also reported six HE at three minutes past one and a similar number of bombs were dropped at Shepperdine, north of Thornbury, at twenty minutes to two.

Nearby Wiltshire also came in for some attention during the hours of darkness. A number of HE bombs were dropped at Wroughton and others fell at Tootshill Farm, Lydiard Tregose. One of the enemy aircraft that had attempted to attack Filton earlier was reported to have been brought down in Dorset. Heinkel He.111H 6N + DK (Werk No.3248) was shot down in flames by a nightfighter.

During the evening the Stroud MP, Mr. Robert Perkins, visited Painswick to meet both Civil Defence personnel and victims of the raid earlier in the day.

Tuesday, 17th June

Four HE bombs were dropped in the grounds of Oaksey Hall just over the Wiltshire border at half-past one in the morning. At around the same time Gloucestershire also began to receive some attention. At Badgeworth 22 HE bombs fell, mainly in open fields but damage was caused to the Cheltenham — Churchdown GWR line. It was to take several hours' hard effort before single line working could be introduced. A house and outbuildings were also damaged. At much the same time 30 HE bombs were dropped at Brockworth near a balloon site. Damage was caused to a house and one person was injured. Nine HE were dropped at Gotherington and an unknown number were reported from both Ashchurch and Bishop's Cleeve. Some damage was caused to farm buildings at Prestbury when three HE bombs fell there at twenty past one. Seventeen HE also fell at Nailsea, demolishing a bungalow near Station road. One person was killed and two injured.

Two of the aircraft sent to attack Brockworth were shot down within 20 minutes of each other. The first of the ill-fated pair to be dealt with was Heinkel He.111H2 6N+CH (Werk No.5462). It was attacked by a 604 Squadron Beaufighter, crewed by Pilot Officer Gossland and Sergeant Phillips. After being vectored onto the bomber, Gossland closed in to within 120 feet before opening fire. After a short burst the Heinkel began to burn. Gossland closed in a second time and hit the doomed bomber with a second accurate burst. Almost immediately it began to go down out of control. The Heinkel crashed to earth in a welter of broken and flaming wreckage at Stourton Towers, near Mere in Wiltshire. The crew, Ofw. Ittner, Uffz. Koster, Gefr. Porada, Uffz. Berwig and Gefr. Keul, were all killed.

The second raider fell to the guns of another Beaufighter, although in this instance the nightfighter was from "A" Flight of 68 Squadron and it was crewed by Flight Lieutenant Pain and Flying Officer Davies. Pain chased the Heinkel for some time before finally closing to about 150 feet. He was behind the bomber and some 20 feet below when he opened fire. The bomber exploded and began to disintegrate as it tumbled earthwards. This raider was Heinkel He.111H3 6N+CL (Werk No.5633) and the only crew member to escape with his life was the pilot, Fw. Georg Deininger. Lady Luck was certainly keeping an eye on Deininger for it was he that had survived a close shave on the 23rd December 1940, following a raid on Bristol. He came down by parachute in a cornfield near Edington in Wiltshire and the aircraft crashed nearby at Bratton. Deininger reached the ground minus a flying boot and with burns to his face and hands. After treatment in Westbury hospital he was taken to the local police station to await interrogation. The other crew members all perished; they were Oblt. Pohner, Fw. Ott, Fw. Hertzberg and Fw. Engels. Valuable target maps and papers dealing with Luftwaffe navigational beacons were picked up from both wrecks.

Sunday, 22nd June

Ten HE bombs were reported from Barrow Elm Farm at quarter to one in the morning. Crops and windows were damaged but there were no human losses.

Tuesday, 1st July

Two parachute mines were dropped at Winford, six miles south-west of Bristol, during the early morning. One house was destroyed, a bungalow damaged and two people injured.

Saturday, 5th July

A house was demolished and many others were damaged when two HE bombs fell in the Central division of Bristol at five minutes past two in the morning. Two people were killed, roads were blocked and water and gas mains were ruptured.

Wednesday, 9th July

Shortly before two o'clock in the morning several bombs, identified as HE, were dropped around the airfield at Hullavington in Wiltshire. However, at least one report suggests that the two items that fell at Littleton Drew to the west of Hullavington were, in fact, landmines.

Saturday, 12th July

At twenty minutes to seven in the evening a lone enemy raider, a low-flying Heinkel, struck at Staverton airfield between Cheltenham and Gloucester. Mr. E.O. Edwards, Chief Flight Engineer of the Rotol Test Flight at Staverton, had just run his car up to the pumps at Chambers garage, when he heard the sound of unfamiliar engines. He could not quite believe what he was seeing as the Heinkel passed low overhead. Within minutes the crump of exploding bombs could be heard from the airfield. The raider dropped three HE bombs, one of which clipped the end of the Rotol Test Flight hangar. The other two fell amongst barrack huts used by the RAF personnel and a number of airmen were killed. During the night there was a heavy fall of rain, very welcome after five weeks of drought.

Thursday, 24th July

A strange event occurred at twenty past six in the morning at Lulsgate Bottom airfield south of Bristol. An enemy aircraft, a Junkers Ju.88, apparently short of fuel, approached the airfield, lowered its undercarriage and landed. The German crew were taken into custody and the aircraft commandeered. It was later flown to Farnborough for tests before joining No.1426 Enemy Aircraft Flight some months later.

Wednesday, 6th August

The Home Office issued Home Security Circular 174/1941, announcing the formation of the Fire Guard. It was also considered that there was a serious threat to crops at harvest time. It was quite possible that the enemy would attempt to set fire to wheat and other cereals. Accordingly, hundreds of people were enlisted for crop fire-fighting and watching, and as a result besoms for fire-fighting were to be in great demand. It proved an unnecessary step as the harvest period of 1941 turned out to be one of the wettest on record and the enemy made no attempt to fire cereal fields.

Wednesday, 13th August

Approximately 100 small bombs of the anti-personnel type fell in open fields three miles north-west of Lechlade half-an-hour after midnight.

Saturday, 6th September

Ten HE bombs fell at Courtfield alongside the Tetbury — Cirencester road at ten minutes past eleven in the evening. Some 30 houses were damaged but there were no human casualties.

Monday, 14th September

On this date the first registration of men for Fire Guard duty was held.

Monday, 24th November

Weston-super-Mare was rocked by a huge explosion during the early hours. A suspect parachute mine had fallen at about eight o'clock the previous evening between New Pier and Knightstone Baths and had lain undiscovered in the mud. When it exploded 37 houses were damaged.

Tuesday, 25th November

Two HE bombs were dropped near Hawkesbury Upton at twenty past seven in the evening but they caused little real damage. Five minutes later a parachute mine fell only 30 yards away from Desert Cottage at Oldbury Naite, north-west of Thornbury. The cottage was virtually destroyed and Mr. Jesse Screen was killed. His son-in-law, Mr. Hall, was badly injured and his wife severely shocked. Three children in the cottage were injured and a fourth was badly shocked. A barn was set on fire and a hayrick that had been covered with oil from the mine later burst into flames, apparently because pieces of the mine were embedded in it.

1942

Thursday, 5th February

On this date all personnel over the age of 18 in the Civil Defence Services were "frozen" in their particular service. This meant that they could not resign except for exceptional reasons and that they were liable to do 48 hours duty every four weeks.

Friday, 6th March

New regulations were brought in to permit Regional Commissioners to declare a Civil Defence Region an "Operational Area". In effect, this allowed the Commissioner to conscript anybody and everybody for work dealing with the results of enemy action. He could not, however, conscript people for combat duties.

Saturday, 4th April

At least two, probably three, raiders carried out a daring and devastating attack on the Gloster Aircraft Co.'s works and the surrounding area of Brockworth — Hucclecote during the late afternoon and evening. It was Easter weekend and the day shift was just leaving the factory at a few minutes after four-thirty when the enemy struck first. Many people were out in the open, boarding buses. Six bombs were dropped and one of them scored a direct hit on a bus in the car park. The carnage was terrible and the whole area was showered with glass and debris from the explosions. A second attack took place at twenty-five past five, and the probable third raider attacked at ten past six. In one incident a house near the factory was hit and all five occupants, including an eleven-month-old baby, were killed. The raiders made off into the low cloud layer that was covering the county and apparently got away without a scratch. The official figures show that ten men, five women and three children were killed. Another 150-200 people suffered varying degrees of injury, some requiring hospitalisation.

A good deal of damage was done to the factory itself. No.1 Canteen was wrecked, as was No.8 shop, and there was blast damage to the machine shop. A block-house was also destroyed and the fires that were raging in the factory were not brought under control until shortly before half-past eight in the evening. Two houses to the east of the aerodrome were also damaged in the third attack.

Friday, 17th April

Just before three in the morning an HE bomb fell into the mud on the foreshore at Avonmouth Docks. A second bomb demolished the Merchant Seamen's Defence Equipment Office, causing two slight casualties. Another damaged a hydrant and electric cables at Royal Edward Dock Passenger Station. By a strange twist of fate parts of the Station were being demolished prior to the attack; thus the Luftwaffe's skill in 'demolition' was put to beneficial use for a change.

Saturday, 25th April

A few minutes after eleven o'clock in the evening bombs began to fall on the Bedminster, Brislington and Knowle districts of Bristol. Major fires broke out at the Smith's Crisp Factory, a timber yard and the Top Dog Factory. Gas, water and electricity services were seriously disrupted but everything was repaired and working again within 48 hours. A Warden's Post received a direct hit, but incredibly there were no casualties. However, in the city as a whole 16 people were killed and 28 injured. In addition some 320 were rendered homeless. A total of 1,200 houses were damaged in the attacks. Two HE bombs fell near the National Smelting Company's premises at Avonmouth and HE bombs were also reported from Dudmore Farm, Westerleigh, six miles north-east of Bristol. At Hanham Green to the east of Bristol several HE bombs damaged electricity cables. Other HE bombs came down at Coalpit Heath, Rock Park, Marshfield, Hunter's

Hall and Horton, north-east of Chipping Sodbury.

Further to the south, Bath, the architectural treasure of the South-West, was struck a severe blow by the black-crossed predators of the Luftwaffe. Shortly after eleven o'clock, just as Bristol was coming under attack, the enemy appeared over the city. Incendiaries showered down, followed by the inevitable HE bombs. Train services were disrupted and within minutes over 20 fires had broken out. LMS railway buildings were hit heavily. The passenger station, offices and signal boxes were all damaged. The Bath Goods Shed was hit and 18 trucks loaded with coal were set on fire and burnt out completely. The Central Telephone Exchange was hit and had to be evacuated. The main power station was hit but managed to maintain output. It was estimated that over 50 HE bombs and 1,000 incendiaries were dropped on the city. Casualty figures given two days later state that 50 people were killed and another 200 injured. However, later unofficial reports put the number of fatalities much higher. Rescue and salvage teams were despatched to the city from many parts of Gloucestershire. This attack was one of the so-called "Baedeker Raids", apparently launched against Britain's cathedral cities Exeter, York, Norwich and Bath as reprisals for an RAF attack on the Baltic port of Rostock. It was thought at the time that the targets had been selected from one of the famous pre-war Baedeker guide books.

Sunday, 26th April

The rescue and salvage teams worked flat out through the day in Bath city. Teams from Cheltenham, Stroud, Thornbury and Chipping Sodbury had been sent in to assist. The Stroud team was heavily involved and in one incident made the macabre discovery of 13-15 bodies in a shelter which had received a direct hit. Despite the carnage, Bath's waters were apparently still thought to be efficacious, that is, at least by the 25 rheumatic patients that turned up during the morning at the Royal Baths.

The city came under attack again during the evening. The gas works at Tiverton was hit and 40 houses in the locality were damaged. More damage was caused to residential areas throughout the city; hundreds of houses were demolished and several thousand damaged. Rest centres had to be opened for the homeless and an emergency feeding centre was set up in the famous Pump

Room. It was estimated at the end of April that 142 people had been killed and up to 800 injured. This figure was later raised in some reports and there is at least one story of a mass grave containing over 300 bodies. There was great confusion for several days and indeed for some time it was impossible to enter the city from some directions because of the damage. In circumstances such as these, the true casualty figure is often difficult to determine with any real degree of accuracy.

Sunday, 28th June

An unidentified enemy aircraft was reported to have struck barrage balloon cables at Weston-super-Mare. Apparently, it did not suffer damage serious enough to prevent it returning to base.

Monday, 27th July

A layer of cloud covered the country at dawn. It was ideal sneak attack weather and the Luftwaffe launched at least 30 aircraft against a mixture of targets, including factories, airfields and rail junctions. The first attack in the area took place at quarter-past six in the morning when a lone raider strafed the Swindon to Westbury mail train. Quarter of an hour later, another single intruder machine-gunned the streets of Cirencester. Several small fires were started and many early risers had narrow escapes. In one house a kitchen copper was struck by a machine-gun bullet and, as is the way of things, the incident gave rise to a rumour that a policeman had been wounded. In fact, there were no human casualties.

This latter raider may well have been one of three Dornier bombers that dived out of the cloud over South Cerney at about the same time. They machine-gunned the aircraft standing in the dispersals and released some incendiaries to the west of the airfield at Culkerton. At twenty-five minutes to seven four HE bombs were dropped near the Cross Keys pub at Hardwick. Several houses nearby were damaged but, once again, nobody was injured. At quarter to seven another lone raider struck at Swindon, dropping four HE bombs and strafing the streets. Over 20 people were injured and GWR property was damaged. Yet another raider was apparently briefed to attack the GAC works at Brockworth but was driven off by anti-aircraft fire. Choosing the next likely-looking target, the intruder released its bombs over Cheltenham at eight minutes to seven. One of the bombs fell in Brunswick Street,

A well ventilated Dornier provides testimony to the accuracy of Fighter Command's gunnery. Unfortunately this one made it back to France.

(Bundesarchiv)

demolishing six houses, damaging many others and killing ten people. In total, twelve houses were destroyed and a further 400 were damaged. In addition, a water main was fractured in Swindon road.

Another bomb fell in a garden at Dunally Parade, causing damage to the Fire House. In all, eleven people were killed and 25 injured. One of the bombs fell behind the old Ritz Cinema and turned out to be a UXB. It was defused by a Home Guard Bomb Disposal Squad, led by Ivor Edmunds. It proved to be a difficult job but once it was finished the Squad was provided with tea by the cinema staff. It is probable that the casing of this particular bomb will be put on public display in Cheltenham in the near future.

The Bomb Disposal Squad of 'K' Company (Dowty) of 1st Gloucestershire Battalion Home Guard, stand behind the UXB which they dealt with behind the old Ritz Cinema in Cheltenham on 27th July 1942.

Tuesday, 28th July

An intruder attacked Moreton-in-Marsh airfield during the early morning with four HE bombs.

Several Anson aircraft were damaged but there were no human casualties. Some minutes later, at quarter to three, over 500 incendiaries were dropped at Cockberry Butts Farm, Langley Hill, setting hayricks alight.

Friday, 31st July
A fire was discovered at Tidenham Chase Farm, three miles north of Chepstow, at twenty past two in the morning. It was thought that the fire had been caused by a new type of incendiary.

Monday, 17th August
Late in the evening a number of UXBs were dropped at Staple Hill, together with four unignited parachute flares. Some rather more effective hardware was dropped minutes later at Randalls Farm, Stockend, Harescomb. Several buildings were damaged and a cow was injured.

Tuesday, 18th August
Swindon, Wilts came under attack during the evening when a number of HE bombs were dropped. Northern Road, Kembrey Street and Ferndale Road were all hit and some 20 houses were demolished. Twenty people were killed and 35 injured.

Friday, 28th August
During the morning the Luftwaffe despatched several individual, high-altitude Junkers Ju.86P aircraft against specific targets. These special high-altitude bombers were capable of reaching heights above 40,000 feet which gave them a fair degree of immunity from fighter attack.

Just after twenty past nine in the morning two aircraft were spotted over the City of Bristol at an altitude of between 30,000 and 32,000 feet. There can be little doubt that they were Ju.86Ps. One of the aircraft released a single bomb which fell in the centre of the city. Three buses were hit, two of them bursting into flames. Nearby buildings were also damaged. Twenty-eight people were killed and 36 seriously injured.

Saturday, 29th August
An HE bomb fell near Groundwell Road, Swindon, just before nine o'clock in the morning, killing eight people.

Sunday, 6th September
Another "high-flyer" was spotted passing over Aston Down airfield during the day at an altitude

of 30,000 feet. The aircraft was identified as a Ju.88 and it was probably on a reconnaissance sortie.

1943

Friday, 9th April
A Home Office Circular established the Fire Guard as a service in its own right.

Tuesday, 18th May
A "hit and run" raider dropped four HE bombs at Aust at quarter to four in the morning. No damage or casualties were reported.

Thursday, 16th September
On this date the King approved a flag for the Civil Defence Services.

Sunday, 31st October
Two HE bombs were dropped near Folly Farm and Thompsons Farm at Aston Blank, south-west of Bourton-on-the-Water, just before quarter to eleven in the evening. Damage was minor, some windows being shattered.

1944

Friday, 4th February
At quarter to six in the morning hundreds of incendiaries fell around Upper Slaughter, causing numerous fires and damaging farm buildings. The village school and several private houses were also damaged.

Monday, 27th March
The inhabitants of Hill, Berkeley and the surrounding area awoke to the sound of gunfire and explosions around midnight. An enemy raider had been downed by a Mosquito nightfighter at Woodlands Farm, Clapton. The four crew members baled out in a hurry and were taken prisoner. They were Uffz. Tutschek, Gefr. Bauch, Uffz. Wirth and Obgefr. Wiedener. As the intruder was being pursued it jettisoned its bombload. The crater left by the bombs was 60 feet wide and 24 feet deep. The aircraft itself set fire to a hayrick as it crashed to earth. Target maps were discovered amongst the wreckage that

Special Police Sergeant John Hancock of Berkeley, Glos. who as a Special Constable on the night of 27th March 1944 captured two German Airmen and was awarded the Gloucestershire Special Constabulary Commendation for his actions.

(Severnside Aviation Society Collection)

showed Sharpness ringed in red with the time 23.58 hours written alongside, suggesting that this may have been the target. The aircraft was a Ju.88A4 of KG.6, coded 3E+FT (Werk. No. 55021).

Tuesday, 28th March

A 1,000 kilo parachute mine was dropped in a field near Tetbury during the night.

Thursday, 11th May

Enemy aircraft were over Filton and some flares were dropped. Heavy anti-aircraft fire seemed to have the required effect however, and the raiders left the district without dropping any bombs.

Monday, 15th May

Three HE bombs were dropped in the Bedminster district of Bristol and a single HE bomb was dropped at Kings Weston. Other HE bombs fell at St. Briavels, Iron Acton, Wickwar and Rangeworthy. Fourteen HE bombs were

dropped at the latter location and fell right across the village. Fortunately, nobody was killed.

Tuesday, 16th May

During the night reports came in of HE bombs at Avonmouth, Dodington, Doynton, Kingscote, Thornbury and Tytherington.

By mid-1944 the Allies had landed in France and the threat of air attack began to recede, at least as far as Gloucestershire was concerned. Further east, of course, there was still sporadic enemy air activity and the scourges of the V1 Flying Bombs and V2 Rockets were yet to come. Christmas was celebrated with much more gusto than usual and by mid-February 1945 most ARP posts and controls were no longer being manned full-time.

On 2nd May 1945 the Ministry of Home Security announced that the National Air Raid Warning System was to be discontinued from mid-day. Restrictions on vehicle and domestic lighting were to be lifted in most areas except for a five-mile coastal belt. The lifting of the "Blackout" was a tangible sign for the man in the street that the end was in sight. It was lighting with a vengeance however in Gloucester on 5th May, when the city tested its VE Day lighting. Floodlights were used, plus several hundred red, white and blue bulbs. On Tuesday, 8th May, at three o'clock in the afternoon Winston Churchill officially announced the Nazi surrender. VE Day had arrived at last. Celebratory bonfires were lit across the county. A torchlight procession was held at Nailsworth and in many places Hitler was burned in effigy. A sense of relief was apparent everywhere and at last people could begin to think of the future with some confidence. At many locations throughout the county Farewell parades were held by the Civil Defence Services during June.

For many the prospect of a return to normality was not something that they entirely relished. A great sense of comradeship and togetherness had developed, but it would inevitably fade with the increasing materialism and selfishness likely to manifest itself in post-war peacetime Britain. For those who had lost kith and kin it would take a long time to come to terms with the new situation. It had been total war in its most terrible sense, but the victory belonged to the ordinary men and women as much as to the soldiery. Together they had overcome the trials and tribulations of war and vanquished the scourge of Nazism.

Chapter 3

The Airfields

The year 1935 was a crucial one for the history of military airfield construction, not only in Gloucestershire and the Cotswolds but throughout the whole of the British Isles. It should, of course, be said that the origins of several of Gloucestershire's military or quasi-military airfields can be traced back to the years of the First World War or even earlier. No examination of the military scene prior to the outbreak of the Second World War would be complete without taking into consideration these early aerodromes, some of which were positioned on the sites of later Second World War establishments.

The expansion scheme for the RAF, drawn up in 1935, fuelled a programme of development that was to lead to the construction of over 120 new airfields during the peak year of 1942. This was a major achievement when one considers that the RAF had only 170 airfields at the outbreak of hostilities in 1939. Many major contractors were involved in the programme under the control of the Air Ministry Directorate of Works, such as Wimpey, McAlpine, Laing and Taylor Woodrow. Some of the sites chosen were on or near old World War One dromes whilst others were sites previously picked out and used by Sir Allan Cobham or even the Automobile Association, who at that time had a considerable interest in aviation.

The availability of labour and heavy plant was a problem during the late thirties. However, by 1942 some 60,000 men were to be employed on airfield construction, many of them Irish. An ocean of concrete was laid. To begin with, standard thickness for runways was six inches, although this was later increased to eight inches.

By the end of the war it was estimated that enough concrete had been laid to build a road 30 feet wide and 9,000 miles long. The names of many of the hangars and buildings that appeared became almost household words, the most famous being probably the Nissen Hut and the "T" type hangar. Other lesser types, however, like the Orlit Hut (similar to the Nissen but with a concrete roof), the Romney, Iris and Maycrete Huts, plus Bellman, Blister, "C" type and Lamella Hangars were also well known. The British construction effort was boosted during 1942 by the arrival of the first U.S. Aviation Engineer Battalions which were destined to work on many sites throughout the United Kingdom. Over 500 airfields were constructed in Britain between 1938 and 1946, turning the whole country into a giant aircraft carrier.

Misunderstandings often occur over airfield nomenclature, thus a few words on that subject will not go amiss. One constant cause of confusion is the similarity between the terms "Satellite Airfield" and "Satellite Landing Ground." They are two distinct entities in the sense of their usage and yet many people interchange the two without a thought. A satellite airfield is one that is used by a unit or units as an additional facility, often purely for training purposes. Large Operational Training Units, for instance, were often overloaded with personnel and aircraft and driven by a tight training schedule. In many cases it was simply impossible to have all the unit's aircraft active at the same time around one airfield. Thus an adjacent airfield would be taken over as a "satellite". Circuits and bumps and other activity could then be split between the two dromes. On occasion, a detached flight might take up a more permanent occupancy of such an airfield, thus giving it many of the trappings of the base airfield.

The "Satellite Landing Ground", on the other hand, was simply a fly-in storage facility for aircraft that had been handed over by a factory and were awaiting delivery to a military unit. These landing grounds were usually under the control of a Maintenance Unit (MU). In fact, some MUs had several such airfields under their control. To provide some degree of concealment they were often located in wooded areas where the aircraft could be easily hidden. Similarly, any buildings erected were made to look as innocuous as possible. The control towers were built to resemble bungalows, as can be seen at Barnsley Park in Gloucestershire. Airmen's billets were designed to appear as cow sheds or tractor sheds. At times these landing grounds held large numbers of aircraft spread over wide areas around the actual grass flying strip. It was this type of situation that was undoubtedly the source of the familiar wartime story of people coming upon brand-new aircraft parked, apparently unguarded, beneath trees or in fields miles from anywhere. This was a situation encountered by a young Land Army girl, now Mrs. Nora Radford, during the early war years to the south of Kemble in Gloucestershire. Nora was mystified to see large numbers of new aircraft sitting out in fields, open to the elements and the public. Her experience is by no means unusual because the area around Tetbury was somewhat crowded and contained a set of airfield ingredients calculated to confuse even the most knowledgeable. In a small area you had the World War Two airfield of Babdown Farm, the defunct World War One airfield of Leighterton and the satellite landing ground at Down Farm. Further to the east there was the huge Kemble Maintenance Unit with its outlying parking areas and somewhat closer to Tetbury there was the satellite airfield of Long Newnton. It is my hope that the details given in this chapter will help to clear up some of the inconsistencies that have become established in people's minds over the last 40 years.

Having explained the background of the Satellite Landing Ground (SLG), there is very little else to say about this type of airfield. They never appeared on aeronautical maps: secrecy was, of course, paramount. Once again Sir Alan Cobham's experience was enlisted when it came to choosing sites and by the end of 1940 over 50 sites

had been picked out. In the final analysis a total of 49 satellites were constructed, a number of the nominated sites not being taken up or being abandoned before work was complete. Two of the latter are known to have been in Gloucestershire, one at Calmsden and the other at Macaroni Down. The sites utilised in the county are as follows (all OS refs. are for 1:500,000 Landranger maps):—

SLG No. 14 Overley   OS ref. 163/965046
                      (10 & 20 MUs and
                      RLG for 3 EFTS)
SLG No. 22 Barnsley Park OS ref. 163/075075
                      (5 & 6 MUs)
SLG No. 23 Down Farm OS ref. 163/855906
                      (10 MU and RLG
                      for 15 (P)AFU*)
                      * Also known as
                      Westonbirt

Barnsley Park's bungalow control tower survives in good condition. No doubt it's designers would smile were they to be aware that it is today a smart residential bungalow.
(Rennison Collection)

Two of these SLGs were also used for some active flying as Relief Landing Grounds (RLG). Down Farm served as an RLG during 1944 for No. 15 (Pilot) Advanced Flying Unit from Castle Combe in Wiltshire. Similarly, the Oxfords of No. 3 Flying Training School at South Cerney used Overley as an RLG during the summer of 1942.

Another Castle Combe-based unit made use of a small south Gloucestershire RLG during 1943-45. This was the North Stoke RLG (OS ref. 172/717687) which was on the well-known Lansdown Racetrack to the north-west of Bath, now, of course, in the County of Avon. No. 3 and No. 7 Flying Instructors' Schools operated their twin-engined Oxfords from this RLG until the summer of 1945 when the racetrack once more became a venue for the sport of kings.

The view across the site of Barnsley Park satellite landing ground has not changed much since the war.
(Rennison Collection)

As these pictures show many of the wartime buildings at Windrush survive including the control tower.
(Rennison Collection)

There were other RLGs in the Cotswolds which had brief histories, one of which was at Northleach (OS ref, 163/110155). This airfield came into use in November 1942 and provided a home for a Flight of Master tugs and Hotspur gliders from No. 3 Glider Training School at Stoke Orchard. However, their occupancy was intermittent due to the poor surface of the airfield. During 1944 the field became a fully-fledged satellite for 3 GTS. By the autumn of that year, however, the grass surface was so damaged as to be no longer useful and it was abandoned when the GTS moved to Zeals.

Yet another somewhat more elaborate RLG was located at Southrop (OS ref. 163/190035). The airfield was close to the site of the proposed Macaroni Down SLG, one of the airfield's dispersed sites being located in Macaroni Wood. Southdrop was equipped with two runways, numerous blister hangars and an MT shed. It also boasted a brick control tower. The first unit to make use of the site was No. 2 FTS from Brize Norton in August 1940. During July 1942 No. 3 (P)AFU from South Cerney took over the used the airfield as a satellite until January 1945. The site was also used briefly as an RLG in December 1945 by No. 6 SFTS. The Ansons of 27 Group Communication Squadron also used the airfield for a short while before the end of the year.

Perhaps the most famous Cotswold RLG is Windrush. It was used from mid-1940 by No. 6 SFTS at Little Rissington and No. 15 SFTS at Kidlington. It was here on 18th August, 1940 that Sgt. Bruce Hancock of 6 SFTS rammed and destroyed a Heinkel bomber that had attacked him, losing his own life in the process. The story is told in detail in the section dealing with Little Rissington.

Pupil pilots and ground crew from the training units were quartered in Nissen huts on the airfields. In 1942 6 SFTS became No. 6 (P)AFU but it still maintained its hold on Windrush. The site was improved during that same year when steel mesh runways were put down and huts and blister hangars erected. Rissington finally gave up the site in July 1945. A considerable number of buildings still remain intact, giving a reasonable impression of wartime days.

Another source of much mystery is the decoy airfield, a subject about which even official records are sketchy. A decision was taken shortly after the outbreak of the war to construct decoy or dummy airfields in the vicinity of major airfields likely to come under attack. The decoys were divided into two types, so-called "K" and "Q" sites. The "K" sites had dummy aircraft and buildings and were intended as daytime decoys. The "Q" sites, on the other hand, were intended to attract enemy intruders at night and were less comprehensively equipped in the sense of foolproof decoy aircraft and trucks. At night, however, they were capable of mounting an impressively effective display of lighting intended to simulate an airfield conducting night flying operations. An aircraft-shaped frame with lights mounted upon it could be propelled at over 50 miles an hour along a simulated flarepath by a cordite charge, giving a fair imitation of an aircraft on the move. The night decoys were very convincing, as were their daytime counterparts, so much so that it was not unusual for our own aircraft to attempt to land at such sites if they were in trouble. In some instances this led to fatal accidents and the loss of valuable lives and aircraft. There is no doubt, however, that these sites were effective, for by the end of July 1940 over 60 attacks had been made on decoys whilst their parent airfields had suffered only ten assaults. By mid-1942 such sites had absorbed over 370 attacks whilst actual airfields had suffered slightly less. The "Q" sites were much more economical in terms of manpower as they only required two men to operate them; on the other hand, a "K" site needed a team of 24 men to run it. By the end of 1940 the Luftwaffe appeared to have had most of the "K" sites located and thus their value was eroded. "Q" sites, however, continued to be useful well into 1942-43. The actual location of some of the sites is still obscure but at least three numbered sites are known to have existed to cover Gloucestershire airfields. They were as follows:—

Decoy No.56 at Ashton Keynes, cover for South Cerney;
Decoy No.57 at Horsley, cover for Aston Down;
Decoy No.73 at Farmington, cover for Little Rissington.

In addition, there was at least one other site at Long Newnton as cover for Kemble.

Rumours persist of some form of decoy site to the south of Birdlip at Blacklains Farm. Certainly there are traces of military occupation and local witnesses attest to the fact that there was a decoy; however, there is, for the moment at least, no documentary evidence to confirm this. There are similar stories about a small landing strip at Temple Guiting which was apparently used as a private landing strip by the Peachey brothers who were local farmers. It is possible that the strip was utilised by the RAF as an emergency landing ground or a decoy, although there appears to be no documentary evidence to support this suggestion either. The story often receives further embroidery because of an incident which occurred after the war. On New Year's Eve, 1952 an Oxford trainer crashed in the area whilst en route from Thorney Island to Wellesbourne Mountford, killing a member of the crew. The information regarding decoy airfields is at best fragmentary and additional detail is always welcome.

Worthy of mention at this juncture are two other locations which, whilst they are not airfields, certainly have undeniable aeronautical connections. The first of these is the Balloon Centre at Pucklechurch (now, of course, in the County of Avon). This base was the home of Nos. 927, 928 and 929 Squadrons of Balloon Command. Balloon barrages of various sorts had been used during the First World War but recruitment for the balloon squadrons did not begin until 1938 and was organised by a Group Headquarters under the control of Fighter Command of the RAF. The first Air Officer Commanding was Air Commodore J.G. Hearson and under his leadership a separate Balloon

A 'Column' of balloons being warmed up, a regular sight around Pucklechurch during the war.

Several of the barrage balloon sheds remain in good repair at Pucklechurch. Today they are still of use supporting various commercial organisations.
(via Dr. Winbolt)

Command was established. The normal type of barrage balloon in use was a streamlined bag of rubber-proofed cotton fabric with a hydrogen gas capacity of 19,150 cubic feet, a length of over 60 feet and a height of just over 31 feet. The approximate weight of the balloon was 550 pounds and it was, of course, anchored to the ground by means of a flexible steel cable. Balloon depots have their own distinctive, high-roofed hangars and several of these remain standing at Pucklechurch although they are now in commercial use.

The second location that deserves a place in this narrative is the RAF station at Innsworth Lane (now known simply as RAF Innsworth). The station was the base of No. 7 School of Technical Training which was responsible for training large numbers of RAF ground crew: airframe riggers and fitters, and so on. One of the "erks" who went through the mill at Innsworth was "Sam" Masters who now lives at Winchcombe. "Sam" recalls his eight-week riggers' course at the school with great clarity. It was a whirlwind of technical lectures on fabric and metal repairing, corrosion treatments, locking devices, hydraulics, brakes and so on. Relaxation for the trainees inevitably meant a visit to the local pubs, the "Hare and Hounds" or the "Bat and Ball" being the favourites. The

Aircrew trainees including a number of Canadians, pictured with one of their instructors. The picture was possibly taken at Staverton or Innsworth.
(via Paul Aston)

local "scrumpy" was consumed with gusto by most, although following one particularly harrowing experience "Sam" decided to give it up permanently. After a fairly heavy session he set off to walk back to camp with another airman. It was some time before they realised that their "footpath" was the main Gloucester to Cheltenham railway line and, to make matters worse, they discovered that they were walking in the wrong direction. Innsworth later became a WAAF depot and a Training and Receiving Centre for the south of England. The station is still going strong today, providing the base for the RAF Personnel Management Centre. Many of the original 1930/40 wooden buildings are still standing, including the Station Headquarters.

During the period 1939-45 there were eighteen military operational airfields within or just upon Gloucestershire's borders. Some live on to this day as military establishments whilst others have vanished almost without trace, but all have earned their place in history.

NB: all OS references are for 1:50 000 Landranger maps.

'Sam' Masters now living at Winchcombe was one of the many airmen trained at RAF Innsworth.

Aston Down (OS ref. 163/912010)

Upon its opening on 12th October 1938 the airfield at Aston Down included within its boundaries the whole of the former World War One airfield of Minchinhampton; indeed, one or two of the old buildings were adapted and revamped to serve the new base. The site was, however, considerably enlarged to the south, beyond the road running up from Minchinhampton through Burnt Ash (which had earlier crossed the older airfield unhindered) which was, as a result, closed and blocked off. At its southern extremity the site encroached upon Aston Farm and a good deal of the farm land was requisitioned for wartime use. The first unit to move in was No. 7 Aircraft Storage Unit which was redesignated No. 20 Maintenance Unit within a few days. The unit's association with the station was to be a long one: Aston Down was to be "home" for more than 20 years. Although the camp was officially open, a good deal of building work was still in progress during late 1938 and one of the main firms involved was Wilson Lovatt & Sons Ltd. Construction work of this sort was not without its dangers, as Wilson Lovatt had discovered earlier in the year. One of the firm's employees, Ivor John Wixey, had fallen to his death whilst working on one of the hangars. The "D" type hangars constructed on the station were used initially to store only equipment but by early 1939 this had been replaced by aircraft.

The Munich crisis of September 1938 had forced the RAF to review its organisation and, as a result, the formation of Mobilisation Pools was ordered. Under this scheme Aston Down was designated a Pool Camp for No. 12 Group of Fighter Command on 23rd August 1939. This decision was to lead to more construction work which was to continue well into 1940. With the outbreak of hostilities in September 1939 the station was inundated with personnel and accommodation problems became acute. Local billets were sought to take the overspill and one particularly comfortable selection was the George Hotel at nearby Nailsworth. The hotel was run by Mr. C.D. Brooks and he agreed to let the RAF have the use of the dining-room and ante-room as an Officers' Mess. Some twelve officers were accommodated and the all-in tariff was six shillings a day! The Pool Camp's job was to train new pilots, intended for the squadrons of 12 Group, in fighter tactics. Gladiator biplane fighters and the more modern Blenheim and Harvard aircraft were used for this training. The transportation needs of the unit were satisfied by the collection of a batch of vehicles from Waddington, Ruislip and Wembley, including beacon and petrol tank trailers.

During mid-November 1939 the unit suffered its first casualty. Sgt. pilot Linton was killed while collecting a Gladiator fighter from Little Rissington, when the aircraft mysteriously caught fire during take off and crashed in flames. Before the month was out the unit suffered a second tragedy when Pilot Officer Masterson lost control of his Harvard trainer near Oakridge. The aircraft went into a spin and crashed to the ground, killing the pilot.

A Yugoslav Air Force crew standing in front of their brand new Blenheim bomber during 1940.

Some strange uniforms were in evidence on the airfield early in the new year of 1940. On 6th February Wing Commander Hinko Dragic of the Royal Yugoslav Air Force arrived on the station and was greeted by the C.O., Wing Commander Caswell. He had arrived with several other Yugoslav airmen to take delivery of a number of Blenheim bombers. A further group of Yugoslavs arrived six days later under the command of Wing Commander Miodrag Lozic and another group arrived two days after that with Flight Lieutenant

A Royal Yugoslav Air Force crew pose before their Blenheim bomber.

Bosko Stanslovic in charge. A fourth group appeared on the scene nine days later under the command of Squadron Leader Milan Mandrasevic. After familiarisation training with the aircraft, during which one of the bombers, registered YU-BAF (RAF serial L6817), crashed on the airfield, the Yugoslavs readied the aircraft for the trip home. They departed in their four groups between 1st and 14th March, 1940. Their route home lay via Bordeaux, Marseilles and Milan. The 20 aircraft all carried Yugoslav civil registrations and included the repaired YU-BAF. These aircraft supplemented those already in service with the R.Yug.A.F., some of which had been acquired in 1937 whilst others had been built under licence at a factory in Zemun, Yugoslavia.

The Blenheims were later to play a gallant part in defending Yugoslavia against the Nazi invasion in April 1941. Aircraft of the 1st Bomber Regiment made daring low-level attacks on the advancing German columns, often below rooftop height. The unit's commander was so low on one occasion that his aircraft was destroyed by the detonations of his own bombs. Other Blenheims of the 8th Bomber Regiment made bombing attacks against Vienna, by then a major city of Hitler's Third Reich.

In March 1940 the Pool was redesignated No. 5 Operational Training Unit. A mix of fighter and training aircraft was to be used, including Spitfires, Hurricanes and Miles Masters. It was one of these Spitfires that was involved in the shooting down of a Ju.88 bomber at Oakridge on 25th July 1940, details of which can be found in the chronological section of the book. During August 1940 the station was visited by Air Commodore Wilkinson, Inspector of Camouflage, who pronounced himself satisfied with the station's efforts at concealment.

One of the construction firms still working on the camp during late 1940 was Walter Lawrence & Sons Ltd. which had begun work on a lecture room and an extension to the armoury. During early September they also completed work on a very important addition to station facilities, the WAAF lavatories! By the middle of the same month the firm had begun to contribute even more to the hygienic needs of the station, having commenced work on a bath-house for the Sergeants' Mess. The 8th October was something of a "Red Letter Day" as the station received a Royal visit from HRH Group Captain the Duke of Kent.

The famous outline of the Spitfire was often seen in the circuit at Aston Down after arrival of 52 OTU in August 1941.

Bristol built Blenheims were stock-in-trade at Aston Down during the early war years. (via B. Rijnhout)

No.9 Ferry Pool pilots line up for the camera at Aston Down in front of a Fairchild Argus.

Women pilots of the Air Transport Auxiliary. There were no operational women pilots during the war but female members of the ATA regularly flew combat aircraft such as Spitfires, Hurricanes and even large four engined bombers on delivery flights. (Rennison Collection)

was often rather unjustly interpreted to mean "Ancient and Tattered Airmen" by their opposite numbers in the RAF. In fact, "airmen" was not a term that applied at all in the general sense because many of the ATA pilots were women. A number of them were pilots of great experience, such as the famous Amy Johnson (or Mollison, as she became after her marriage to record-breaking pilot Jim Mollison). These Ferry pilots flew just about

"You can fly my Spitfire anytime". One can almost hear the airman on the ground thinking aloud as this attractive ATA pilot climbs aboard the fighter.

November 1940 brought with it a change of nameplate for 5 OTU which was redesignated 55 OTU but remained a fighter training unit. The work of building runways began during 1941 but the process was a slow one. During the early part of that year 55 OTU departed. One of the other units based on the airfield at this time was the quasi-military No. 9 Ferry Pool which was staffed by members of the Air Transport Auxiliary, or the ATA as it was known. The No. 9 Pool was under the command of Captain Hugh Bergel and had been formed as an offshoot of No. 2 Pool at Bristol. A typical Ferry Pool consisted of about 50 pilots and 30 ground crew plus support personnel, drivers, clerks and so on. The abbreviation ATA

anything, anywhere, and the sight of a slight feminine figure descending from the massive bulk of a four-engined bomber was guaranteed to raise eyebrows among RAF personnel at the station of delivery.

A new Operational Training Unit, No. 52, arrived on the scene in August 1941. It was equipped with Spitfires, Hurricanes and Miles Master trainers. Almost inevitably, accidents became the order of the day. Flying training was undoubtedly a risky business and many seasoned pilots considered operational flying less dangerous.

Posed on a Fairey Battle of 'X' Gunnery Training Flight 52 OTU are left to right on wing; Sgt Portas & Sgt Franks, Sgt Furness is in the cockpit.
(Severnside Aviation Society Collection)

Sgt's Furness and McKinley (an American in the RAF) front a Fairey Battle of 'X' Flight 52 OTU Aston Down in 1942.
(Severnside Aviation Society Collection)

One of the instructors with "X" Air Firing Flight of the OTU was Squadron Leader P.W. Lefevre DFC. He had joined the unit fresh from a fairly hectic time defending Malta against German and Italian air attacks. Few were better qualified to pass on their knowledge of air combat techniques. After his spell on training Peter Lefevre returned to operational flying as the CO of 266 (Rhodesia) Squadron. He was killed in February 1944 whilst leading his squadron on a ground attack sortie.

In December 1941 81 Group Communications

Flight arrived on the station. The Group HQ was located in an old manor house at Avening and Aston Down was the most convenient airfield for the Flight to use. The unit remained until its disbandment in April 1943.

The station was certainly well into the sheep-owning traditions of the Cotswolds. During early April 1942 45 ewes and 61 lambs were purchased, bringing the strength of the station flock to 600! On 14th May, 1942 one of the OTU's Spitfires came to grief near Lydney as a result of an attempt to underfly the Severn Bridge. The aircraft struck the water, was damaged and crashed about a mile from the river. An amusing "service coincidence" occurred about three weeks after this somewhat nautical event. A Squadron Leader Crusoe was posted to the unit as Chief Flying Instructor. Presumably the RAF felt that the OTU pilots were in need of some instruction on the subject of survival in (or over) hostile waters. During August some elements of the OTU began to move out to a satellite airfield at Chedworth. There was some excitement on 6th September when a Ju.88 reconnaissance aircraft was spotted overhead at 30,000 feet but, fortunately, no attack was made on the airfield.

Foreign uniforms once again appeared on the airfield during October 1942 when Squadron Leader Huang, the Chinese Air Attache, arrived to undergo familiarisation training on the Spitfire. Aircraft from the OTU were to be involved in a number of tragic incidents prior to the unit's disbandment in August 1943. Perhaps the worst of these occurred during October 1942 when one of the unit's Spitfires crashed into sheds at RAF Quedgeley, killing a female civilian worker.

Hawker Hurricane I V7754 of 55 OTU 'Lydia' seen in 1942.
(Photo Map)

Miles Master III W8647 PA—M of 55 OTU also marked
'Lydia' on the engine cowling probably pictured in 1942.
(Photo Map)

Hawker Hurricanes I's 1) AG122 (PA—F), 2) V7754 (PA—
X), 3) ?3039 (PA—J), probably overhead Aston Down
during 1942. *(Photo Map)*

Upon the disbandment of the OTU in 1943 the Fighter Leaders' School took up residence for some five months. The work of 20 MU continued throughout all these movements and was chiefly concerned with such types as Spitfires, Typhoons and Mustangs. The station's farming activities also continued apace, the main occupation during late 1943 being haymaking and pig-keeping.

Flying under the Severn Bridge was still very much in vogue during 1943, so much so that in August three pilots were court-martialled for indulging in this rather foolhardy pursuit. All were found guilty and reduced to the ranks.

For a short time during September a detachment of Mitchell bombers from 180 Squadron used the airfield. Another new unit arrived during May 1944 when No. 1311 Ambulance Flight brought their Ansons to the airfield. They in their turn were followed by 84 Group Support Unit which arrived in June. The purpose of this highly mobile unit was to provide replacement aircraft for the Group's squadrons operating on the Continent. As the invasion forces moved deeper into France, the Support Unit followed. It departed from Aston Down on 14th July 1944. The next day the advanced elements of No. 3 Tactical Exercise Unit (TEU) arrived from Annan, although the main party did not arrive until the 17th via Chalford railway station. By the 21st the unit had an aircraft strength of 2 Masters, 20 Typhoons, 6 Mustangs and 16 Hurricanes. No. 3 TEU's purpose in life was to provide pilots with specialised training in ground attack techniques. Once again, accidents became an everyday occurrence, as the incident log will show. At the end of 1955 the unit was redesignated 55 OTU and as such survived until its disbandment on 14th June 1945.

ATA pilots had been much in evidence at the station during June 1944 with the formation of an "Invasion Pool". However, with the end of the war 20 MU found itself the sole occupant of a very busy airfield. Aston Down became a gathering place for surplus aircraft and large numbers of Lancasters, Typhoons and other types arrived to suffer the ignominy of the scrapman's hammer. The mass destruction that followed left a legacy of aircraft components that can still be found on local farms even today.

Babdown Farm (OS ref. 162/845938)

This airfield came into use during July 1940 as a relief landing ground for the Hawker Audaxes and Harts of No. 9 Flying Training School at Hullavington in Wiltshire. A small party of airmen were despatched each day to set out flares for nightflying.

At quarter-past ten in the evening of 3rd August 1940 a lone enemy raider dropped 18 bombs in the Beverstone area, most of which fell on the edge of the airfield. The nightflying training that was in progress at the time was hurriedly curtailed; however, no physical damage was caused. The airfield continued in use as a training facility for No. 9 FTS and for the Overseas Aircraft Delivery

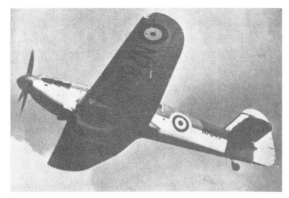

The Miles Master trainer was used No.3 FIS at Babdown Farm.

Flight from Kemble throughout 1940.

Babdown came under attack again on 26th March 1941 when a lone raider dived out of low cloud and shot up the airfield. Fortunately, no damage was caused despite the fact that a number of aircraft were out in the open. The FTS was re-designated No. 9 (P)AFU (Pilot Advanced Flying Unit) early in 1942 and moved further south to Castle Combe. For a while the airfield was left empty and a number of improvements were put in train. Sommerfeld steel tracking was put down to create three runways and blister hangars were built. A large amount of building was carried out in an effort to improve the instructional and domestic accommodation.

From a flying point of view, the station was re-opened during August 1942 but rebuilding work was still in progress. Two Flights of No. 3 Flying Instructors' School took up residence with Oxford and Miles Master trainers. Equipment for Beam Approach Training was installed during 1943 and in June of that year No. 1532 BAT Flight began training with it. This blind approach technique was mainly taught for the benefit of bomber crews and with the amount of night and all-weather flying rising continually there was great demand.

Improvement work continued during the year and when officers of No. 15 (P)AFU inspected the station in August new hangars and a maintenance site were under construction. They obviously liked what they saw, however, for by January 1944 personnel from the unit had begun to move onto the station. Hangar lighting was still incomplete at that time and a temporary system was rigged up. Similarly, much of the accommodation was only half-finished. Squadron Leader Danby was appointed the CO of 3 Squadron of the Advanced Flying Unit and training got under way.

Oxford trainers were constantly circling Babdown Airfield and its environs throughout the war years.

Babdown became a temporary home for a number of French Navy airmen and their Anson aircraft during this period, but, unfortunately, there were disciplinary difficulties which resulted in four of the trainees being suspended. The situation was made worse when one of the trainees was killed in an accident and the trainees were posted out.

Heavy rainfall caused problems during May 1944 and restricted flying considerably. Medical personnel were also under training on the station and a number of them were detached to Tetbury Hospital during the year. Just before Christmas 1944 their skills were put to practical test when a

Typical of the breed, Warrant Office Don White was a Pilot Instructor on Oxfords at Babdown Farm from August 1944 to May 1945. *(via P. Aston)*

Remains of wartime buildings were still visible at Babdown Farm in the early 1980's.   *(Rennison Collection)*

Mosquito aircraft crashed at Dursley and the station ambulance was sent to the scene.

By the beginning of 1945 it was obvious that the war in Europe was coming to an end and flying training began to run down. By May it was all over and flying at the station had ceased. Although the base was to remain in use as a storage facility for 7 MU for some time to come its days as an active RAF airfield were over.

87 Squadron brought their Hurricanes to Bibury in 1940 to strengthen the defences of the West Country.

Bibury (OS ref. 163/115095)

Having been picked out in 1939 as a likely landing ground to cater for overspill from South Cerney, the airfield was in use by the spring of 1940. The Oxford trainers of No. 3 Flying Training School from South Cerney became constant visitors. Between early August and December of 1940 the airfield was home to detachments from 92 and 87 Squadrons, flying Spitfires and Hurricanes respectively, which were acting as part of the defence of the west of England. Among the personnel of 92 Squadron often seen at Bibury was the famous Flight Lieutenant Brian Kingcome (later Group Captain DSO DFC). The insignia painted on his personal Spitfire was a single hand with the fingers raised in a "Victory" salute.

The 87 Squadron Hurricanes rotated through the airfield in two flights, each doing a week about. The pilots of the squadron spent time at nearby Walton House and amongst them was the well-known Roland "Bee" Beamont. "Bee" finished the war as a Wing Commander and went on to become Chief Test Pilot of English Electric at Warton in Lancashire. Still very much an aviation enthusiast, he is involved in a number of aeronautical organisations, including the local

A Hurricane gets its ammo replenished.

A delayed action bomb explodes at Bibury during 1940 but life goes on although one airman has taken the precaution of hiding beneath a lorry.

Cotswold Aircraft Restoration Group, of which he is a patron.

Shortly after the arrival of the first 92 Squadron Spitfires the Luftwaffe made a call. A Junkers Ju.88 bombed and strafed the airfield and one Spitfire was destroyed, a second damaged and three were hit by shrapnel and stray bullets. Two Spitfires managed to get off the ground and set off in pursuit of the raider. One of the aircraft was flown by Flight Lieutenant T.W. Wade who later became well-known as a Test Pilot for Hawkers. The enemy aircraft was caught and shot down over the Solent. Revenge was not all that sweet, however. Flt. Lt. Wade had problems and had to make a forced landing himself. He rapidly vacated his burning aircraft and only just managed to get clear before it exploded.

By the end of 1941 the fighters had departed and the Oxfords of 3 FTS had returned. Because of this constant use the surface of the airfield began to deteriorate although it remained usable. The Flying Training School continued with their circuits and bumps into 1942. In March of that year 3 FTS was redesignated No. 3 (P)AFU but Bibury was still retained as a satellite. During mid-July another selection of Oxfords arrived on the scene. These aircraft belonged to No. 1539 Beam Approach Training Flight and it was this unit that took over the airfield and used it as its base. To begin with the BAT Flight was forced to operate from South Cerney until problems with the beacon could be sorted out. However, a Link Trainer was installed on 9th July and the unit

moved in on 13th July, although there were problems with the transport. Many of the vehicles were the worse for wear and breakdowns were frequent.

Work continued on the development of the airfield during 1942-43. Two Sommerfeld Matting runways were laid and five blister hangars plus one "T" type hangar were erected. In fact, the erection of the latter had far-reaching consequences for it was found during the summer of 1943 that this hangar was reflecting the signal of the main beacon. This had had the effect of putting it one degree out of alignment and causing many unnecessary problems for the trainees.

Accidents were not, perhaps, so common as on some training units but the mid-air collision which occurred between the two Oxfords (DF277 and MP402) on 11th September, 1943 was horrific enough to make a lasting impression. Three airmen were killed and two others barely escaped with their lives by taking to their parachutes. During January 1944 continual rain and the resultant problem of a water-logged airfield caused the unit to move to the only dry area, the north side of the landing ground. The continual bad weather made the airfield almost useless and pupils and instructors alike found themselves "tidying up" dispersals and doing other distinctly non-aeronautical tasks.

Flying got under way again during the spring but weather was to be a recurring problem at Bibury. During September 1944 the whole unit donned their gas masks and tested them in the gas

Vestiges of Bibury Airfield can still be found; a blister hangar used for farm storage, a derelict hut and a decaying peri-track. (Rennison Collection)

chamber. This sort of "diversion" was never a popular pursuit with the airmen and it could be that the degree of disenchantment was the reason for the unit holiday that was announced the following day. By the end of the year a combination of high winds and heavy snow had, once again, rendered the airfield unusable. This was of no real consequence, however, as both 1539 BAT Flight and 3 (P)AFU had ceased to use the airfield to any extent by this time. The site was taken under the wing of 7 MU for storage purposes and its flying days were over.

Brockworth/Hucclecote
(OS ref. 162/882160)

Although not strictly a military airfield, Brockworth has more than earned the right to be included amongst the ranks of airfields that served the RAF during World War Two. Its origins go back much further, however, back, in fact, to the first world-wide conflict of 1914-18.

An Aircraft Acceptance Park and Mobilisation Station was set up on the site by the Air Board in 1915. This was certainly due in no small measure to the large-scale manufacture of aircraft and components by H.H. Martyns of Sunningend Works in Cheltenham. The company had initially begun manufacturing components for Farman aircraft and by the end of the war it was turning out DH.6 and DH.9 fuselages plus complete Bristol F.2B's, FE.2B's and Nieuport fighters. The completed aircraft were towed out to the airfield by truck for their acceptance tests. To begin with the work was done under contract to the Aircraft Manufacturing Company but in 1917 the two firms got together and formed the now famous Gloster Aircraft Company Ltd.

By 1918 the Aircraft Acceptance Park covered 140 acres, including 20 acres of buildings. The latter consisted of five aeroplane sheds (170 x 100 feet), 21 storage sheds (200 x 60 feet), an MT shed, an ammunition store and several other small buildings. The military staff numbered 357 and amongst the available transport was a "wing carrier", a mobile body workshop and an aeroplane trailer.

At least two RFC squadrons passed through during the latter part of 1918. The first, 90 Squadron, arrived from Shotwick during July but was disbanded less than a month later when its personnel were used as replacements for other units. The second, 86 Squadron, began to re-form at Brockworth during October 1918 but the signing of the armistice caused this activity to be suspended and personnel were posted to other units. After this brief flirtation with active flying units the airfield became a storage base under the control of No. 7 Group.

In 1921 GAC began to rent hangar space on the airfield and the company's involvement with the site began to expand. The whole airfield was purchased by the firm in 1928 for £15,000 and within two years the complete GAC operation was based at Brockworth.

Following a take-over bid by Hawker Aircraft Ltd. in 1934, the Hucclecote factory was

One of Gloster's most famous products was the Gladiator fighter. (*Rennison Collection*)

considerably expanded and construction of a shadow factory, incorporating a further 24 acres of floor space, was started in 1938. During this period the company built a number of Hawker designs, including the Hardy, Hart and Audax, in addition to their own Gloster Gauntlet and Gladiator fighters.

The new factory was completed in November 1940, and became involved with the production of Hurricanes, Typhoons and Albemarles. Despite enemy air attacks and the more general difficulties

Views of the heavily camouflaged Glosters factory taken by the RAF Camouflage Unit. (*Rennison Collection*)

A ground view of the Gloster's factory across a Typhoon wing showing an Albemarle in the background.

of the wartime environment, Glosters and its sister company, A.W. Hawkesley, made a major contribution to the war effort. By the time production of the Hurricane fighter ceased in March 1942 some 2,750 had been built. In addition, by the end of 1945 over 3,000 Typhoons had been produced by GAC and some 600 Albemarles by Hawkesleys. Many elements of the factory were dispersed around the locality to reduce the threat from enemy air attack,

The Albemarle was not a success as a bomber but more than earned its keep as a glider and paratrooping aircraft.

premises being taken over at a number of locations. A drawing-office was established in the Manor House at Bishop's Cleeve and another was set up in the Savoy Billiard Hall in Cheltenham. Numerous garages were taken over as spray shops, assembly shops, rolling mills and stores. New dispersal factories came into being at Ledbury,

Stoke Orchard, Uckington, Bentham and Newent.

Work on Britain's first jet aircraft, the Gloster E28/39, was moved to a dispersal factory at Regent's Motors in Cheltenham. From here the finished aircraft was conveyed back to Brockworth during April 1941 for taxi trials. During these trials the aircraft became airborne in a series of "short hops", covering distances of 100 to 200 yards, and during which the aircraft rose to a height of about six feet. After these tests the aircraft was returned to Cheltenham, this time to Crabtree's Garage, for some adjustments to the undercarriage. Whenever parts were required they were transported from Brockworth by local man Jimmy Townsend. He remembers that the garage was guarded by an armed policeman and that the mystery aircraft was carefully screened from prying eyes. From Carlton Street the aircraft was conveyed to Cranwell where it made its first official flight in May 1941.

By 1944 the twin-jet Meteor fighter was in production at Brockworth. The line was to continue running well into the post-war years and

The Gloster E28/39 experimental jet seen in uncharacteristic surroundings.

(Rennison Collection)

H.M. King George VI and H.M. The Queen visit the Gloster factory 10. Feb. 1940.

(Rennison Collection)

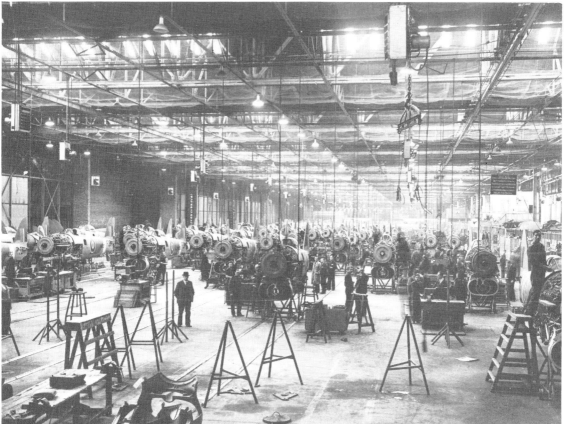

Construction of the Hawker Typhoon became a major undertaking by Glosters.

(Cheltenham Newspapers)

The E28/39 displays its well known lines whilst chocked and quiet.

the Meteor was to be followed into service by its more powerful descendant, the Javelin. Unfortunately, the company did not survive beyond the 1960's and since then the airfield has fallen into disuse. Much of it is still intact and in reasonable condition, creating the illusion of use when viewed from the air.

The Spitfires of 52 OTU were the first residents of Chedworth.

Chedworth (OS ref. 163/042131)

The airfield at Chedworth was constructed by the Landing Grounds Corporation and was officially declared open during April 1942. A single long north-south runway was completed, followed by a shorter east-west runway. The airfield did not become active until August when No. 52 Operational Training Unit at Aston Down began to use it as a satellite. The OTU's "E" Flight moved into the airfield with its Spitfires during August 1942.

During early September Sgt. Freel, an American pilot on No. 20 Course, caused some excitement when he flew over the airfield and dropped his Mae West with a note attached. The note read: "Wheels don't work, radio don't work. Love, Steve". As he flew low across the drome his Spitfire struck a stationary Miles Master trainer which was severely damaged. The Spitfire later made a forced landing near Aston Down. Crashes were frequent during this period, particularly when night flying was in progress. Constable Ian Hughes, based at Chedworth, considered the sight of a "bent" Oxford sitting at the end of the runway as something of an everyday thing.

In January 1943 a Fighter Leaders' School was opened as part of 52 OTU with a section at Chedworth. The school provided a three-week course for potential fighter squadron commanders.

The first week dealt with section tactics, the second with tactics for larger formations up to wing size and the third week was dedicated to the niceties of army support. During February the Chedworth section of the school became the Fighter Command School for Tactics and on completion of the first training course it moved away further south to Charmy Down in Somerset. By the end of the month Chedworth had become a satellite airfield for South Cerney, serving the Oxford trainers of the Advanced Flying Unit based there. Circuits and bumps by pupil pilots were very much the order of the day until October 1943 when the air gunnery elements of two Operational Training Units, Nos. 60 and 63 moved into the airfield and combined to become 60/63 Gunnery Squadron. This unit, with its Mosquitos and Martinets, remained "in situ" until early 1944. A quiet period then ensued although during the summer No. 125 Liaison Squadron of the US 9th Air Force operated their Stinson L5 Sentinels from the airfield.

By mid-July 1944 the airfield was once more under the control of nearby Aston Down. No. 3 Tactical Exercise Unit with Mustangs and Typhoons had needed more room and Chedworth was ideally placed. It was not long before the Mustang element was permanently based on the airfield. The unit certainly made a

Mustang fighters were much in evidence at Chedworth during the Summer of 1944.

No.3 TEU brought Typhoons to Chedworth in mid 1944.

Most of Chedworth has disappeared but odd buildings could still be seen in the early 1980's. (Rennison Collection)

dramatic debut when on the 28th July a Mustang III struck a lorry on take-off. Fortunately, no-one was killed but both machines were more than a little scarred.

During December 1944 the TEU was redesignated No. 55 Operational Training Unit. In its new guise the unit moved some Typhoons onto the station, although Mustangs were still to be seen in the circuit. Flying activity had ceased by the end of May 1945 and the airfield was put on to care and maintenance. Although it was to have a brief rebirth in the 1950's the site has been gradually decaying ever since. Most of it has now been returned to farm land and the only aircraft to be seen overhead now are models flown by local enthusiasts.

Down Ampney (OS ref. 163/100965)

This airfield was opened early in 1944 under the control of No. 46 Group Transport Command. During the last few days of February advance parties and aircraft from 48 and 271 Squadrons began to arrive. Twenty of 271's twin-engined Dakota transports arrived before lunch on 29th February and by early March the airfield was full of Dakotas and Horsa gliders. Unfortunately, much of the construction work on the station was still incomplete and conditions were somewhat primitive.

In the weeks that followed the squadrons embarked on an intensive training programme involving glider towing, navigation, formation flying and paradropping exercises. Such training could be hazardous, as evidenced by the collision that took place between two Dakotas on 25th March 1944. The Dakota of Sgt. Moody collided with that of his fellow 271 Squadron pilot, Flight Sergeant Anderson. Moody managed to regain control and returned to base. Anderson's aircraft crashed, killing the six airmen aboard. Only two nights later an Oxford trainer, again of 271 Squadron, crashed into buildings at Little Rissington during a night exercise, killing its crew.

By the early part of June 1944 both squadrons had built up enough expertise to enable them to take part in "D" day. "Operation Tonga" took place on the night of 5th/6th June and involved seven Dakota/Horsa glider combinations and nearly 40 aircraft with paratroopers. "Operation Mallard" followed during the evening of 6th June when 37 Dakota/Horsa glider combinations operated. Only one aircraft was lost on both these

A Dakota transport striped for D–Day.
(B. Rijnhout Collection)

A Horsa glider is towed aloft. (Rennison Collection)

David Lord V.C. (B. Rijnhout Collection)

missions. On 13th June Squadron Leader Pearson of "A" Flight landed his Dakota at Bazenville, making it the first British transport aircraft to land in France since 1940. Lt. General Browning was a passenger on this historic trip. On the return journey the aircraft was loaded with wounded personnel.

Both units became heavily involved in casualty evacuation work over the next few months. By early August 1944 the number of personnel evacuated by the Down Ampney squadrons had risen to 20,000. Queen Mary visited the station whilst the evacuation was in full swing and impressed everyone with her bearing and warm demeanour. In addition to the casualty work both units ferried a considerable number of 2nd Tactical Air Force personnel "the other way" to units based in France.

The Dakotas were once more in the firing line in September when they took part in "Operation Market", the airborne assault on Arnhem. The first foray from Down Ampney took place on 17th September 1944 when 49 Dakota/Horsa combinations set out for Holland. A further mission was flown in similar strength the following day. A third re-supply mission was flown on 19th September and this time the Dakotas really came in for a pasting and three aircraft were lost. One of those that failed to return was the aircraft of Flight Lieutenant David Lord of 271 Squadron. As his aircraft approached Arnhem it was hit twice by anti-aircraft fire and an engine was set on fire. Having ascertained that his crew were uninjured, Lord decided to press on to the Drop Zone, which was only some three minutes' flying time away, and drop his precious cargo. Trailing a plume of flame and smoke behind it, the stricken aircraft struggled on towards Arnhem at the dangerously low height of 900 feet, a prime target for anti-aircraft fire. The crew managed to drop all but two of their parachute containers over the DZ. Having accomplished the mission, David Lord ordered the crew to bale out while he tried to hold the aircraft in level flight. Before all the crew could get clear the aircraft crashed in flames and only one member of the crew survived. In recognition of his gallantry David Lord was awarded a posthumous Victoria Cross. Another now famous personality was piloting a Dakota on that day and narrowly escaped with his life. The aircraft of Flight

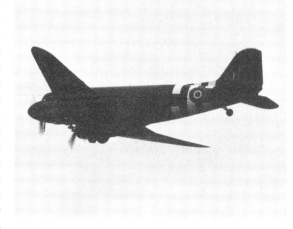
Taken at Fairford in 1985 this picture shows a surviving Dakota painted to represent David Lord's aircraft.
(R. Smith)

100

Jimmy Edwards the famous post was comedian flew Dakotas from Down Ampney and won the D.F.C. whilst with 271 Squadron. *(B. Rijnhout Collection)*

Lieutenant Jimmy Edwards was attacked by fighters and shot down in flames. Jimmy was thrown clear as the aircraft struck the ground but suffered burns and an injured left arm.

Back at Down Ampney Sergeant Harry Hodgson, a member of 271 Squadron ground crew, looked across at Flight Sergeant Charlie Outhwait. Three missing and one of them was David Lord's aircraft. He would not be needing the new identity card photos that had arrived for him shortly after take-off for Arnhem. There were two photographs and Harry and Charlie kept one each, not knowing that in the years to come Lord was to become one of the central characters of the Arnhem saga.

Through October and on into the New Year of 1945 the Dakotas were kept busy airlifting casualties from the Continent. In March 1945 Dakotas of both units left Down Ampney for airfields in Essex, in order to participate in "Operation Varsity", the crossing of the Rhine. Following "Varsity", the Dakotas continued to operate from Gloucestershire until July/August 1945 when they moved away. Before the end of the year, however, they were replaced by more Dakotas. This time, though, the aircraft belonged to Nos. 435 and 436 Squadrons of the Royal Canadian Air Force. By early the following year

The window of Down Ampney Church records the exploits of the airmen and soldiers that were based on the airfield during World War Two. *(B. Rijnhout Collection)*

Not much remains of Down Ampney in the 1980's except some concrete acreage and a small memorial. (P. Aston)

they too had departed and the land around Down Ampney began to return to something like its former rural tranquillity. Today there is not much remaining of the airfield except one or two crumbling buildings and a single memorial stone. The nearby church has a splendid memorial window which recalls the exploits of David Lord and the other personnel who served at Down Ampney. It is here each September that former members of the squadrons and their support gather for a small service of rememberance.

Fairford (OS ref. 163/150990)

On 17th January 1944 Squadron Leader R.G. Taylor arrived at Fairford in his capacity as Officer Commanding the Opening-up Party (one Flight Sergeant and 24 airmen) and officially took over from the site engineer, Mr. Graham. Much of the domestic site was still incomplete and for the first few days the airmen were based at Southrop.

Construction work continued throughout January although it was subject to delays. One of the major problems was concerned with the laying of steel plates at dispersal points. However, by the end of the month things were much improved and service personnel moved onto the station from Southrop.

In mid-February two officers from 26th Signals Construction Battalion US Army visited. The unit was in the process of installing telephone lines in the area and needed accommodation. They were allocated eleven huts and opted to take care of their own messing. The station water supply was source of difficulties due to the presence of "suspended matter" in the system. The problem became so bad during February that a 350 gallon water tanker had to be brought in from Lechlade to supply the station's needs.

The giant black-bellied Stirling bombers of 620 Squadron began to arrive in mid-March, some towing gliders. Within two days they were involved in operation Bizz-1, a parachute-dropping exercise. Before the end of the month more Stirlings and gliders had arrived, this time from 190 Squadron. This unit was also exercising within two days of its arrival. In the weeks that followed both squadrons began to carry out clandestine missions to France in addition to their glider activities. These operations were often mounted from Tarrant Rushton airfield in Dorset. They were carried out in support of the Special Operations Executive, or SOE, as it was known. Glider and parachute training up to the end of May 1944 included exercises with such undistinguished names as Posh, Mush, Dingo 1, Dingo 2, Drongo and Exeter. Several accidents occurred during this period, including one particularly horrific one which happened as aircraft were returning home following exercise Exeter. Two of the Stirlings (LJ880 and EF244) collided in mid-air over the tow rope dropping area near Kempsford. The collision took place at 400 feet. Both aircraft crashed, killing their crews.

With the approach of "D" Day all personnel were confined to the station. It was a nerve-jangling time for everyone and in order to ease the tension an "outdoor gang show" was held. The station also received a visit from Air Chief Marshal Sir Trafford Leigh Mallory. Matters came to a head at half-past eleven on the evening of 5th June 1944 when an armada of 45 Stirlings took off for Normandy, carrying 887 men of 6th Airborne Division. "Operation Tonga" was under way. The men were dropped to the east of the River Orne, their objective being to secure a bridge near Drop Zone "N". Three of the Stirlings were shot down and many of the others were found to be

Horsa Gliders being 'towed off'. (Rennison Collection)

Some members of 620 Squadron at Fairford in July 1944. The crew of Stirling LJ566 'Yorkshire II' survived a total of 33 Ops including D–Day 5th & 6th June and four trips to Arnhem between 17th & 23rd September 1944, all from Fairford.

(Severnside Aviation Society Collection)

Back Row:
    F/S Brian Garwood   F/O Ben Crocker   F/S Frank Pearman   F/O Derek De Rome
           AB   NAV   FE   PILOT RAAF
Front Row: W/O Noel Chaffey   F/S Pete Griffin
               W/OP RAAF   AG

badly damaged upon their return. The following evening 36 Stirlings with Horsa gliders in tow clambered into the air to begin "Operation Mallard". This operation was intended to convey elements of 6th Air Landing Brigade to France. The equipment carried consisted of 33 jeeps, 29 trailers, 11 motorcycles, eight 75mm guns and 254 troops. Thirty-five gliders landed safely; however, Horsa 158, piloted by S/Sgt. Turvey, was forced to ditch in the Channel when the tow rope snapped.

Throughout the next two months training continued interspersed with sorties on behalf of the SOE and the Special Air Service. One unusual night exercise involved the positioning of a Eureka beacon at Clun in the Black Mountains. Six aircraft from 190 Squadron then homed in on the beacon and dropped sand bags. The aircraft were able to pick up the beacon at a range of over 40 miles. In addition to Horsa gliders, the squadrons also made use of the American Waco glider and it was one of these that made an emergency landing at Bibury during July 1944.

The station was treated to two ENSA shows during August and in early September it came under the scrutiny of the press. A group of five newsmen, including John Yoxall of "Flight" and Edmund Townsend of the "Telegraph", toured the camp and spoke to airmen with their cameras ever at the ready. Clandestine operations on behalf of the SOE and SAS continued throughout August and into September.

A garishly decorated Stirling at Fairford.
(B. Rijnhout Collection)

Operation "Market", the airborne assault on the Arnhem bridges, got under way in mid September. Fifty aircraft were despatched to Arnhem from Fairford (25 from 620 Squadron and 25 from 190 Squadron) on the 17th. A further 43 aircraft made the trip in daylight on the 18th and 34 aircraft set off on the 19th. On the latter date one of the Stirlings crashed on take-off and two others failed to return. Twenty-nine out of the 34 despatched on the 20th got through. They managed to drop 696 containers and 116 panniers to the encircled troops. Five aircraft were lost on this occasion. Additional sorties were carried out on the 21st and 23rd of September. The CO of 620 Squadron, Wing Commander Lee DFC, was shot down on the 23rd but managed to evade capture and returned to Fairford some days later.

The scene at Fairford 17th September 1944 first day of the Arnhem landings. The Stirling in the centre is V—Victor Pilot F/O Ross Bunce. Men of the First Airborne Division are waiting to embark in Horsa gliders in foreground.
(Severnside Aviation Society Collection)

Horsas of 620 Squadron at Fairford during September 1944. (*B. Rijnhout Collection*)

Stirling Mk IV's of 620 Squadron RAF returning to Fairford from Arnhem September 1944. 'E' Easy — F/O G. F. Smith.
(*Severnside Aviation Society Collection*)

During early October 1944 elements of the squadrons and station staff began to move out to Great Dunmow. The move was to be a protracted one. The main party of station personnel did not leave until the 18th of the month, although the squadrons and their servicing echelons had departed the day before in the case of 620 Squadron, and three days earlier in the case of 190 Squadron.

By the end of 1944 Fairford had become a satellite airfield for No. 21 Heavy Glider Conversion Unit based at Keevil. This unit later moved to Blakehill Farm but continued to use Fairford as an outpost. However, by the end of 1945 the HGCU had moved away and Fairford had been put on care and maintenance. The airfield had certainly earned a rest but the respite was to be a brief one. The last 40 years have brought much activity and involvement with both the USAF and the RAF. Today's occupants are the giant silver KC135 tankers of the USAF, and it is currently the home of the 'International Air Tattoo' which takes place every two years.

Filton (OS ref. 172/595802)

The famous Bristol businessman, Sir George White, was responsible for bringing aviation to Filton. In 1910 he registered the British and Colonial Aeroplane Company. Transportation was one of White's great interests. He had virtually become the king of Britain's tramways and his bus services ran far and wide. Thus aviation was perhaps the next logical step.

A Clyde-trained engineer named Frank Barnwell was brought in to run things and the firm began to thrive. It became a major producer of aircraft during the First World War and an Aircraft Acceptance Park was established at Filton to deal with the newly-produced machines. Many well-known types were to be seen on the airfield, including Bristol's own Bristol Fighter and DH.9s built by the Westland Company further south. Average throughflow for the Acceptance Park was 80 aircraft a month.

Filton was also a mobilisation station for the RFC and many squadrons arrived, took over their aircraft and after a few weeks training departed for France. These units included Nos. 19, 20, 33, 42 and 66 Squadrons. At least two squadrons, Nos. 100 and 101, were disbanded at Filton after the Armistice in 1919.

Inevitably, there was a change of tempo after the end of hostilities, but in 1923 the company was given a contract to establish a Reserve Flying School at the airfield. Six years later No. 501 (Gloucester) Special Reserve Squadron was formed at Filton with Avro 504N trainers. Frank Barnwell was still producing excellent designs for the company and during the thirties he began to design and later build a very streamlined all-metal, twin-engined bomber, known as the Bristol Type 142. The assembled fuselage of this aircraft was displayed at the Paris Air Show of 1935. It was there that it came to the notice of Lord Rothermere (Britain's first Air Minister in 1918) who had been looking for a British aeroplane that could rival the latest American machines. He bought the aircraft when it was finished and after naming it "Britain First" he presented it to the Air Ministry. Within a year the Ministry had placed an order for the new aircraft which was now known as the Blenheim. Frank Barnwell was killed in 1938 when he crashed in a light aircraft of his own design. The country had lost one of its best designers at a time when it could ill afford to do so.

By the late thirties the Flying School had

The Blenheim shows its solid looking but attractive outline.

become known as No. 2 Elementary and Reserve Flying Training School but it was still run by the Bristol Company. During January 1939 a Ferry Flight was formed to serve the factory. This flight was later to become No. 2 Ferry Pool. On 1st June, 1939 RAF Station Filton was established under the command of Wing Commander H.D. O'Neill AFC. A few weeks later on 24th August a general mobilisation was ordered and 501 Special Reserve Squadron was embodied into the regular RAF as a fully-fledged fighter unit. The squadron's Hurricanes were officially declared operational on the fateful 3rd September, 1939. Twelve days later the Blenheims of 25 Squadron arrived from Northolt to assist in the defence of the Bristol area. During October the Blenheims returned to Northolt and No. 263 Gladiator Squadron was formed at Filton under Squadron Leader Donaldson. This was the "Phoney War" period and everything seemed strangely quiet. There was, however, some excitement on 4th October when Flying Officer Rayner of 501 Squadron was scrambled to intercept a drifting barrage balloon. He eventually caught it and shot it down in the Welsh mountains. There were one or two more abortive scrambles before the year's end and 501 Squadron moved out to Tangmere in November.

The station had some rather unusual visitors during January 1940: 24 airmen from Finland under the command of Captain Eskola. At nine o'clock on 11th January they set off on the first

A Finnish Airforce Blenheim with its blue swastika national markings.

stage of their trip home with twelve Blenheims, purchased for the Finnish Air Force. They were escorted north to Scotland by four RAF Blenheims. The air defences were itching for some action and were somewhat "trigger-happy". This, added to the fact that the Finnish Air Force markings consisted of a blue swastika on a white circle, suggested that an escort would be wise!

Early in February the station had a day to remember when HRH King George VI and the Queen visited. More strange aircraft markings were to be in evidence during the latter part of the month. Westlands requested permission to test fly two Lysander aircraft in Turkish Air Force markings in the Bristol area from late afternoon to dusk at a height of 20,000 feet.

Tragedy struck 263 Squadron on 29th March 1940 when two of the unit's Gladiators collided in mid-air and crashed. The incident took place over Marlwood Farm, Thornbury and was seen by Royal Observer Corps personnel at post K.4. A car was sent to the place where both aircraft had crashed, near Alveston, but nothing could be done for the pilots.

On 1st April there was almost a gala atmosphere in the station when 450 personnel involved in

Westland Lysanders in RAF colours were a common enough sight, but in 1940 a pair with the red squares of the Turkish Air Force emblazoned on their fuselage circled over Bristol.

local anti-aircraft defence arrived. They were given a demonstration of friendly aircraft types which included a flypast by Anson, Hampden, Lysander, Battle, Whitley, Wellington and Hudson aircraft.

The Ferry Pool moved out to Cardiff during April, becoming No. 4 (Continental) Pool, and 263 Squadron took their Gladiators to Norway that same month. June 1940 brought an increase in enemy activity and both Cardiff and Avonmouth were bombed during the month. Throughout the rest of 1940 and 1941 the airfield and the Bristol Aircraft Co. premises were bombed repeatedly (details of these incidents are given in the section on air attacks).

During April 1941 263 Squadron returned to Filton. After the ill-fated Norwegian campaign the unit had had to be reformed. The losses suffered in Scandinavia had been heavy and the final straw had come on 8th June, 1940 when the aircraft carrier HMS *Glorious* had been sunk with 263 Squadron personnel and aircraft on board. Thus it was a completely new unit that arrived at Filton ten months later: new personnel and new equipment. This time the squadron had the distinctively-shaped Westland Whirlwind fighter bomber.

The main runways were extended in late 1941 and early 1942, the airfield becoming the base for a large Overseas Aircraft Preparation Unit. A Ferry Flight was also formed to support the OAPU during February 1942 under the command of Squadron Leader Shaw. At this time the station also received several engineering liaison visits from a Colonel Borisenko, the Soviet Air Attache. Before the end of the year the OAPU had been redesignated No. 2 Aircraft Preparation Unit. During the spring and summer of 1942 several defence exercises were held on the airfield which involved mock attacks by the Somerset Light Infantry.

The "Red Air Force" also invaded the station in some strength during the middle of the following year when a group of six Soviet officers was attached to the Bristol Aircraft Company to study engineering methods and so on. In June 1943 No. 528 Squadron was formed on the airfield with Blenheims and Hornet Moth aircraft for calibration duties. It was decided in late 1943 to base several USAAF Mobile Repair and Reclamation Squadrons at Filton. Accordingly, in November Brigadier-General Knerr of the US 8th Air Force visited to inspect the site of USAAF Station 803, as the new base area was to be called.

Pilots of a Whirlwind fighter squadron pose before one of Westland's shark-like fighters.

No. 21 MRR Squadron was the first to arrive on 28th November, followed by No. 22 on the 29th. Early in December a third unit, No. 33 MRR Squadron, set up shop at Filton. A number of Butler hangars were built to provide premises for aircraft assembly. Many of the airmen, however, were put "under canvas" to begin with. The main task of the units was the reassembly of P47 Thunderbolt and P51 Mustang aircraft that had been shipped from the USA.

The "Yanks" made sterling efforts to fit in, holding several parties at local pubs during their first few weeks at Filton. Early in the spring they were given a demonstration by the Station Military Police Dog Team. This had a salutory effect on many of the late night revellers. The number of late returns by young airmen via the perimeter fence dropped remarkably! During May 1944 Station 803 assembled its 500th aircraft which was named "Flying Panther" and had been sponsored by a high school in East Orange, New Jersey. The MRR Squadrons began to prepare for departure in May and June and it was whilst these preparations were under way that a serious accident occurred. One of the hangars collapsed as it was being dismantled and injured 16 airmen. By

20th June 1944 all three MRR squadrons had departed. They had suffered only one fatal casualty during their time at Filton. This had occurred during February 1944 when 2nd Lt. Alva W. Leeper was killed when the aircraft he was test-flying crashed near the airfield.

The departure of the MRR squadrons went almost unnoticed, for Fate had provided an "American diversion" that attracted the undivided attention of the "locals". Flying Fortress bombers were arriving regularly during June 1944 and disgorging batches of crisp, attractive-looking American nurses. They were destined to serve in No. 94 General Hospital in Bristol. A huge medical support operation was under way, backing up the "D" day bridgeheads, with hospital and convalescent units spread throughout south Gloucestershire. By the end of 1944 a continual stream of Dakotas was bringing wounded personnel into Filton from France, whilst other Dakotas brought in precious cargoes of plasma and medicines to supply the hospitals.

With the cessation of hostilities in Europe things became considerably quieter. One organisation still using the airfield regularly at this time was the Bristol Aircraft Company's Centaurus Test Flight.

Mustang fighters were amongst the types 'put together' by the Mobile Repair and Reclamation Squadron at Filton.
(B. Rijnhout Collection)

USAAF Dakotas were a familiar sight at Filton during 1944 as they brought back wounded soldiers from Normandy.

Filton was to continue its association with test-flying and the aircraft industry through the post-war years up to the present day. Of course, the factory installations are now controlled by British Aerospace and Rolls-Royce (Bristol) but they have never quite shaken off the "feel" of the old Bristol Aircraft Company. The traditional RAF involvement is still kept alive by the presence of the Bulldog trainers of the Bristol University Air Squadron, an association which should continue into the foreseeable future.

Percival P.3 Gull six AX866 (EX G–ADPR Impressed) seen at 'C' Site R.A.F. Kemble during the war. (via B. Kedward)

Kemble (OS ref. 163/960965)

The first occupant of the airfield at Kemble was an Aircraft Storage Unit that took up residence during mid-1938. By early 1939 "H" Maintenance Unit had arrived from Waddington and was redesignated No. 5 MU under the control of 41 Group. Life for the MU went along fairly quietly until the outbreak of war in September 1939, when the station was placed on war footing. Three days after the declaration of war a number of Wellington bombers from 37 Squadron at Feltwell were dispersed to Kemble for a couple of days. This unit had already been in action against the enemy. Six of its Wellingtons had carried out an anti-shipping sweep in the area of the Heligoland Bight only seven hours after the expiration of Britain's ultimatum to Germany.

The following month additional land was acquired to accommodate the ever-growing number of aircraft being stored by the MU. The number had risen to over 500 by early 1940. During the spring of 1940 a Ferry Pilot Pool came into being on the station although it was not as well-equipped as it might have been. Some of the personnel were given very rudimentary

Wicko G.M.I. 'Warferry' HM574 (EX G–AFKS Impressed) 'poses on the grass at Kemble during the mid war years.
(via B. Kedward)

Percival 'Verga Gull' T–TEC X9340 (G–AFBC Impressed) near the B2 Hangar at Kemble. (via B. Kedward)

accommodation. An airfield defence flight was formed during July and was in action almost straight away. One of the Flight's Hurricanes was scrambled to intercept an intruder during the

Taylorcraft 'Auster' 1 LB319 seen at Kemble with other assorted aircraft types.   *(via B. Kedward)*

A.S. Airspeed A.S.5. Courier X9437 (EX G–ADAX Impressed) at Kemble cira 1943.   *(via B. Kedward)*

afternoon of 25th July 1940. The pilot of the Hurricane, Pilot Officer Bird, had already acquired something of a reputation for allegedly shooting down an enemy aircraft in France whilst delivering a Hurricane. He was at the time of the scramble in the grip of a very fatalistic mood. He felt quite strongly that he would not survive the war. Only the day before he had walked around Cheltenham with his young wife and with the feeling of foreboding stronger than ever. In a book shop he had come across a poem entitled "Wings" which, with some slight alteration, he felt was appropriate to himself. He asked his wife to ensure that, if anything happened to him, the last verse of the poem would be put on his gravestone.

ᵛᴸᴱ ᴴᴰᴱ   ᴴᴱ ᴵᵁᴿᴺᴵ)

WINGS

HE

M~~xxxxx~~ had wings. On many a windy day,
  A plaid fixed firmly to his tiny back,
With arms outstretched he danced his happy way
  Running, half flying, down the mountain track.

HE

M~~xxxx~~ had wings, for when no more a boy
  Nothing would serve him of our mundane things,
But with the birds and winds he took his joy,
  And soon he proudly came to earn his wings.

HE

M~~xxxx~~ had wings, and when the war swept near
  And he was called, gladly and swift he sped
To meet outnumb'ring foes, and without fear
  Fell crashing to the ocean's icy bed.

- -

HE

M~~xxx~~ has wings, for as the plane dived deep,
  His spirit, free within the realms of space,
On new-found wings flew with a swifter sweep,
  Fearless and laughing, to the Throne of Grace.

Last verse on his grave stone. A.C.L
at Hotel. – wings carved also.

A copy of the poem discovered in Cheltenham by Alec Bird and altered by him the day before his death.

The intruder for whom he went hunting on that July afternoon was brought down, albeit in somewhat confused circumstances. The sad irony is that shortly afterwards, Bird's Hurricane also crashed, killing its pilot. The tragic circumstances of that summer so long ago are still remembered with great clarity by the young woman whom he had married on the day that war broke out less than a year earlier.

By October the station had some 15 hangars, seven of which were of the small Robin type. At this point in time the airfield ground defences boasted four 2-pounder Vickers guns, four Hispano guns and four twin Vickers guns. On 2nd November 1940 a disaster was narrowly averted when a Mohawk and a Hurricane collided in mid-air without the expected result. The two Ferry Pool pilots managed to get their aircraft down safely. The airfield was continually being upgraded and despite the wintry weather work was still under way in December 1940. Hard core was being put down at the entrance to two new hangars on "D" site and steel wool camouflage was being used in an unexplained manner at "C" site. On Christmas Day the CO and other station officers served lunch to the airmen in keeping with RAF tradition.

There was some extremely poor weather during January and February 1941 which served to lower morale somewhat. The situation was not helped by the court martial on 11th February of eleven airmen accused of stealing petrol. On 1st April the Ferry Pool was reorganised and the majority of the pilots were transferred to No. 4 MU. The remainder formed the Service Ferry Training Squadron which had two detached Flights: No. 10 (Polish) Ferry Flight at nearby Hullavington and No. 11 Ferry Flight based at Dumfries. HM Queen Mary made an unofficial visit to the station during the afternoon of 17th April 1941. She was accompanied by the Duchess of Beaufort and her Private Secretary, Major Wickham.

The station continued to develop and during September work began on new runways. Kemble was at this time home to elements of a Lancaster Conversion Unit, mainly based at Northolt. Life continued steadily through to the end of the year, by which time the station had been taken over by Ferry Command and was under the control of 44 Group. By early 1942 Kemble was the parent station for SLGs at Berrow (No. 4), Beechwood (No. 12), Bush Barn (No. 44) and Barnsley (No. 22). An assembly facility for Horsa gliders was set up in No. 1 hangar during June and No. 3 hangar became a Miscellaneous Aircraft Supply Centre. The Luftwaffe provided a diversion on 27th July when three Dorniers strafed the airfield and dropped incendiaries. Only minor damage resulted fortunately.

Exercise "Boomerang" was held early in August. The scenario for this test of the station defences required the 30th Battalion of the Gloucestershire Regiment to recapture the station from hostile forces. They must have managed the task because the station was available for visitors the following month! Sir Stafford and Lady Cripps arrived on 19th September, at the same time as a large group of civilian employees from RAF Quedgeley. The civilians were given air experience flights in Whitley, Oxford and Blenheim aircraft. The glider assembly operation had by the end of September taken over six hangars and flight testing of Horsa and Hotspur gliders was an almost everyday occurrence. Prior to the end of the month a stranger-than-fiction event occurred which the station diary does not adequately explain. On 23rd September an unidentified aircraft was reported as having crashed nearby during a storm. This aircraft was eventually found in a field a few miles from the drome. It was on fire and although a search was carried out there was no sign of the crew. The following day "fragments of a body" were found near the aircraft wreckage. These were preserved in formalin for four days, at which point permission was given for a burial. The diary says no more about this incident. Neither the aircraft nor the mysterious "casualty" is identified. A strange incident altogether.

The Overseas Aircraft Preparation Unit which was now working on a variety of aircraft in addition to large numbers of Lockheed Hudsons was redesignated No. 1 OAPU in December 1941.

As the end of the year approached the weather

A Hudson of the type handled by No.1 AOPs in 1941.

once again began to worsen. An excellent Christmas lunch, however, raised the spirits of one and all. Despite wartime rationing, the menu offered celery soup, turkey and pork with apple sauce, brussels sprouts and baked potatoes, followed by Christmas pudding. It had been a busy year for the OAPU. They had handled 269 Hudsons, 661 Wellingtons, 17 Halifaxes, four Beaufighters, two Marylands and a Beaufort: a total of 954 aircraft with an average monthly output of 79.6 aircraft. Despite all the work on the station facilities, the airmen's quarters were still in a poor state. One medical report put forward during 1942 described huts 20 to 24 as "incredible". They were built of plasterboard, which was broken in many places. The roof leaked and the huts were unbelievably cold. The air was constantly full of dust blown around by the draughts.

January 1943 brought tragedy for No. 1 OAPU when Halifax W7844 crashed with eight personnel from the unit's Despatch Flight on board. The bomber had taken off on a routine test flight and a number of ground crew from the Flight had gone along for the ride. The pilot was 24 year-old Flight Lieutenant Frederick Harrison, the CO of the Test and Depatch Flight. Another aircraft seen in the vicinity at the time is variously identified as a Spitfire or a Blenheim. There is no doubt that this second aircraft is associated with the incident that followed but the details are obscure. What is known for certain is that the Halifax went into a steep turn at about 2,000 feet, stalled and spun in. This was something the Halifax was prone to do off a steep turn. Harrison was comparatively inexperienced on this type of aircraft and may have been taken unawares. The aircraft came down at Oaksey Woods to the east of Kemble striking the ground vertically. One of those that saw the Halifax "go in" was a local man, Bill Sherwood. He was one of the first to get to the crash scene. The aircraft was a blazing inferno; crash recovery vehicles sped to the crash

A Halifax bomber. An aircraft of this type crashed near Kemble early in 1943 whilst on a test flight.

site across fields but could do nothing more than contain the fire.

During 1943 the station became heavily involved with such types as Warwick, Whitley, Oxford, Master and Typhoon. Towards the end of the year an extension to runway 09/27 was begun and more taxiways were built. The year closed with a "workers' playtime concert" which was attended by the AOC No. 41 Group, Air Vice-Marshall Laing, and more than 300 personnel. The show was compered by Bill Gates and featured Kenway & Young, Pat Hyde, Robert Easton, Bruce Merry and George Myddleton.

Emphasis during early 1944 was placed on the production of such types as Lancasters, Warwicks, Hurricanes, Oxfords and Lysanders. With the approach of "D" Day the need was for Typhoon fighter bombers. Production was upped dramatically, with "E" site being turned into an extra production site. Total output of aircraft during 1944 rose to 1,100. Typhoon production continued into the New Year and by June 1945 the total output of this aircraft alone had risen to 750. In addition, a number of Lancasters were produced for Canada and at the other end of the size scale a number of the diminutive Cierva Autogyros were taken into store. Kemble satellites began to run down with the end of hostilities and No. 22 SLG at Barnsley Park closed in September. American Dakotas brought 1945 to a close with a massive tow-off of over 100 gliders. Kemble was destined to carry on in its Maintenance Unit role right through the post-war years up to the present day. Although there have been one or two alterations along the way the station looks today much as it did during the war years, and now services A10 'Warthogs' of the USAF.

112

Little Rissington (OS ref. 163/215190)

This station, with an elevation of 730 feet above sea level, was one of the highest operational airfields in the RAF when it opened during August 1938. The advance party of No. 6 Flying Training School arrived on 11th August 1938 from Netharavon. The unit was equipped with a somewhat tired assortment of Hawker biplanes and one or two Anson trainers. The flying side was modernised slightly just prior to the move with the addition of some new Harvard trainers.

The first station commander was Group Captain A. ap Ellis CBE who is well-remembered locally because he added a Cotswold flourish to the military austerity. He authorised the building of a Cotswold stone wall along the roadside adjacent to the Sergeants' Mess and married quarters and made a concerted attempt to preserve the tree population of the station.

During October 1938 No. 8 Maintenance Unit under Squadron Leader W. Dean set up on the station. The initial task of the unit was vehicle storage but this was soon to change. The increasingly tense situation in Europe during early 1939, culminating in Hitler's seizure of what was left of Czechoslovakia, made changes inevitable. As a consequence the unit's role was changed to one of aircraft preparation and storage and the build-up that followed was a rapid one. By September 1939 over 250 aircraft, mainly Spitfires and Wellingtons, were in storage. A month earlier 41 Group had ordered the unit to apply wartime finish to the aircraft in its charge in anticipation of the hostilities to come.

A new unit established itself at Rissington during September: the Equipment Training School for Officers under Squadron Leader B.W. Hemsley. By the end of 1939 No. 6 FTS was bulging at the seams with called-up reservists and members of the Royal Auxiliary Air Force. After elementary training the unit's programme was divided into two parts: an intermediate stage, completion of which meant the award of pilot's wings, and an advanced stage, followed by posting to an Operational Training Unit. With the outbreak of war the unit was redesignated No. 6 Service Flying Training School.

The winter of 1939/40 was a particularly severe one and flying training was drastically curtailed. Rissington suffered a good deal from rain and snow and in January 1940 "E" and "G" Flights made a brief foray to Kidlington, Oxfordshire in hope of finding better conditions. Things proved to be little better and both flights returned after only a few days. The thaw that followed the cold weather did not really help matters either and through February and March only parts of the airfield were usable. By the middle of 1940, however, the yellow-bellied Oxford trainers of the SFTS were constantly overhead, doing their "circuits and bumps". In order to improve pilot throughput the course had been reduced from 14 weeks to 12 weeks, with a new group of trainees arriving every three-and-a-half weeks.

It was during the long, hot summer of 1940 that one of Rissington's trainees earned himself a place in local and RAF folklore. Sgt. Bruce Hancock was making his final night approach to the satellite airfield at Windrush before completing his course and heading off on a well-earned leave, when events took a completely unexpected turn. Unknown to Bruce, the airfield had just been bombed by a Heinkel intruder and as the Anson approached, the enemy aircraft slid into line behind it. Suddenly the spark-like flicker of tracer was seen by airmen on the ground as the Heinkel opened fire on its helpless target. Bruce Hancock could have only had seconds to realise what was happening and make a decision. He had previously said to his brother-in-law if anything like this should happen and he was defenceless, he would ram his attacker. The airmen on the landing strip watched in horror as the Anson seemed to slow down, allowing the Heinkel to overshoot, and then, seemingly with absolute deliberation, it pulled up and crashed into its adversary. The two aircraft fell to the ground close to each other at Blackpits Farm, Aldsworth. Sgt. Hancock and the crew of the Heinkel perished in the crash. One of the first to the scene was Constable Taylor, of Bibury, together with

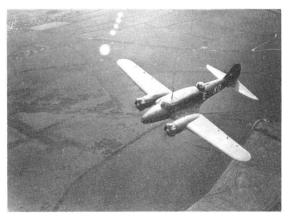

A splendid view of an Anson 'exercise bound'. (H. Hodgson)

Constable Kendal. They found wreckage scattered over a wide area. They helped the ambulance crew look for casualties and almost missed one of the German airmen who was still slumped in the rear part of the smashed Heinkel. "A very young, ginger-haired fellow", as PC Taylor described him.

The station civilian staff formed their own unit of the Home Guard for ground defence duties during August 1940 and manned a network of strongpoints around the base. The flying training programme was still gathering momentum despite the occasional attention of the Luftwaffe. The ever-increasing demand for pilots brought about a further cut in the length of the course from twelve to ten weeks by the autumn. The MU was also at full stretch, turning out hundreds of aircraft for operational and training units alike. The pressure to increase the pilot output was continuous during 1941/42 and, as a result, the "Gordon-Dean" scheme was introduced to maximise the use of all available resources. Flying hours increased dramatically and the SFTS achieved first place in the hours league table during July 1941 by reaching a total of 9,000 hours. Things could not continue at such a pace, however, and the total fell back when the experiment ended. A start was made on runway construction prior to the end of 1941 — long overdue.

During the spring of 1942 the SFTS was redesignated No. 6 (Pilot) Advanced Training Unit. Its task as a (P)AFU was mainly the familiarisation of pilots trained abroad with conditions in the United Kingdom. Another Oxford-equipped unit had arrived on the scene earlier in the year, No. 1523 Beam Approach Training Flight. A new, non-flying organisation also appeared during July 1942 when the station anti-aircraft defences were taken over by No. 417

AA Flight of the newly-formed RAF Regiment. At this time the MU was heavily involved in the assembly of Hotspur and Horsa gliders. These "wooden warriors" were towed aloft on test flights by ageing Whitley bombers. In addition, the unit continued to work on Spitfires, Wellingtons, Oxfords and Hampdens. By 1943 the mixture had become a rather more exotic one and included Halifaxes, Typhoons and American Kittyhawk and Mohawk fighters.

The Duke and Duchess of Gloucester visited the station and the MU in the early part of 1943. The Duchess showed particular interest in the work done by the station's airwomen. It was in August 1943 that a former pupil at Little Rissington, Flight Sergeant A.L. Aaron DFM, earned the country's highest gallantry award. He was one of the pilot's of 218 Stirling Squadron who were briefed to bomb Turin on the night of 12th August. As his aircraft approached the target it came under fighter attack. Three engines were hit, the front and rear turrets were put out of action and the cockpit was severely damaged. Aaron, with half his face shot away and with wounds in his arm and side, fought to control the aircraft.

F./Sgt. A. L. Aaaron V.C. D.F.M. who was trained at Little Rissington.

Other members of the crew had also been wounded in the onslaught and the navigator had been killed. Aaron could not regain control; he was too weak and unable to speak. He gestured to the Flight Engineer to take over the controls. The Bomb Aimer also came to assist and together they managed to keep the stricken bomber aloft. After resting, Aaron made several attempts to take over the controls of the aircraft as its makeshift pilot, the Bomb Aimer kept it on course for North Africa, but he was too weak from loss of blood. The aircraft managed to reach Bone airfield on the North African coast and the Bomb Aimer set about the hazardous business of making a belly

landing. Aaron gathered his remaining strength and insisted on helping but even so five attempts at a landing were made before the bomber finally managed to get down. Some nine hours later Aaron died of exhaustion and loss of blood. He had shown incredible courage and fortitude as well as the utmost concern for his crew and was justly awarded a posthumous Victoria Cross.

The MU empire was still expanding during 1943 and the unit took over No. 34 SLG at Woburn Park for extra storage plus a number of storage facilities at other locations, including RAF Northolt. Throughout 1944 the MU was a major repository for Wellington bombers, having over 750 in hand at the end of the year. More storage was needed during 1945 and as a consequence No. 107 Sub-storage Unit was set up at Honeybourne in Worcestershire and No. 188 at Long Marston in Warwickshire.

November 1945 saw the end of No. 6 (P)AFU's training activities. The unit had done its job well and a total of 5,444 pilots had received their training at its hands. It was disbanded on 26th November 1945, only to be reformed three weeks later, once again under the title of 6 SFTS, equipped with the distinctive-sounding Harvard trainer. Little Rissington was to have a distinguished post-war history but the part played by the station in providing pilots and aircraft at a time of dire need should never be underestimated.

A formation of Harvard trainers over Little Rissington.

114

A selection of photographs showing typical scenes from Little Rissington during the mid war years. Harvard trainers and trainee aircrew being prepared for a sortie.
(All photos W/Cdr. G. Hamer via B. Kedward)

Long Newnton (OS ref. 163/929920)

This airfield site hovers on the Gloucestershire — Wiltshire border and was almost certainly in use by the military as an air-ground firing range during World War One. The locally-based Australian Flying Corps certainly made use of the range during 1918-19 to train Australian pilots for the Western Front. The fresh outbreak of hostilities in 1939 meant a new lease of life for the site and it was chosen as the location for a "Q" site dummy to cover nearby Kemble. The basic

grass surface was also used as an RLG by the Harvard trainers of No. 15 SFTS from Kidlington in Oxfordshire. South Cerney's Oxford trainers took over the usage during 1941 and they were followed by more Harvards, this time from 14 SFTS at Lyneham.

By early 1942 the site had been developed into a fully-fledged satellite airfield with a control tower and blister hangars to serve No. 3 (P)AFU at South Cerney. Oxford trainers were based on the airfield and the facilities continued to expand with more blisters and a T.1 hangar being erected. No. 15 (P)AFU took over the airfield during the autumn of 1943. The surface of the airfield was poor and during the winter of 1943/44 the weather conspired to keep 15 (P)AFU on the ground most of the time until the spring arrived. The training round was interrupted in August 1944 when a B.25 Mitchell bomber (FR190) of No. 320 (Dutch) Squadron tried to get down on the small airfield during a cross-country training flight from Dunsfold. Lt. Collee, the pilot, touched down on the small landing area and began treading heavily on the brakes. The ground was wet and the aircraft careered across the airfield skidding violently, crashed through the boundary fence and ended up in a potato field with its back broken. Most of those watching breathed a sigh of relief; it could have been much worse. Collee and his four crew members, Jaap Boom, the observer, trainee navigator Sgt. Van Berkum, and the two gunners, De Jong and Muller, disembarked a little shakily. Fuel had spilled from the split tanks but fortunately no fire ensued. Collee later became a

A line up of B−25 Mitchell bombers form 320 (Dutch) Squadron during the latter part of the war. One of these aircraft came to grief at Long Newton during the summer of 1944.

Lt. Collee the pilot of Mitchell FR190 is 3rd from the left (standing) and Jaap Boom the observer is kneeling on the extreme right. (J. Boom)

bank manager in his native Holland after the war and often recalled his brief flirtation with Long Newnton's grassy surface.

Bad weather during the latter part of 1944 once again restricted flying activities and things did not improve in the New Year. In April 1945 15 (P)AFU was disbanded and the airfield was put on care and maintenance, being used for storage by 11 MU at Chilmark. The site has now largely been returned to agricultural use although several buildings can still be seen, giving some indication of the wartime activity.

Moreton-in-Marsh (OS ref. 151/230350)

Construction of this airfield began in 1940 and was still incomplete in January 1941 when the first RAF elements began to arrive. Pilot Officer Turner from Headquarters Bomber Command was first to arrive with three SNCO's and 15 airmen on 21st January. He was appalled to find the whole station a sea of mud, with runways and peri-tracks still incomplete. Contractors were still busy on the foundations of two "T" type hangars and had only erected the framework for two others.

On 11th February 40 soldiers from the Gloucestershire Regiment arrived to take over station defence duties. Ten days later Wing Commander R.A.A. Cole became station commander and the airfield received a flying visit by the Air Officer Commanding, Air Commodore MacNeece-Foster. Three days after this the first Wellington and Anson aircraft of 21 OTU began to arrive.

By 1st March 1941 No. 1 Course, consisting of six pilots, three observers and nine air gunners, was ready to commence. Two aircraft from "C" Flight inaugurated the flying training programme on 3rd March 1941 when they took off on a training flight at 10.30 hours. On its very first approach one of the aircraft struck the tops of some trees on the edge of the airfield. The instructor immediately took over from the pupil pilot and landed safely.

No. 2 Course began on 18th March and the training programme was well under way. The unit's main purpose in life was to train bomber crews up to the required standard for operational flying. Not an easy task, and one further complicated by the fact that there were no dual-control Wellingtons on the unit strength. As a stop-gap, two dual-control aircraft were

V for Victor a Wellington of 'E' Flight and personnel of 21 OTU at Morton-in-Marsh in 1941
(Severnside Aviation Society Collection)

'E' Flight personnel of 21 OTU at Morton-in-Marsh, in 1941

(Severnside Aviation Society Collection)

"borrowed" from 15 OTU at Harwell. By the end of March a dozen aircraft had been fitted with the extra set of controls and the situation eased.

Although 21 OTU was a training unit it frequently despatched aircraft on operational sorties. Typical of this type of activity was a leaflet or "Nickel" raid, as it was known, carried out on the night of 27th/28th March. A leaflet drop was to be carried out by four Wellingtons of the unit in the Paris area. All four aircraft returned safely from this "taster". During June the station defences were improved by the addition of twelve Lewis and 25 Vickers guns. Unfortunately, they were not as lethal as they looked since the consignment had been despatched without gun sights or mountings.

OTU aircraft were worked extremely hard and consequently there was a high attrition rate due to basic wear and tear. Typical of the sort of incident that occurred as a result of this overworking was what happened on 23rd July 1941. Sgt. Anderson had just touched down when the tail wheel of his aircraft collapsed. The verdict of the inquiry was that the wheel had given way as a result of the cumulative effect of many heavy landings. That same month a BBC recording party arrived on the station to record for posterity the sounds of an OTU at work and play. The ever-expanding workload created a requirement for more space and in September 1941 the OTU took on Edgehill as a satellite airfield.

HRH the Duke of Kent visited the station during October. A few days later an Anson and a Wellington had a pile-up on the peri-track. Apparently, the Anson pilot had not switched on his tail light and the Wellington pilot did not see him until it was too late. In November two

Lysander aircraft were taken on strength, adding to the 58 Wellingtons and one "instructional airframe" already "owned" by the unit. Accidents frequently occurred on OTUs and Moreton was to have its fair share as Christmas 1941 approached. There were two accidents late in December; the first involved Wellington DV422 which dived into the ground at Chipping Norton on the 23rd. The pilot of this aircraft was the highly experienced and popular Squadron Leader Williams DFC AFM. All six crew members perished as the aircraft crashed in flames.

The second incident occurred during the small hours of 24th December. Flight Sergeant Fryer touched down in Wellington DV425 and the undercarriage collapsed. The aircraft ground to a halt on its belly but, fortunately, there were no casualties.

Early in the New Year of 1942 the famous Jim Mollison, now an ATA pilot, landed in a Stirling bomber whilst on a delivery flight. The reason for his visit is not recorded but it is possible that he

The OTU's Christmas Party in 1941 at Morton-in-Marsh.
(Severnside Aviation Society Collection)

was intending to visit Stoke Orchard to the north of Cheltenham where his wife, the equally famous Amy Johnson, had been living before the war. By this time the OTU was training crews for the Middle East Air Force. Once their training was complete the crews would depart with their bombers via France for North Africa. By the spring the number of crews heading south was 15 a month and by the summer this had risen to 20. The despatch of these crews was managed by No. 1446 Ferry Training Flight which had been formed at Bassingbourn and later moved to Moreton.

On the night of 30th/31st May 1942 the RAF mounted its first 1,000 bomber raid against Cologne. These attacks were the brainchild of Sir Arthur Harris, the new chief of Bomber Command and a native of Cheltenham. The RAF was required to put up every possible aircraft, including those drawn from training units. The OTU provided 19 aircraft for this raid from Moreton itself and from the satellite at Edgehill.

Wellingtons from the OTU also participated in the 1,000 raids that followed against Essen and

A number of Hurricanes were in evidence at Moreton for gunnery training purposes during 1944.

A Wellington crew ready for 'the off'.

Many of the young airmen that died at Moreton remain 'in situ' in the village's small cemetery.

(Rennison Collection)

Bremen. Throughout the remainder of 1942 and into 1943 the unit continued to train crews and provide aircraft for raids on Continental targets. On 29th January 1943 five Wellingtons were detailed for a "Nickel" raid on Nantes. Two aircraft dropped their leaflets on Brien and one dropped on Lamballe. One of the remaining two had to land at Colerne with a malfunction and the second aircraft, W5705, was reported as missing. It was later found that this aircraft had come down at Ruscombe, near Stroud, killing its crew.

In May 1943 the Ferry Training Flight became No. 311 Ferry Training Unit, although its role of Middle East supply did not change. The previous month Moreton had relinquished the Edgehill satellite and by May the OTU was making use of Enstone, across the border in Oxfordshire. The unit's Wellingtons made quite a number of leaflet raids during late 1943, along with some bombing operations against targets in France. In fact, 21 OTU was one of the last units to use the obsolete Wellington Ic on operational missions and these aircraft were still in use well into 1944. An all-ranks Christmas dance was held in the NAAFI on Christmas Day attended by some 2,000 people.

In the spring of 1944 the unit received some additional aircraft when 35 Wellingtons were transferred because of the disbandment of 15 OTU at Harwell. Several Hurricane fighters were also taken on charge to assist in training gunners, replacing the Miles Martinets that had previously been employed in this role. Operational flying by the unit's Wellingtons ceased in July 1944. The

Morton-in-Marsh main runway is now full of fire training buildings and the like. (Rennison Collection)

Traces of Moreton's old dispersals could still be clearly seen during the early 1980's.

Part of Moreton's old wartime HF/DF site has survived into the 1980's in a field close to the station.
(Rennison Collection)

Moreton Valence (OS ref. 162/796104)

Initially known as Haresfield, this airfield opened in an incomplete state in November 1939. It was first used by the Anson trainers of No. 6 Advanced Observer Navigation School at Staverton. To support these activities an ambulance with medical crew was despatched daily from Staverton when flying was in progress. One of the medical orderlies who carried out this duty was Mr. G.J. Jenkins, who now lives in South Wales. He recalls that on several occasions the auxiliary ambulance driver was a well-to-do lady racehorse owner from Cheltenham. The medical orderlies and other ground personnel would often be flown back to Staverton in a Rapide piloted by Wing Commander Barlow, the CO.

The Armstrong Whitworth Albemarle bomber was under test on the airfield at this time. The aircraft was still on the secret list and was being built at nearby Brockworth by Hawkesley Ltd. It was something of a disappointment as a bomber but established a good reputation as a glider tug. The airfield was revamped during 1941 and emerged with runways, extra hangars and a new name: Moreton Valence. By the end of the year two Flights from Staverton were permanently based on the station. Servicing, however, was done on a pool basis at Staverton by Airwork personnel. A Pilot Refresher Training Unit was formed on the airfield during the early part of 1942. Its tenure was brief, however, and within a few weeks it had moved out, leaving the airfield to Staverton's Ansons.

training activity continued until the end of hostilities in May 1945 and beyond.

There was some excitement during April 1945 when no less than 17 Lancasters were diverted to Moreton, together with two American B.24 Liberators. The OTU was finally to leave Moreton in 1946; however, the station was retained by the RAF into the 1960s. It is now the home of the Fire Service Technical College but many of the wartime buildings survive and can easily be seen.

Amongst this group of aircrew trainees photographed at Moreton Valence in February 1943 is LAC W. Halpern (extreme right back row) who was to be killed within weeks when his Anson crashed during March.

In 1943 Gloster Aircraft Company was given permission to take over the airfield for use as an aircraft assembly and testing facility. The runways were extended and new buildings were erected. By the end of the year the company had taken up residence. A good deal of the work on the new jet fighter, the Meteor, was transferred to Moreton. Comparative tests were conducted between the new Gloster aircraft and its American counterpart, the Bell YP-59A.

The Advanced Flying Unit closed down during December 1944 but this did not mean the end of military flying at the airfield. South Cerney took on Moreton as a satellite and its Oxfords replaced the Ansons of the AFU. In the spring of 1945 this unit closed down also and, as a result, Moreton was passed to Little Rissington as a satellite. It continued to be used in this way up to the end of 1945.

Post-war, the Gloster Company continued to occupy the site and several record-breaking flights were made from the airfield during the late 1940s. Nowadays the old airfield is an industrial estate bisected by the M5 motorway.

South Cerney (OS ref. 163/045985)

The first signs of activity occurred on this airfield site in 1936 when employees of Chivers & Sons from Devizes began pegging out the locations of hangars and other buildings. It was envisaged that the station would provide a permanent home for No. 3 Flying Training School which was at that time based at Grantham, Lincolnshire.

The FTS began to move in with its Audax biplanes in August 1937 although the station was far from complete. Indeed, Kier & Company of London were still involved in hangar construction work a year later. By the end of 1938 the Audax biplanes had given way to twin-engined Oxford trainers. It was about this time also that the Headquarters of No. 23 Group moved onto the station, again from Grantham.

The number of Oxfords on the strength rose steadily until Airspeed's attractive twin became synonymous with the airfield. The CO during these early years was Group Captain Iron OBE, a much respected officer who later achieved air rank. Following the outbreak of war in September 1939 the tempo of training moved up and the station received a visit by HM King George VI on 10th February 1940. In June of that year elements of No. 15 Service Flying Training School arrived

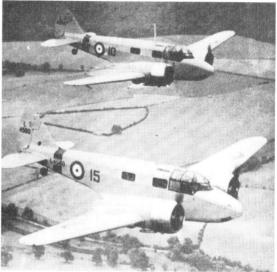

Pre war Oxford trainers from South Cerney pose for the camera.

from Middle Wallop. They were greeted by the Luftwaffe a few days later when a Heinkel bombed and strafed the airfield.

The FTS continued its repetitive but highly important training tasks through into 1942 despite numerous interruptions by the Luftwaffe and the numerous accidents that were so much a feature of life on any training unit. One of the worst accidents occurred during August 1940 when two Oxfords (P1821 and P1955) collided during a formation flying exercise. As a result P1821 crashed near the airfield, killing its crew. The pilot instructor of P1955 managed to get the aircraft down safely in spite of the fact that a sizeable chunk of one wing was missing. Early in 1942 the FTS was redesignated No. 3 Pilot Advanced Flying Unit and more emphasis was placed on refresher training and acclimatisation for pilots trained abroad under the Empire Training Scheme.

During April 1943 No. 1539 Beam Approach Training Flight arrived. They were to operate from South Cerney pending the availability of Bibury airfield which required amongst other things a beacon installation. By May it appeared that all was ready at Bibury and then it was found that a stone wall was reflecting the beacon signal. An attempt was made to retune the beacon and then it was found that the wet grass of the airfield was acting as a reflector. The difficulties were eventually overcome and No. 2 Course was able to commence training on 13th May, 1943.

The BAT Flight finally moved to Bibury in mid-July. Two other BAT units spent time at South Cerney before the war's end, No. 1532 and No. 1547 Flights, which did not depart until 1945.

With the end of the war 3 (P)AFU began to run down and on 4th December 1945 it was disbanded. However, like a phoenix from the ashes a new unit arose, designated No. 3 FTS, and it was formed on 11th December. Its stay was to be brief for in May of the following year it moved away to Feltwell in Norfolk. South Cerney continued to be used by the RAF up to 1971 when it was handed over to the Army. RAF gliders still operate from the airfield on occasions and the odd Hercules transport can be seen in the circuit from time to time. The semi-deserted airfield is maintained in good condition and still retains much of its wartime appearance.

Staverton (OS ref. 162/887218)

Staverton airfield opened in 1936 but its origins go back to a somewhat earlier date. In the early 1930s a small landing strip came into use just across the road from the present airfield site, known as Down Hatherley landing ground. It had been set up under the auspices of a Major Blood and a Mr. A.W. King who ran the Westgate Motor Company. They had become agents for De Havilland in 1930 and had needed somewhere to display the aircraft. A visit by Sir Alan Cobham in 1933 sparked off much interest in the possibility of a local airport proper and many eyes were cast across the road where there was what appeared to be an ideal site.

There was much local support for such a scheme and finally during 1934 Gloucester and Cheltenham Town Councils farsightedly agreed to purchase the 160-acre site for development as a municipal airport.

The official opening date was 16th July 1936 but the weather intervened and caused a delay. However, by November the airfield had an operating licence and Railway Air Services became the first commercial users when they began staging

Aircraft of Cobham's Flying Circus were amongst the first users of the Down Hatherley landing ground.
(Rennison Collection)

through the new airport on their Bristol to Birmingham run. Representatives of the Air Ministry visited the airfield during 1937 and recommended its use as a military base. Negotiations then took place between the two corporations and the Ministry, together with Westgate Motor Company which was administering the airport. As a result of these talks the Ministry granted the right to use the airfield as a training base for twelve years. The Ministry was to extend the airfield as required, erect its own buildings and install night flying equipment.

In 1938 the Cotswold Aero Club, based at the airport, was asked to train pilots under the new Civil Air Guard scheme. The club was overwhelmed with applications for training as soon as the scheme was publicised. The cost of the training was extremely low, being set at between five and ten shillings (25p-50p) an hour. This was less than a quarter of the normal flying school rate.

RAF involvement began during May 1939 when Martins School of Air Navigation arrived from Shoreham. The school was renamed the Airwork Civil School of Air Navigation, although the title was to change again in August to No. 6 Civil Air Navigation School. In September the name was to undergo yet another change when it became No. 6 Air Observer Navigation School, and the following month the airport itself changed its name from Cheltenham to Staverton. New hangars were erected to accommodate the new unit and its Dominie trainers (the military equivalent of the De Havilland Rapide). The aircraft were to be serviced by Airwork Limited under Government contract. Trainees were to be billeted in two houses at Lansdown Place and in the former Thomas's Hotel in Cheltenham.

A fatal accident occurred during the evening of

A number of Polish personnel were trained by the 6 AONS at Staverton. Here a group of armourers are dismounting the gun from the turret of an obsolete bomber frame.

15th July 1939, involving one of the Civil Air Guard trainees flying with the Cotswold Aero Club. Mr. C.H. Pitt, a garage owner from Beckworth, was flying solo in a red Gipsy Moth biplane when the aircraft got into a spin and crashed at Deans Farm, Brockworth. Although the aircraft was smashed to pieces and the fuel tank was split apart there was no fire.

Frank Pool from Brockworth was first on the scene. He found the unconscious pilot still strapped into the cockpit and pinned beneath the wreckage. He managed to cut the injured airman free with his penknife. A second CAG aircraft, flown by a Mr. Walwin, circled briefly overhead and then sped off to Staverton to summon help. Dr. J.J. Foster reached the scene some time later but Pitt died shortly after his arrival. Perhaps it could be said that the imminent conflict had claimed its first airman casualty two months before it began.

By the end of 1940 the Dominies of No. 6 AONS had been largely replaced by the radial-engined Anson. On the 3rd August 1940 No. 2 Elementary Flying Training School moved in

from Filton. This unit was to remain, with its Tiger Moth biplanes, until April 1942 by which time it had been redesignated No. 6 Flying Instruction School. In February 1941 "A" Flight of the AONS became a Polish Flight, reflecting the influx of these hardy East Europeans following the fall of France the previous summer. They seemed impervious to the cold and insisted on

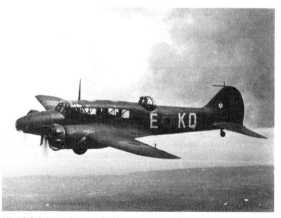

'Faithful Annie' provided basic training for many wartime air-crew and is remembered with affection far and wide.
(H. Hodgson)

122

Airwork servicing personnel line up before one of Staverton's Anson trainers.

keeping the doors of the Flight hangar open no matter what the weather. The AONS had expanded to several Flights by 1941 and they were dispersed at Moreton Valence and Llanbedr in Wales as well as at Staverton itself. By early 1942 the school had 53 Ansons and three Dominies on the strength. One of the personnel employed by Airwork to do the servicing was Mr. J. Butt of St. Mark's, Cheltenham. He recalled that a favourite trick used to unfreeze the hangar's doors on a winter morning was to pour 100 octane petrol into the runners and set fire to it. This apparently backfired on one occasion when one of the engineers accidentally set light to himself.

A typical exercise flown by an Anson would last between 2½ and 3 hours. The aircraft would be crewed by a staff pilot and wireless operator, accompanied by three trainee navigators, who would take it in turns to direct the pilot. All the aircraft were rotated between Staverton, Moreton and Llanbedr, returning to the home base for maintenance work. Other RAF units that used the airfield during the war years were No. 7 School of Technical Training and No. 7 Anti-Aircraft Co-operation Unit with De Havilland Rapides.

Staverton was much used by civilian organisations during the war, including the Rotol Flight Test Department, Folland Aircraft Ltd. and the Gloster Aircraft Company Flight Test Department. The site was highly convenient for Rotol and had probably influenced their decision to build their new factory just over the road on the site of the old Down Hatherley airstrip. The Rotol Test Flight became known locally as "Greenstead's Air Force", after the Chief Test Pilot, Brian Greenstead. As a result of this involvement many interesting and even exotic aircraft passed through the airfield during the war years. They included the first production Spitfire I (K9787), the Folland F3/37's (P1774-P1783), Westland Welkin (DX330) and a host of Hurricanes, Typhoons and Tempests, to mention but a few.

Flight Refuelling Ltd. was based at Staverton from 1942 and did some extremely important

On occasion Lancasters were the cause of some excitement at Staverton, the airfield being a little less than 'Lancaster size'.

development work whilst operating from the station. The company's design office was located at Malvern, Worcestershire, in the Morgan Car Factory. It was one of Flight Refuelling's Lancasters that overshot the runway in August 1945 and blocked Bamfurlong Lane for some time. Amongst the more interesting experiments undertaken by the company were the Fighter Towing Trials conducted under the SB.22 contract. Hurricanes and Spitfires were towed behind a Wellington after having taken off under their own power and then switching off. It was thought that this could be used as a method of providing long range escorts for bombers or as a means of increasing a fighter's ferry range.

By December 1944 the OAFU had closed down. The final flying unit to use the airfield during 1945 was No. 44 Group Communications Flight which operated a mixed bag of aircraft, including a Proctor and a Tiger Moth. There were many crash incidents on and around the station during the war years but perhaps one of the less macabre and more humorous ones that is remembered took place around 1942. Legend has it that a young pilot "pranged" his aircraft behind the Plough Inn and after pulling himself from the wreckage staggered into the pub and asked for a whisky to steady his nerves. Obviously inured to this kind of thing, the landlord stared at him blandly and told him to wait his turn!

Post-war Staverton was home for the RAF Police School and several other ground units before being handed back to the civil authorities in 1950. Today it is a thriving airport, embracing many small business concerns. The wartime hangars can still be seen and the flavour of those times lingers in the atmosphere.

Stoke Orchard (OS ref. 163/925275)

The first RAF personnel to arrive at the Stoke Orchard airfield were airmen detached from Staverton for guard duty. They arrived on 5th February 1941 and were accommodated in some of the newly-completed huts on the station. It was to be another seven months before the first permanent unit appeared on the scene. No. 10 Elementary Flying Training School arrived from Weston-Super-Mare with their Tiger Moths in September 1941.

The Gloster Aircraft Company had by that time established a shadow factory at Stoke Orchard just across the road from the airfield and the newly-

The Tiger Moths of No.10 EFTS were the first occupants of Stoke Orchard Airfield.

assembled aircraft were often to be seen on the drome. During 1942 it was decided to close down the EFTS and, despite the proximity of Cleeve Hill, Stoke Orchard was earmarked for development as a glider training base. In March 1942 a Hotspur glider was test-flown from the airfield and the site was pronounced suitable for a Glider Training School.

The first aircraft and gliders began to arrive in July shortly after the EFTS closed down. The first official glider flight by an aircraft of the new unit, No. 3 GTS, was carried out by the CO on 3rd August 1942 and No. 1 Training Course began flying three days later. Less than two weeks after this the unit suffered its first fatal accident when a fully-loaded Hotspur (HH519) crashed into a tree just after take-off, as a result of being caught in the slipstream of the tug aircraft. The army pilot, Cpl. McQueen, was killed instantly. Before the end of the month the occupants of the vicarage at Bishop's Cleeve gained some first-hand experience of the dangers of gliding. Sgt. J.E. Alexander took off just before 10.00 hours on the morning of 25th August 1942 with a glider in tow. After casting off the glider he headed back towards the airfield, forgetting that the tow rope was still

Hotspur Gliders were constantly overhead at Stoke Orchard from 1942 onwards.

Miles Masters were used to tow Hotspur gliders aloft from Stoke Orchard.

basis. Until quite recently many of the wartime buildings were still standing but during 1985 the site was being cleared. Soon there will be little left to tell the tale of the Glider Training School and the war years.

attached. The tow struck the roof of the vicarage and carried away a chimneypot!

Due to the intense level of training the GTS took over Northleach airfield as a Relief Landing Ground during November. There had been a constant stream of accidents like the one mentioned above involving the non-release of tow ropes and a possible solution to the problem was suggested towards the end of 1942. A device was fitted to one of the Master tugs which gave a warning, indicating that the tow had not been released. The test proved successful and the device was subsequently fitted to other aircraft.

Through the remainder of 1942 and on into 1943 life went on much the same, with the Hotspurs and Horsas being towed aloft and then being released to fly unfettered around the circuit. In August 1943 Sgt. Petre was killed in Master DM404 when he got into difficulties whilst doing aerobatics over Bishop's Cleeve. Sgt. Smart also ran into difficulties during November of that year when he was despatched to Bibury to pick up a glider that had force-landed earlier on. He misjudged the landing at Bibury and overran the landing area, damaging the starboard wing and undercarriage of Master DL520.

Throughout 1944 the Unit was working flat out to produce pilots for the Glider Pilots' Regiment. Many of those trained at Stoke Orchard piloted gliders during the assault on Normandy and later during the attack on Arnhem. The worst incident of 1944 occurred on 26th August when Halifax MZ311 of 78 Squadron crashed nearby on Cleeve Common. The aircraft was returning from an operation against La Rochelle. The seven crew members were all killed.

In January 1945 No. 3 GTS moved further south to Exeter and No. 7 MU took over the blister and Bellman hangars for storage. The airfield itself was put on a care and maintenance

Stoke Orchards buildings were still mainly intact but crumbling slowly away during the early 1980's. By early 1986 most of these buildings had also been demolished although the hangars are possibly to be refurbished as stores buildings.
(Rennison Collection)

125

Chapter 4

Aircraft Incident Log

Compiling a list of this sort is fraught with difficulty, memories can dim with the passage of time and even official records contain inaccuracies. Some of the latter may have been perpetuated here, although every effort has been made to eliminate such errors.

It should not be regarded as a complete record, but I am confident it contains the vast majority of crashes and other similar incidents. Where known, details are given of aircraft types, serials, locations, units, crew names and fates. The log has been arranged in chronological order. The area covered is that encompassed by the pre 1974 county of Gloucestershire, with one or two notable exceptions.

In some instances details remain obscure and thus additional information is always welcome. It should also be said that where specific details of a location are given this does not imply an open invitation to visit a site. Permission should always be sought from the owners of the land involved.

Abbreviations Used.

A&AEE	Aeroplane and Armament Experimental Establishment.	HGCU	Heavy Glider Conversion Unit.
AONS	Advanced Observer Navigation School.	HQSFP	Headquarters Service Ferry Pool.
		(i)	Injured.
AOS	Air Observers School.	(k)	Killed.
ATA	Air Transport Auxiliary.	MU	Maintenance Unit.
CU	Conversion Unit.	OAFU	Observer Advanced Flying Unit.
ECFS	Empire Central Flying School.	OAPU	Overseas Aircraft Preparation Unit.
EFTS	Elementary Flying Training School.	OTU	Operational Training Unit.
ERFTS	Elementary Reserve Flying Training School.	PAFU	Pilot Advanced Flying Unit
		PFNTU	Pathfinder Night Training Unit.
FIS	Flying Instructors School.	(pow)	Prisoner of War.
FP	Ferry Pool.	PRDU	Photo Recconnaisance Development Unit.
FPP	Ferry Pilot Pool.	PRU	Photo Recconnaisance Unit.
FTCCF	Flying Training Command Communications Flight.	RFTS	Reserve Flying Training Unit.
		RS	Radio School.
FTF	Ferry Training Flight.	SFP	Service Ferry Pool.
FTS	Flying Training School.	SFTS	Service Flying Training School.
FTU	Ferry Training Unit.	TEU	Tactical Exercise Unit.
GOTU	Glider Operational Training Unit.	TFU	Telecommunications Flying Unit.
GSU	Group Support Unit.	TURP	Training Unit and Reserve Pool.
GTS	Glider Training School.	USAAF	U.S. Army Air Force.
HCU	Heavy Conversion Unit.		

GERMAN AND BRITISH RANKS

Below officer level Luftwaffe ranks do not equate exactly with those of the RAF. The listing below therefore contains, in some instances, only an approximation to either an RAF or Army rank.

German Rank	Luftwaffe Abbrev.	British Rank	RAF Abbrev.
Oberst	Obst.	Group Captain	Gp.Cpt.
Oberstleutnant	Obstlt.	Wing Commander	W/Cdr.
Major	Maj.	Squadron Leader	S/Ldr.
Hauptmann	Hptm.	Flight Lieutenant	F/Lt.
Oberleutnant	Oblt.	Flying Officer	F/O.
Leutnant	Lt.	Pilot Officer	P/O.
Oberfahnrich	Ob.Fhr.	Senior Officer Cadet	
Fahnenjunker-Oberfeldwebel	Fhj-Ofw.	Cadet Warrant Officer	
Oberfeldwebel	Ofw.	Flight Sergeant	F/Sgt.
		Warrant Officer	W.O.
Fahnrich	Fhr.	Officer Cadet	
Fahnenjunker-Feldwebel	Fhj-Fw.	Cadet Sergeant Major	
Feldwebel	Fw.	Sergeant Major	
Fahnenjunker-Unteroffizier	Fhj-Uffz.	Cadet Sergeant	
Unteroffizier	Uffz.	Sergeant	Sgt.
Obergefreiter	Obgefr.	Corporal	Cpl.
Gefreiter	Gefr.	Leading Aircraftsman	LAC.
Flieger.	Flg.	Aircraftsman	AC.

Main Luftwaffe Unit Designations and Abbreviations

Kampfgeschwader	KG.	Bomber Unit	
Lehrgeschwader	LG.	Operational Training Unit	
Jagdgeschwader	JG.	Fighter Unit	
Nachtjagdgeschwader	NJG.	Night Fighter Unit	
Zerstorergeschwader	ZG.	Destroyer/Heavy Fighter Unit	
Transportgeschwader	TG.	Transport Unit	
Eprobungsgruppe	Egr.	Experimental Group	
Aufklarungsgruppe (Fern)	Aufklr.Gr(F)	Reconnaissance Group	

DATE	'AIRCRAFT TYPE/SERIAL'	DETAILS	
13. 7.36.	Armstrong Whitworth Atlas K1549	Station Flight Andover, crashed on take off Filton.	
30. 4.37.	Hawker Audax K3094	26 Squadron, stalled avoiding radio masts and crashed Filton.	
27. 9.37.	Hawker Audax K5218	No.3 FTS, crashed whilst on approach to South Cerney.	
8.10.37.	Hawker Audax K5219	No.3 FTS, crashed into trees while diving on target Aston Down.	
21.12.37.	Hawker Audax K7443	No.3 FTS, crashed near Stroud at 1030 hours.	Acting P/O M.L. Birch (k). Acting P/O C.L. Taylor (k).
10. 1.38.	Unidentified	Force landed in snow storm near the Stow to Bourton Road in a field owned by Mr. D.N.A. Gifford.	Two crew members safe.
17. 2.38.	Hawker Hind K5501	No.3 FTS, crashed into houses in Cheltenham after pilot abandoned the aircraft due to icing and lack of control. En-route Manchester — Andover.	G. Thompson (pilot) safe.
25. 2.38.	Avro Anson K6233	No.6 FTS, crashed whilst on approach to South Cerney.	
29. 7.38.	Hawker Fury K2058	No.3 FTS, stalled on landing at South Cerney.	
13. 9.38.	Airspeed Oxford L4580	No.3 FTS, spun into the ground near Poulton.	
7.12.38.	Hawker Fury K5673	No.3 FTS, crashed on landing South Cerney.	
12. 1.39.	Hawker Audax K5223	No.3 FTS, undershot whilst landing at South Cerney.	Acting P/O R.E. Winter (k).
9. 2.39.	Fairey Battle K9216	98 Squadron, crashed near Stow-on-the-Wold.	
10. 2.39.	Fairey Battle K9236	40 Squadron, force landed in a field near Hallen after engine failure.	
26. 3.39.	Hawker Hurricane L1869	501 Squadron, stalled on approach and crashed at Filton.	P/O R.H. Jacoby (pilot).
4. 4.39.	Unidentified bomber	RAF Andover, force landed near Upper Slaughter. Came to rest in a field 50 yards from the church.	
4. 4.39.	Airspeed Oxford L4628	No.3 FTS, crashed on landing during night flying practice at South Cerney.	
17. 4.39.	Hawker Audax K7318	No.9 FTS, crashed while landing at Kemble.	Sgt. T.H. Nicholls (pilot).

3. 5.39.	Hawker Hart K4372	No.2 ERFTS, collided with Tiger Moth G—ACBA while on approach to Filton.	
19. 5.39.	Bristol Type 146 K5119	Bristol Aeroplane Co., damaged on landing at Filton and later struck off charge.	
2. 6.39.	Hawker Hurricane L1602	56 Squadron, crashed whilst on approach to Filton.	
11. 6.39.	Miles Magister L6927	No.31 ERFTS, crashed upon landing at Cheltenham?.	
13. 6.39.	Hawker Hart K4976	No.6 FTS, crashed on approach at night at Little Rissington.	
29. 6.39.	Hawker Fury K2035	No.3 FTS, crashed while landing South Cerney.	
5. 7.39.	Airspeed Oxford L9701	No.3 FTS, crashed in forced landing 2 miles south of South Cerney.	
15. 7.39.	De Havilland Gipsy Moth G—ABBV.	Civil Air Guard, went into a spin and crashed in a field at Deans Farm, Brockworth.	Mr. C.H. Pitt (k).
17. 7.39.	Hawker Hart K6550	No.2 ERFTS, collided in mid-air with Anson N5260 whilst on approach to Filton.	
17. 7.39.	Avro Anson N5260	No.2 FP, see above for details.	
25. 8.39.	Avro Anson L7903	No.6 FTS, undershot whilst landing at Little Rissington.	
6. 9.39.	Hawker Fury K3738	No.6 FTS, crashed on landing Little Rissington.	
7. 9.39.	Miles Magister N3909	No.5 MU, collided on the ground with Miles Mentor L4430 at Kemble.	Sgt. F.C. Apps.
7. 9.39.	Miles Mentor L4430	Station Flight Andover, see above for details.	
9. 9.39.	Airspeed Oxford L9696	No.3 FTS, struck an airman on the flare path whilst landing at South Cerney.	Flt.Lt. P.V. Foss (pilot).
12. 9.39.	Airspeed Oxford L4574	No.3 FTS, overshot and turned turtle whilst making a night landing at South Cerney.	F/Sgt. G.A. Clarke (pilot) safe.
16. 9.39.	Bristol Blenheim L6678	25 Squadron, crashed whilst landing at Filton.	
19. 9.39.	Fairey Battle K9448	207 Squadron, flew into hill near Winchcombe in bad visibility whilst on D/F and Homing Exercise.	P/O J.E. Hull (New Zealander) (k).
11.10.39.	Miles Magister P2404	No.9 AOS, crashed in a field between Little Rissington and Warmwell, having struck ground earlier when diving below HT cables.	P/O H.D. Dawlish.
11.10.39.	Hawker Hart K5810	No.6 FTS, crashed whilst on approach to Little Rissington.	

DATE	'AIRCRAFT TYPE/SERIAL'	DETAILS	
11.10.39.	Avro Anson L7905	No.6 FTS, pilots first night solo landing, aircraft hit floodlight and crashed at Little Rissington.	F/O M.N. Hancocks.
16.10.39.	Armstrong Whitworth Whitley K8943	102 Squadron, undercarriage collapsed on landing at Aston Down, delivery flight.	Two injured.
20.10.39.	Airspeed Oxford P1815	No.3 FTS, struck tree whilst on night training flight, and forced landed one mile from South Cerney airfield.	904142 Sgt. M. O'Donovan (pilot) (i). P.C. Elliot (pupil) (i).
21.10.39.	Gloster Gladiator K6145	263 Squadron, crashed in River Severn near Sharpness bridge.	Sgt. Watson-Parker (i).
5.11.39.	Airspeed Oxford L9698	No.3 FTS, landed with undercarriage retracted at South Cerney.	F/O D.S. Pain.
7.11.39.	Fairey Battle K9238	98 Squadron, flew into ground near Stow-on-the-Wold whilst low flying in cloud.	P/O D.K. Robertson.
18.11.39.	North American Harvard P5789	No.10 FTS, undercarriage collapsed while taxying after test flight at Staverton.	Flt.Lt. L.P. Rowley (pilot) safe.
19.11.39.	Gloster Gladiator K7950	12 Group Pool, engine caught fire after take off and aircraft crashed in a field near Little Rissington.	Sgt. K. Linton (k).
19.11.39.	Airspeed Oxford N4802	No.3 FTS, landed wheels-up at South Cerney.	521960 LAC. A.E. Bowes (pilot).
19.11.39.	North American Harvard N7090	No.2 FTS, aircraft made a belly landing after pupil attempted to land with undercarriage up at Southrop.	Acting Flt.Lt. W.N. Sykes (pilot and Instructor).
21.11.39.	Hawker Audax K7361	No.6 FTS, crashed in forced landing near Bourton-on-the-Water.	
21.11.39.	North American Harvard P5871	No.12 Group Pool, aircraft spun-in from 6,000 feet at Chalford.	42069 P/O H.N. Masterson (k).
22.11.39.	Airspeed Oxford L4620	No.3 FTS, forced landing with undercarriage up at South Cerney, during night flying training.	F/O A.M. Crawley (pilot).
24.11.39.	Airspeed Oxford P1820	No.3 FTS, collided with Oxford L4631 on landing. Dual test for first solo by trainee pilot.	363919 Sgt. G.A. Clark (pilot).
24.11.39.	Airspeed Oxford L4631	No.3 FTS, see above.	
29.11.39.	Airspeed Oxford P1807	No.5 FTS, aircraft spun in near Chavenage, Tetbury after stalling in bad weather. Solo cross-country flight.	745332 Sgt. Banks (pilot).

3.12.39.	Fairey Battle K7962	No.12 Group Pool, undercarriage collapsed on landing Aston Down. Ferry flight from Hucknall to Aston Down.	P/O E.A. Allan (pilot).
9.12.39.	Fairey Battle K9467	No.98 Squadron, flew into ground in bad visibility south west of Stow-on-the-Wold. Cross-country flight Upwood to Andover and return via Gloucester.	P/O P.D.B. Stevens (k).
20.12.39.	Bristol Beaufort L4468	Bristol Flying School, crashed in the Severn/Bristol Channel.	F/Lt. Deacon (k), body washed ashore at Avonmouth.
22.12.39.	Blackburn Botha L6108	Torpedo Development Unit, hit house on overshoot in bad weather at Filton.	F/O Gadd (pilot) and three passengers safe.
8. 1.40.	Miles Magister N3903	No.5 School of Technical Training, cross-country from Turnhill to Locking. Force landed in a field at Hallen.	S/Ldr. Greave and passenger safe.
10. 1.40.	Hawker Audax K8332	No.3 FTS, forced landing seven miles west of Tewkesbury.	
26. 1.40.	North American Harvard P5862	No.12 Group Pool, spun-in near Aston Down.	
3. 3.40.	Bristol Blenheim L6817	Royal Yugoslav Air Force, aircraft crashed during training flight at Aston Down.	
3. 3.40.	Airspeed Oxford P1817	No.3 FTS, crashed just north of Cirencester during night training flight.	758046 Sgt. E.C. Warren (pupil) (k).
4. 3.40.	Hawker Audax K8334	No.3 FTS, crashed whilst landing at South Cerney.	
8. 3.40.	Airspeed Oxford L9700	No.3 FTS, crashed on overshoot during night flying at South Cerney.	
8. 3.40.	Avro Anson N5294	No.9 FTS, aircraft struck telegraph wires and force landed two miles south of Nailsworth. Carrying illegal passenger.	Actg. P/O K.V. Palmer (pilot).
8. 3.40.	Airspeed Oxford P1823	No.3 FTS, crashed on approach to South Cerney during night flying.	
8. 3.40.	Bristol Beaufort L4470	No.20 MU. Force landed in a field near Aston Down after engine failure.	Actg. F/Lt. C. Marshall.
12. 3.40.	Avro Anson N9824	No.61 Squadron, aircraft struck a tree whilst low flying at Lechlade.	

DATE	'AIRCRAFT TYPE/SERIAL'	DETAILS	
29. 3.40.	Gloster Gladiator N5588	No.263 Squadron, collided with Gladiator N5960 one mile east of Marlwood Farm Thornbury and came down in flames at Alveston at 12.17 hours.	P/O D.E.D. Mason (pilot) (k).
29. 3.40.	Gloster Gladiator N5960	No.263 Squadron, see above	P/O J. Nettleton (pilot) (k).
5. 4.40.	De Havilland 80A Puss Moth X9439	No.24 Squadron, forced landing near Tewkesbury.	
10. 4.40.	Hawker Audax K5156	No.3 FTS, overturned whilst taxying down-wind at South Cerney.	
15. 4.40.	Hawker Hind K6837	No.1 FP, crashed whilst landing at Aston Down.	
17. 4.40.	Hawker Audax K7308	No.9 FTS, crashed on landing at Babdown Farm.	
18. 4.40.	Bristol Beaufort	Bristol Aircraft Company, crashed at Cribbs Causeway, Filton at 10.00 hours.	Pilot and passengers safe.
22. 4.40.	Hawker Hind K6633	No.1 FTS, aircraft struck a tree whilst making a forced landing two miles north of Pucklechurch.	
24. 4.40.	Bristol Beaufort L4494	No.5 MU, aircraft made a belly landing at Little Rissington and was damaged beyond repair.	
13. 5.40.	Handley Page Hereford L6065	No.14 OTU, crashed on approach to Aston Down.	
16. 5.40.	Supermarine Spitfire P9514	No.5 OTU, aircraft struck wall on take off from Aston Down.	
25. 5.40.	Hawker Audax K7439	No.3 FTS, crashed on landing at South Cerney.	
1. 6.40.	Bristol Blenheim L6643	No.236 Squadron, belly landed at Filton.	
8. 6.40.	North American Harvard P5870	No.5 OTU, crashed on approach to Aston Down.	
8. 6.40.	Airspeed Oxford L4537	No.3 FTS, stalled and crashed on approach to South Cerney.	
19. 6.40.	Bristol Blenheim L1471	No.5 OTU, crashed in the River Severn, off Lydney Harbour, near Woolaston.	
1. 7.40.	Supermarine Spitfire R6640	No.5 OTU, caught fire and crash-landed at Kemble.	
3. 7.40.	Bristol Blenheim K7112	No.5 OTU, crashed on take-off from Aston Down.	
7. 7.40.	North American Harvard N7070	No.15 FTS, crashed on landing at Bibury.	
13. 7.40.	Fairey Battle L5133	No.5 OTU, crashed on landing at Aston Down.	
19. 7.40.	Handley Page Hereford L6023	Unit unknown, crashed on take-off from Kemble.	
20. 7.40.	Airspeed Oxford R6320	No.3 FTS, crashed on landing at Bibury.	

20. 7.40.	Fairey Battle L4959	No.12 OTU, crashed two miles east of South Cerney.	
22. 7.40.	De Havilland Tiger Moth T5624	No.2 EFTS, flew into ground near Upton on Severn at night.	
22. 7.40.	Bristol Blenheim L6652	No.5 OTU, aircraft made a wheels up landing in a field at Tetbury after engine failure.	
23. 7.40.	Bristol Blenheim L1105	No.5 OTU, crashed in an orchard at Bakers Mill, Frampton Mansell.	
25. 7.40.	Junkers Ju.88A (9K—GN)	KG.51, brought down by a Hurricane of No.4 FPP at Oakridge Lynch at 14.25 hours.	65120 Uffz. Theiner (k), other crew members; Uffz. Dorner, Gefr. Treue and Uffz. Hugelschafer were POW's.
25. 7.40.	Hawker Hurricane P3271	No.4 FPP, spun-in after collision with Ju.88 near Aston Down. See above.	P/O A.C. Bird (k).
25. 7.40.	North American Harvard P5901	No.15 FTS, crashed on take-off at night from Windrush.	
30. 7.40.	North American Harvard N7190	No.6 FTS, aircraft struck trees whilst low flying at Turkdean.	
30. 7.40.	Airspeed Oxford P1874	No.15 FTS, crashed just after take off at night from Windrush.	
31. 7.40.	Handley Page Hereford N9057	Unit unknown, aircraft landed with undercarriage retracted at Aston Down.	
1. 8.40.	Airspeed Oxford N6323	No.15 FTS, aircraft hit trees on approach to Windrush.	
1. 8.40.	Bristol Blenheim L1308	No5 OTU, crashed at Chalford, whilst on approach to Aston Down. Aircraft burnt out.	Crew killed.
1. 8.40.	Handley Page Hampden P1266	No.16 OTU, landed on one engine and swung, undercarriage collapsed in soft ground, Babdown Farm.	
3. 8.40.	Airspeed Oxford P1821	No.3 FTS, collided with P1955 during formation flying exercise near South Cerney and crashed.	Sgt. Mitchley (pilot) (k).
3. 8.40.	Airspeed Oxford P1955	No3 FTS, see above. After collision pilot managed to land the aircraft with one wing almost destroyed.	Sgt. Sly (pilot & instructor).
5. 8.40.	North American Harvard P5793	No.15 FTS, undershot while landing at Bibury.	
6. 8.40.	Airspeed Oxford P1869	No.15 SFTS, dived into the ground shortly after take off from Windrush for night flying exercise.	P/O D.J. Young (k).

DATE	'AIRCRAFT TYPE/SERIAL'	DETAILS	
6. 8.40.	Airspeed Oxford R6332	No.3 FTS, crashed after take off from Bibury for night flying exercise.	
10. 8.40.	Supermarine Spitfire L1063	No.5 OTU, collided with Blenheim L6799 on take off from Aston Down.	Sgt. Wilson (k).
10. 8.40.	Bristol Blenheim L6799	No.5 OTU, see above.	P/O G.G. Crawford (New Zealander) (k). Sgt. J.M. Oxtoby (pupil) (k).
12. 8.40.	Airspeed Oxford N4803	No.3 FTS, aircraft broke up in the air over Hankerton.	
13. 8.40.	Supermarine Spitfire R6880	No.4 FPP, struck balloon cable at Brockworth and crashed.	
17. 8.40.	Avro Anson L7907	No.6 FTS, hit trees whilst low flying and crashed at Lodge Park, Eastington.	Sgt. D. Duncan (k). Sgt. E.W. Osborne (k).
18. 8.40.	Avro Anson L9164	No.6 FTS, collided with or rammed He.III near Windrush at 23.50 hours. Struck the ground near Aldsworth at Blackpits Farm.	Sgt. B. Hancock (k).
18. 8.40.	Heinkel He.III Werk No.1408 See page 113	KG.27, collided with or was rammed by Anson L9164, see above. Crashed and burnt out at Blackpits Farm near Aldsworth.	Ofw. Dreher (k). Uffz. Schmidt (k). Uffz. Rave (k). Uffz. Cohrs (k).
19. 8.40.	De Havilland Tiger Moth T7032	No.2 EFTS, aircraft hit telephone wires and crashed at Lower Lode Lane, Tewkesbury.	918024 Sgt. W.N. Davis (instructor), LAC P.W. Spencer both severely injured, Davis later died.
19. 8.40.	North American Harvard P5788	No.6 FTS, hit ground whilst low flying and crashed at Northleach Lane Field, Hazleton.	754390 Sgt. J.S. Bell (k).
25. 8.40.	Bristol Blenheim L6733	No.5 OTU, struck trees on high ground at Chase House Farm Tidenham. Site examined by the Severnside Aviation Society in 1982 and some parts recovered.	748790 Sgt. D.E. Paul (k). P/O D.M.M. Bell.
26. 8.40.	Hawker Hurricane N2606	No.5 OTU, spun-in under full power near Stroud at 07.05 hours.	36256 P/O R.S. Magee (New Zealander) (k).
26. 8.40.	Hawker Hurricane V6563	No.4 FPP, crashed whilst on approach to Kemble.	
29. 8.40.	Fairey Battle L5283	No.12 OTU, crashed whilst on approach to Aston Down.	
4. 9.40.	De Havilland Tiger Moth T5627	No.2 EFTS, crashed in forced landing at Hesters Way, Cheltenham.	LAC Williams (pilot) (i).
7. 9.40.	Hawker Hurricane P2962	No.242 Squadron, reported shot down near Cheltenham.	

29.10.40.	Avro Anson N5285	No.6 FTS, see above.	922600 LAC Allen (k).
9. 9.40.	North American Harvard P5885	No.15 FTS, spun in near Brockworth.	7540975 Sgt. W.G. Lane (k). 754410 Sgt. E.A. Hares (k).
10. 9.40.	Hawker Hurricane	No.87 Squadron (B Flight), crashed whilst landing at Bibury.	P/O J.F. Stepien (Polish) (k).
20. 9.40.	Miles Master N7987	No.5 OTU, broke up in the air and crashed at Cherrington at 11.15 hours.	LAC Hugh (k).
20. 9.40.	Airspeed Oxford P9039	No.2 FTS, collided with Anson N9821 to the south of Little Rissington.	968378 LAC Sturgis (k). 903457 LAC Sutherland (k).
20. 9.40.	Avro Anson N9821	No.6 FTS, see above.	F/Lt. R.G. Coventry (k). Sgt. J. Lane (safe). Sgt. G. Wilcox (safe).
23. 9.40.	Bristol Blenheim L8797	No.17 OTU, crashed in a field at Tuffley after engine failure.	758037 Sgt. Keatley (pupil) (k). 745795 Sgt. Harry (instructor) (k).
24. 9.40.	Airspeed Oxford N1192	No.3 FTS, hit power lines and crashed at Frampton on Severn at 16.00 hours. Aircraft caught fire on impact.	
25. 9.40.	Bristol Beaufort L9856	No.22 Squadron, damaged beyond repair during an air raid on Filton.	
25. 9.40.	Bristol Beaufort L9880	No.22 Squadron, damaged beyond repair during an air raid on Filton.	
25. 9.40.	Bristol Beaufort L9827	No.22 Squadron, damaged beyond repair during an air raid on Filton.	
25. 9.40.	Bristol Beaufort N1157	Bristol Aeroplane Co., damaged beyond repair in an air raid on Filton.	
26. 9.40.	Airspeed Oxford	No.3 FTS, landed with undercarriage retracted at Bibury, aircraft extensively damaged.	LAC Robinson (pilot) (safe).
27.9.40.	Messerschmitt Bf.110 (U8—FK) Werk No.2162	ZG.26, shot down by a Hurricane of 504 Squadron at Stapleton Institution, Fishponds, Bristol at 11.45 hours.	Ofw. H. Tiepelt (k). Uffz. H. Brosig (k).
27. 9.40.	Bristol Beaufort L4507	No.42 Squadron, destroyed in an air raid on Filton.	
30. 9.40.	Hawker Hurricane P2987	No.504 Squadron, force landed at Filton following combat with enemy aircraft over Yeovil at 17.00 hours.	P/O E.M. Frisby (safe).
30. 9.40.	Hawker Hurricane P3774	No.504 Squadron, force landed at Filton following combat with enemy aircraft over Yeovil.	Sgt. W.H. Banks (safe).
1.10.40.	Hawker Hurricane L1946	No.5 OTU, dived into the ground near Aust.	F/Sgt. D.V. Hayter.

DATE	'AIRCRAFT TYPE/SERIAL'	DETAILS	
24. 3.41.	Hawker Hurricane P3603	No.9 FTS, spun into the ground while attempting to land at Babdown Farm at 12.45 hours.	1168888 LAC D.C. Hopkins (k).
26. 3.41.	Glen Martin ? (prob. Maryland)	Unit unknown, overshot and crashed on landing at Kemble.	Crew safe.
26. 3.41.	Supermarine Spitfire X4820	No.118 Squadron, aircraft landed at Filton with undercarriage not locked down. Main wheels collapsed at the end of the runway at 13.30 hours.	P/O Milne.
26. 3.41.	De Havilland Tiger Moth R5062	No.3 EFTS, spun into the ground near Lechlade.	
27. 3.41.	Supermarine Spitfire X4675	No.118 Squadron, aircraft swung on landing at Filton and struck an air raid shelter.	P/O J.C. Robson.
8. 4.41.	Supermarine Spitfire P7835	No.609 Squadron, collided with a compressor pump on landing at Filton.	F/Lt. R.H.M. Richie.
14. 4.41.	Hawker Hurricane V7190	No.501 Squadron, dived into the ground near Frampton on Severn after circling at low altitude.	P/O R.W. Waine (k).
14. 4.41.	Vickers Wellington	No.21 OTU, undercarriage collapsed on the runway.	Crew safe.
15. 4.41.	Airspeed Oxford L4558	No.2 FTS, hit house whilst low flying near Dursley.	Sgt. G.E. Ffitch (pilot).
17. 4.41.	Hawker Hurricane P3263	SFP, crashed after engine fire at Kemble. Cockpit full of fumes and pilot was unable to see properly.	794077 Sgt. E. Wojezynski (Polish) broke finger.
22. 4.41.	Armstrong Whitworth Whitley T4278	No.502 Squadron, struck water tanker whilst landing at Staverton.	
22. 4.41.	Miles Master T8468	No.9 FTS, crashed on take off from Babdown Farm.	
25. 4.41.	Hawker Hurricane L1867	No.9 FTS, undercarriage retracted by trainee pilot whilst taxiing at Babdown Farm.	1257667 LAC H.E. Spain.
30. 4.41.	Vickers Wellington T2905	No.11 OTU, struck balloon cable and crashed at St. Andrews Park, Bristol.	
1. 5.41.	Airspeed Oxford R6229	No.6 FTS, crashed on landing at Little Rissington.	
4. 5.41.	Hawker Hurricane	No.1 FPP, pilot braked to avoid excavation rubble and aircraft flipped on its nose at Aston Down.	P/O A. Paszkowski (Polish).
7. 5.41.	Hawker Hurricane P2968	No.9 FTS, undercarriage collapsed after heavy landing Babdown Farm.	1257535 LAC C.R. Tapp.

16. 5.41.	Hawker Hurricane V7444	No.9 FTS, crashed four miles south west of Stroud at 12.25 hours. Cockpit full of smoke, pilot unable to see.	1255522 LAC L. Eate.
21. 5.41.	Hawker Hurricane P3320	No.9 FTS, undercarriage collapsed after heavy landing at Babdown Farm.	934540 LAC E.T. Griffith.
27. 5.41.	Hawker Hurricane P3807	No.9 FTS, crashed in a field on approach to Babdown Farm after engine cut out at low altitude.	1285910 LAC L.W. Daniel.
28. 5.41.	Vickers Wellington	No.21 OTU, force landed at Southrop after oil leak in port engine, aircraft had no flaps.	S/Ldr. Williams DFC, AFM (pilot).
30. 5.41.	Hawker Hurricane V6605	No.52 OTU, spun into the ground at Elburton near Bristol.	
1. 6.41.	Airspeed Oxford P1952	No.3 FTS, crashed after collision near South Cerney.	
3. 6.41.	Airspeed Oxford R6114	No.3 FTS, crashed on overshoot at Bibury.	
7. 6.41.	Avro Anson N9733	No.11 AONS, crashed in forced landing north west of Lechlade.	
12. 6.41.	Westland Whirlwind P7045	No.263 Squadron, crashed on landing at Filton and burst into flames.	P/O Ferdinand (k).
15. 6.41.	Handley Page Hampden AD938	No.8 MU, force landed at Little Rissington at 12.00 hours.	
16. 6.41.	Vickers Wellington T2910	No.21 OTU, struck trees on approach and crashed Moreton in Marsh, after engine failure. Night flying training.	Sgt. Smiles (Instructor) head injuries, rest of crew safe.
18. 6.41.	Hawker Hurricane P3268	No.9 FTS, starboard wheel broke off after heavy landing at Babdown Farm at 11.10 hours.	1192939 LAC K.N. Clark.
24. 6.41.	Hawker Hurricane P4194	No.9 FTS, wing hit ground on landing and undercarriage collapsed at Babdown Farm.	1377542 LAC R.C. Pickering.
24. 6.41.	Hawker Hurricane L1666	No.9 FTS, undercarriage collapsed after heavy landing at Babdown Farm at 17.00 hours.	1062857 LAC P.M. Hamilton.
25. 6.41.	Airspeed Oxford V3839	No.6 FTS, crashed on overshoot at Windrush.	
25. 6.41.	Airspeed Oxford V3939	No.6 FTS, crashed on take off from Windrush.	
26. 6.41.	Airspeed Oxford N4846	No.3 FTS, stalled on approach to Bibury and crashed.	
28. 6.41.	Airspeed Oxford N4782	No.3 FTS, crashed on landing at Bibury.	

DATE	'AIRCRAFT TYPE/SERIAL'	DETAILS	
2. 7.41.	Vickers Wellington	No.21 OTU, overshot landing, swung off the runway and hit stationary truck at Moreton in Marsh.	Sgt. Anderton (instructor).
12. 7.41.	Handley Page Hampden P2064	No.8 MU, forced landing at Westcott near Little Rissington due to engine failure. Aircraft came down at Youngs Farm at 16.00 hours.	P/O R.W. Ritchie (pilot).
25. 7.41.	Miles Master T8547	No.9 FTS, hit tree whilst low flying west of Moreton.	
26. 7.41.	Miles Master N7992	No.9 FTS, crashed whilst taking off at night from Babdown Farm.	
26. 7.41.	Airspeed Oxford W6617	No.6 FTS, crashed on take-off from Windrush.	
3. 8.41.	Hawker Hurricane N2429	No.2 FPP, tyre burst on landing at Aston Down and undercarriage collapsed 19.00 hours.	1st.Off. F.G.S. Wilson ATA.
3. 8.41.	Airspeed Oxford P1813	No.3 FTS, crashed on approach Bibury.	
3. 8.41.	Hawker Hurricane R4183	No.52 OTU, collided with W9194 whilst 'dog fighting', location unknown.	Sgt. Fleming (k).
3. 8.41.	Hawker Hurricane W9149	No.52 OTU, see above.	Sgt. Cheyne (k).
5. 8.41.	Hawker Hurricane	Gloster Aircraft Co., crashed near Park Lane, Woodchester after mid-air collision.	Test Pilot Marshall.
5. 8.41.	Hawker Hurricane N2617	No.9 FTS, undercarriage collapsed on landing at Babdown Farm.	1379308 LAC E.E. Vergette.
7. 8.41.	Hawker Hurricane V7627	No.52 OTU, swerved off runway on landing at Aston Down and hit Hurricane P3702.	Pilot safe.
9. 8.41.	Hawker Hurricane P3588	No.9 FTS, landed with undercarriage retracted at Babdown Farm at 15.00 hours.	925408 LAC R. Farmer.
12. 8.41.	Supermarine Spitfire AB866	No.6 FPP, wheel struck rut whilst landing at Rissington and port undercarriage leg broke, aircraft tipped on its nose.	1st.Off. J.G. Bergel ATA.
17. 8.41.	Miles Master N7780	No.9 FTS, struck tree and crashed near Babdown Farm.	
18. 8.41.	Hawker Hurricane V7002	No.52 OTU, collided in mid-air with V7179, but pilot managed to return to Aston Down with no starboard aileron.	P/O Gallo (American).

18. 8.41.	Hawker Hurricane V7179	No.52 OTU, see above. Pilot parachuted location unknown.	P/O Williams (American).
19. 8.41	Hawker Hurricane V6744	No.52 OTU, force landed at Aston Down with engine trouble.	S/Lt. Bernard (Free French).
19. 8.41.	Boulton & Paul Defiant T4110	No.125 Squadron, abandoned by pilot when lost over the Forest of Dean. Aircraft came down at Lower Lydbrook.	
20. 8.41.	Hawker Hurricane P3106	No.9 FTS, undercarriage collapsed after heavy landing at Babdown Farm.	1382997 LAC C.I. Scott.
20. 8.41.	Airspeed Oxford R6073	No.3 FTS, crashed on landing at Bibury.	
21. 8.41.	Airspeed Oxford N4790	No.2 FTS, crashed in forced landing two miles north of Andoversford.	
21. 8.41.	Miles Master T8631	No.9 FTS, belly landed at Babdown Farm.	
24. 8.41.	Miles Master T8490	No.9 FTS, crashed on landing at Babdown Farm.	
25. 8.41.	Airspeed Oxford R6056	No.15 FTS, flew into the ground just south of Tetbury.	
26. 8.41.	Hawker Hurricane P3148	HQSFP, aircraft landed straight ahead after engine failure on take off 15.10 hours.	1259118 Sgt. F.G. Ford.
28. 8.41.	Hawker Hurricane P2558	No.9 FTS, aircraft was abandoned in the air after catching fire. Pilot was almost overcome by fumes.	1312483 LAC D.D. Smith.
28. 8.41.	Miles Master T8367	No.9 FTS, overshot and hit wall at Babdown Farm.	
29. 8.41.	Miles Master N7632	No.9 FTS, crashed at Calcot Farm near Tetbury.	
29. 8.41.	Hawker Hurricane P5172	No.52 OTU, landed with undercarriage retracted at Kemble at 20.00 hours.	1377544 Sgt. R. Penteney.
29. 8.41.	Hawker Hurricane V7176	No.52 OTU, undercarriage collapsed after a heavy landing at Aston Down.	P/O Gallo (American).
30. 8.41.	Hawker Hurricane W9136	No.52 OTU, undercarriage collapsed after aircraft ran onto soft ground whilst landing at Aston Down.	P/O Gallo (American).
2. 9.41.	Hawker Hurricane R2684	No.52 OTU, landed with undercarriage retracted following aileron failure at Aston Down at 13.15 hours.	1256363 Sgt. G.E. Simms.
3. 9.41.	Hawker Hurricane V6942	No.52 OTU, landed with undercarriage retracted following engine failure at Cherrington cross roads near Aston Down at 15.45 hours.	1258665 Sgt. G.P. Hanson.

DATE	'AIRCRAFT TYPE/SERIAL'	DETAILS	
3. 9.41.	Hawker Hurricane V7176	No.52 OTU, crashed into trees during at attempted forced landing at Oldbury on Severn following engine failure.	41164 F/O H.C. Baker.
3. 9.41.	Supermarine Spitfire P8199	No.1 FPP, undercarriage collapsed after heavy landing (aircraft dropped from 15 feet) at Kemble.	1st Off. C. Dutton ATA.
4. 9.41.	Hawker Hurricane V2647	No.52 OTU, undercarriage collapsed after heavy landing at Aston Down.	1264979 Sgt. F.H. Pelham.
4. 9.41.	Vickers Wellington L7894	No.21 OTU, landed with undercarriage retracted Moreton in Marsh.	
9. 9.41.	Vickers Wellington X9698	No.21 OTU, abandoned after aircraft became uncontrollable in cloud, to the east of Moreton in Marsh.	
10. 9.41.	Hawker Hurricane L1822	No.9 FTS, abandoned after catching fire in the air. Aircraft crashed near Owlpen, Dursley. Pilot landed in a tree in a wood at Uley.	1252826 LAC D.E. Pike.
13. 9.41.	Hawker Hurricane N2712	No.52, OTU, lost height, stalled and crashed whilst attempting to make a forced landing at Chafford.	1264979 Sgt. F.H. Pelham.
13. 9.41.	Hawker Hurricane V6732	No.52 OTU, swung on landing at Aston Down and struck stationary Miles Master, both aircraft severely damaged.	P/O Cicurel.
16. 9.41.	Hawker Hurricane L1956	HQSFP, forced landing one mile west of Kemble.	1378396 Sgt. K.S. Whitehead.
20. 9.41.	Airspeed Oxford AB693	No.6 FTS, lost hatch and crash landed at Bourton on the Water.	
23. 9.41.	Handley Page Hereford N9091	No.5 MU, belly landed in a cornfield near Rodmarton at 18.08 hours. Aircraft was on transfer to 20 MU at Aston Down.	40378 F/Lt. R. Ferguson.
25. 9.41.	Vickers Wellington	No.21 OTU, hit trees on approach to Moreton in Marsh at night and crashed.	Four killed two injured.
25. 9.41.	Airspeed Oxford AP396	No.3 FTS, hit trees on take off from Bibury, aircraft completely wrecked.	F/O Willoughby (k).
27. 9.41.	Supermarine Spitfire X4503	No.1 PRU, struck a telegraph pole and crashed near Yate after windscreen became obscured by oil.	84696 F/O B.J. McMaster.
28. 9.41.	Bristol Beaufighter R3206	No.600 Squadron, spun into ground at Acton Turville.	

29. 9.41.	Airspeed Oxford N6378	No.3 FTS, crashed on landing at Bibury.	
30. 9.41.	Supermarine Spitfire P8392	No.401 Squadron, undercarriage collapsed on landing at Little Rissington.	C1172 F/O J.B. McColl (Canadian).
30. 9.41.	Hawker Hurricane V6605	No.52 OTU, spun into ground from a height of 7,000 feet at Elberton near Bristol, during an air combat practice. Pilot parachuted and came down at Bushey Grove, Elberton at 15.45 hours.	1058906 Sgt. E.S. Locke.
30. 9.41.	Hawker Hurricane V3086	No.52 OTU, undercarriage collapsed after heavy landing at Aston Down 17.00 hours.	R79676 Sgt. D.P. Blyth (Canadian).
30. 9.41.	Hawker Hurricane L1695	No.9 FTS, undershot and hit a wall at Babdown Farm.	1165207 LAC W. Albery.
3.10.41.	Hawker Hurricane V7508	No.52 OTU, belly landing after engine failure at Water Lane, Bisley.	P/O Cicurel.
6.10.41.	Hawker Hurricane W9175	No.50 OTU, dived into the ground after being caught in the slipstream of other aircraft in formation. Aircraft came down at New Grounds, Slimbridge.	A407250 Sgt. P.B. Quint (Australian).
10.10.41.	Hawker Hurricane V7509	No.52 OTU, forced landing after engine failure near Coates. Aircraft then struck a wall.	R62817 Sgt. R.F. Mcdermid (Canadian) taken to Station Sick-Quarters at Aston Down with head injuries.
10.10.41.	Airspeed Oxford W6623	No.6 FTS, flew into cables on overshoot at Windrush.	
12.10.41.	Airspeed Oxford P1810	No.3 FTS, crashed while landing at night at South Cerney.	
13.10.41.	Miles Master T8681	SFP, spun into the ground four miles west of Cirencester after taking off from Kemble.	
16.10.41.	Miles Master T8317	No.9 FTS, crashed on approach to Babdown Farm at night.	
22.10.41.	Hawker Hurricane W9263	No.52 OTU, dived into River Severn near Severn Bridge whilst low flying.	
23.10.41.	Hawker Hurricane P2798	No.87 Squadron, abandoned after engine failure near Marshfield.	
25.10.41.	Airspeed Oxford V3234	No.14 FTS, crashed on overshoot at Long Newnton.	R75859 Sgt. A. Cooper (Canadian).
25.10.41.	Airspeed Oxford R6072	No.3 FTS, crashed whilst landing at night at South Cerney.	

DATE	'AIRCRAFT TYPE/SERIAL'	DETAILS	
26.10.41.	Vickers Wellington T2844	No.23 OTU, crashed at Swindon Farm, near Cheltenham. Wings broke away in a dive, possibly due to the dinghy being released.	402435 F/O T.N.G. Boyd (Australian) (k).
27.10.41.	Airspeed Oxford V3644	No.3 FTS, hit tree and crashed at Oldbury on Severn.	78169 Sgt. P.E. Lacey (Canadian) (k). LAC W. Skrzypek (Polish). LAC E.R. Janowicz (Polish).
31.10.41.	Hawker Hurricane P3021	No.52 OTU, out of control in cloud and crashed near Washingpool Hill, Almondsbury.	R77479 Sgt. H.C. Cotnam (Canadian) (k).
31.10.41.	Airspeed Oxford N4570	No.2 FTS, crashed on approach to Windrush.	
7.11.41.	Westland Lysander P9183	No.10 Gp. AAC Flt, crashed on take-off from Staverton.	
11.11.41.	Miles Master T8670	No.9 FTS, crashed on night approach to Babdown Farm.	
12.11.41.	Airspeed Oxford V3786	No.6 FTS, crashed on overshoot Windrush.	
12.11.41.	Vickers Wellington L7894	No.21 OTU, crashed on landing and caught fire at Moreton in Marsh.	S/Ldr. Williams (pilot) and crew safe.
27.11.41.	Handley Page Hampden AE440	No.144 Squadron, struck high ground at Birdlip, whilst descending through cloud to pinpoint position. Aircraft was returning from ops.	1008479 Sgt. G.H. Cornish (k). One crew member also injured.
5.12.41.	Miles Master AZ317	No.52 OTU, aircraft burst into flames after heavy landing at Aston Down. Pilot was trapped 911802 LAC L. Payne, a nursing orderly, dashed forward and tried to force the cockpit hood open, first from the port side and then from the starboard side. He managed to get the pilot out of the burning aircraft and was later awarded the George Cross.	P/O Verach (pilot).
5.12.41.	Supermarine Spitfire N3229	No.52 OTU, crashed on landing at Aston Down.	
6.12.41.	Hawker Hurricane Z2989	No.2 FPP, crashed in forced landing south east of Ross on Wye.	P/O Cukr.
6.12.41.	Supermarine Spitfire	No.52 OTU, struck Master on runway during night landing at Aston Down.	
6.12.41.	Miles Master	RAF Hullavington, see above.	F/Lt. Mould (instructor) (i). P/O Murray (pupil) (k).

7.12.41.	Airspeed Oxford P1930	No.2 SFTS, dived into the ground during a snow storm at Boughton Heath near Moreton in Marsh at 10.00 hours.	
8.12.41.	Airspeed Oxford R6017	No.3 FTS, crashed on overshoot at Bibury.	65700 LAC J.C. Cann (k).
9.12.41.	Airspeed Oxford T1249	No.15 FTS, dived into the ground at full power, whilst on solo cross country flight. Aircraft came down 1½ miles south of Aston Down, near Avening.	
10.12.41.	Airspeed Oxford L9643	No.3 FTS, struck tree whilst low flying near Cirencester.	
11.12.41.	Airspeed Oxford V3856	No.6 FTS, caught fire on the ground at Windrush and damaged beyond repair.	
13.12.41.	Hawker Hurricane Z3050	No.87 Squadron, crashed at Almondsbury, spun into the ground out of cloud.	Sgt. Robinson (k).
14.12.41.	Westland Whirlwind P7044	No.263 Squadron, crashed after loss of control near Coleford.	
16.12.41.	Supermarine Spitfire R7212	No.52 OTU, crashed on take-off from Aston Down.	
18.12.41.	Supermarine Spitfire R7061	No.52 OTU, struck ground after take-off from Aston Down at France Lynch.	R77460 Sgt. R.P. Owen (American)(k).
29.12.41.	Vickers Wellington X9694 (ED—Q)	No.21 OTU, belly landed in a field after engine failure, near Bledington. Aircraft struck light pole on approach.	
31.12.41.	Vickers Wellington DV425	No.21 OTU, undercarriage collapsed on landing at Moreton in Marsh at 01.11 hours.	F/Sgt. Fryer and crew safe.
2. 1.42.	Bristol Blenheim L6837	No.604 Squadron, caught fire in the air and crash landed at Staverton.	
3. 1.42.	Airspeed Oxford L9699	No.3 FTS, dived into the ground at Shorncote.	Cpl. Gmiter (Polish) (Pilot).
5. 1.42.	Supermarine Spitfire X4608	No.52 OTU, force landed at Aston Down and struck Hurricane BN224.	
10. 1.42.	Supermarine Spitfire X4925	No.53 OTU, landed in bad weather at Staverton with undercarriage partially retracted.	404982 Sgt. D.L. Boyd (Australian).
23. 1.42.	Avro Anson N5324	No.6 AOS, struck HT cables in bad weather and crashed near River Severn ?	1270838 Sgt. P. Pantoock. 1330641 AC.2. H. Amoore. 1336457 LAC R.W. Banks. 656298 LAC. R.S. Palmer.

DATE	'AIRCRAFT TYPE/SERIAL'	DETAILS	
24. 1.42.	Supermarine Spitfire X4162	No.52 OTU, force landed after engine failure 1½ miles south of Aston Down.	F/O S.A.H. Whitehouse.
28. 1.42.	Supermarine Spitfire P9326	No.52 OTU, belly landed after engine failure near Aston Down.	R54494 Sgt. J.M. Sabourin (Canadian).
29. 1.42.	Airspeed Oxford V3322	No.15 FTS, lost in snow storm, circled at low altitude and struck a fence at Hoffmans football ground, Stonehouse.	657094 Cpl. Letts (Pilot).
4. 2.42.	Vickers Wellington L7893	No.21 OTU, struck trees on take-off from Moreton in Marsh at night. Aircraft came down ½ mile north east of the airfield.	107518 P/O J.H. Kirk (pilot) (k). 107516 P/O H. Waugh (k). 1104350 Sgt. W.J. Harrison (k). 989009 Sgt. R. Marshall (i). 407164 Sgt. W.J.A. Brook (Australian) (i).
5. 2.42.	Vickers Wellington X3212	No.21 OTU, tyre burst on take-off from Moreton in Marsh.	Crew safe.
6. 2.42.	Vickers Wellington R1047	No.21 OTU, port propeller and reduction gear fell off near Moreton in Marsh and whilst making single engined circuit the aircraft struck a tree and crashed.	
6. 2.42.	Vickers Wellington R1610	No.300 (Polish) Squadron, flare exploded in the bomb bay. Front gunner baled out and struck a propeller causing severe damage to engine and aircraft force landed at Bibury.	
6. 2.42.	Supermarine Spitfire X4932	No.52 OTU, crashed at Aston Farm, near Aston Down at 14.10 hours.	R78841 Sgt. B.H. Cassidy (Canadian) (k).
8. 2.42.	Supermarine Spitfire R7135	No.52 OTU, crashed at Oldbury Sands, River Severn. Incident witnessed by pilot of second aircraft Sgt. Foster.	R78852 Sgt. J.R. Pierce (Canadian ?) (k), body washed ashore on 7.4.42.
8. 2.42.	Vickers Wellington T2608	No.21 OTU, hit obstruction whilst low flying 2 miles north of Eastleach.	
8. 2.42.	Miles Master T8506	No.9 FTS, crashed on take-off from Babdown Farm.	
10. 2.42.	Miles Master AZ311	No.52 OTU, crashed near Berkeley.	R83133 Sgt. Arn (American) (k).
11. 2.42.	De Havilland Tiger Moth T7850	No.6 FIS, collided with Master N7766 and crashed at Pardward Mansions, Cheltenham, near Shurdington Road.	88652 F/O G.G.W. Pledger (k). 413085 P/O S.C. Jones (New Zealander) (k).

No.	Date	Aircraft	Details	Casualties
11.	2.42.	Miles Master N7766	No.9 FTS, see above.	67054 P/O F.W. Buckland (k). R55815 Sgt. A.J. Maher (Canadian) (k).
11.	2.42.	Airspeed Oxford W6620	No.6 FTS, collided with house while low flying at Cold Aston.	
11.	2.42.	Supermarine Spitfire P9546	No.52 OTU, broke up in the air south west of Dymock and crashed near Grange Farm.	R85636 Sgt. G.A. Davies (Canadian) (k).
11.	2.42.	Hawker Hurricane L1951	No.9 FTS, struck hedge and crashed at Park Farm, Chipping Sodbury.	
13.	2.42.	Vickers Wellington R1082	No.21 OTU, crashed after engine failure at Moreton in Marsh ?.	655429 Sgt. E.T.A. Cartwright (k). 655481 Sgt. J.E. Adlam (k). 1325633 Sgt. D.B. Atkinson (k). 986400 Sgt. A.W. McRae (k).
17.	2.42.	Miles Master W8517	No.5 FTS, dived into the ground at Chetwynd Heath.	
17.	2.42.	Westland Lysander V9715	No.4 Squadron, hit ground whilst recovering from a dive near Clifton.	
19.	2.42.	Vickers Wellington X3179	No.21 OTU, crashed on landing at Moreton in Marsh.	
22.	2.42.	Avro Anson AW970	No.12 OTU, ran out of fuel and crashed 1 mile east of Southrop.	
27.	2.42.	Handley Page Hampden P5319	No.16 OTU, dived into the ground 1½ miles south east of Bourton on the Water at 00.25 hours after engine failure.	Three killed.
27.	2.42.	Supermarine Spitfire X4240	No.52 OTU, overshot on landing at Aston Down.	
18.	3.42.	Vickers Wellington X9627	No.23 OTU, crashed after take off from Defford at Woodmancote ? (possibly Worcestershire).	
19.	3.42.	Airspeed Oxford P1988	No.3 PAFU, crashed on take off from South Cerney.	
20.	3.42.	Bristol Beaufort AW301	OAPU, crashed on take-off from Filton.	
21.	3.42.	Airspeed Oxford N6429	No.3 FTS, struck trees whilst attempting to land in fog at Bibury.	
21.	3.42.	Bristol Beaufort	FTF, crashed at Filton.	Sergeant pilot broke leg. P/O Slade safe.
22.	3.42.	Supermarine Spitfire R7250	No.52 OTU, lost engine cowling and crashed in forced landing near Rodmarton. Aircraft hit a stone wall and was badly damaged.	
25.	3.42.	Supermarine Spitfire R7064	No.52 OTU, lost engine cowling and crashed 3 miles south east of Aston Down.	
25.	3.42.	Handley Page Hampden P5398	No.14 OTU, aircraft off track whilst on a training flight, crashed at Whithill Farm, Brockhampton.	Four crew killed.

DATE   'AIRCRAFT TYPE/SERIAL'   DETAILS

DATE	'AIRCRAFT TYPE/SERIAL'	DETAILS	
27. 3.42.	Vickers Wellington N2800	No.21 OTU, crashed after engine fire near Aston Magna at 02.40 hours. Aircraft burnt.	972095 Sgt. E. Dutton (k). 1113754 Sgt. W. Brawd (k). 1196328 Sgt. A.C. Thomas (k). 1354828 Sgt. J.H. Young (k). 1028012 Sgt. H. Wilson (i).
5. 4.42.	Airspeed Oxford V3869	No.3 (P)AFU crashed near Lechlade.	Sgt. B. Jeffery (Canadian)(k).
6. 4.42.	Bristol Beaufighter AW281	FTF, crashed on take-off from Filton.	Sgt. Mason (pilot) safe.
7. 4.42.	Miles Master AZ315	No.52 OTU, crashed on take-off from Aston Down, just east of 'B' site.	F/O H.K. Smith (k). R98142 Sgt. L.N. Brown (Canadian) (pilot) (k).
8. 4.42.	Supermarine Spitfire R6686	No.57 OTU, collided with L7818 and crashed at Cold Aston in a rainstorm.	Two killed.
8. 4.42.	Vickers Wellington L7818	No.15 OTU, see above.	
10. 4.42.	Bristol Beaufort L4444	No.5 OTU, stalled just to the north of Kemble, whilst on approach and spun in. Aircraft burnt out.	
12. 4.42.	Supermarine Spitfire R7114	No.52 OTU, struck by Spitfire R6806 whilst parked at Aston Down.	
13. 4.42.	Airspeed Oxford T1111	No.6 FTS, dived into the ground at night, whilst in the circuit at Little Rissington.	Two killed.
20. 4.42.	Handley Page Hampden P1297	RAF Croughton, crashed 1 mile from Little Rissington. Aircraft burnt out.	
24. 4.42.	Supermarine Spitfire R7124	No.53 OTU, crashed whilst low flying over the Severn, near Newnham.	
25. 4.42.	Lockheed Hudson AM953	No.1444 Flight, taxied into water main excavation alongside unfinished peri-track at Kemble.	
25. 4.42.	Lockheed Hudson V9059	No.1444 Flight, swung on take-off from Kemble. Port wheel collapsed and aircraft caught fire.	P/O J. Conway-Hunt (pilot) safe.
6. 5.42.	Vickers Wellington T2848	No.21 OTU, stalled and crashed on landing at Moreton in Marsh.	Crew safe.
14. 5.42.	Supermarine Spitfire P8169	No.52 OTU, struck River Severn whilst flying in formation at low level, crashed 2 miles ENE of Lydney at 11.00 hours. Flew under Severn Bridge after making contact with water. Site investigated in 1982 by Severnside Aviation Society nothing found.	P102255 P/O Livingstone (Canadian) safe.

No.	Date	Aircraft	Details	Casualties
15.	5.42.	Avro Tutor K3322	No.1 RFTS, crashed on landing at Moreton Valence.	
20.	5.42.	Avro Anson AX430	No.21 OTU, taxied into Wellington DV811 at Moreton in Marsh.	
21.	5.42.	Avro Anson N5259	No.21 OTU, struck HT cables and crashed near Kingham (possibly Oxfordshire).	Two killed.
22.	5.42.	Airspeed Oxford W6555	No.3 FTS, collided with Oxford R6321 and crashed at South Cerney.	
22.	5.42.	Airspeed Oxford R6321	No.3 FTS, see above.	
23.	5.42.	D.H. Tiger Moth R4894	No.10 EFTS, spun into the ground whilst in the circuit at Stoke Orchard.	
24.	5.42.	Airspeed Oxford	No.3 (P)AFU, crashed in the woods at Bathurst Park, Cirencester.	
26.	5.42.	Miles Master AZ256	No.52 OTU, crashed on landing at Aston Down.	
26.	5.42.	Vickers Wellington DV657	No.1446 Flight, tyre burst on take-off and aircraft swung into X9934, which was subsequently destroyed by the explosion of bombs.	
26.	5.42.	Vickers Wellington X9934	No.21 OTU, see above.	
30.	5.42.	Supermarine Spitfire P7968	No.52 OTU, crashed in forced landing ¼ of a mile south west of Nympsfield.	
2.	6.42.	Supermarine Spitfire N3065	No.52 OTU, spun in after pilot lost consciousness and then abandoned the aircraft near Longhope on Main.	Sgt. S.G. Haines (pilot) (k). AC T. Smith (fitter) (k).
2.	6.42.	Vickers Wellington DV658	No.1446 Flight, overshot at Moreton in Marsh and crash landed.	
7.	6.42.	Handley Page Halifax V9977	TFU, caught fire and crashed 8 miles south south west of Ross on Wye.	
9.	6.42.	Miles Master AZ332	No.52 OTU, crashed on overshoot at Aston Down.	
14.	6.42.	De Havilland Tiger Moth R5029	No.101 GOTU, dived into the ground near Innsworth.	
17.	6.42.	Supermarine Spitfire K9929	No.52 OTU, overshot landing and crashed at Aston Down at night.	
22.	6.42.	Hawker Typhoon R7590	No.8 MU, landed with undercarriage retracted at Little Rissington.	
26.	6.42.	Supermarine Spitfire P8093	No.52 OTU, stalled on landing after probable engine failure and crashed at Aston Down.	1391657 Sgt. J.E. Kent (i).

DATE   'AIRCRAFT TYPE/SERIAL'   DETAILS

DATE	'AIRCRAFT TYPE/SERIAL'	DETAILS	
2. 7.42.	Supermarine Spitfire ?8031	No.52 OTU, crashed in a wheatfield near Aston Down.	Sgt. P.R. Cole.
10. 7.42.	Blackburn Botha L6436	No.6 (P)AFU, crashed in forced landing 1 mile south of Hawling.	68805 F/O N. Buchanan.
15. 7.42.	Airspeed Oxford ED115	No.3 (P)AFU, crashed 1 mile east of Aston Down, after colliding with a hay elevator (40 feet high) on low level cross country.	
15. 7.42.	Supermarine Spitfire P7353	No.52 OTU, crashed in forced landing near Rockhampton.	
19. 7.42.	Airspeed Oxford AT674	No.3 (P) AFU, crashed 1 mile north of Bibury after engine failure whilst overshooting.	
21. 7.42.	Miles Master	Unit unknown, crashed at Babdown Farm.	F/O A.K.C. Holder (k). P/O White (k). Sgt. Henderson (k).
21. 7.42.	Airspeed Oxford AT603	No.3 (P)AFU, struck trees and farm buildings on take-off from Southrop and crashed at Homeleigh Farm.	
23. 7.42.	Supermarine Spitfire ?7509	No.52 OTU, dived into the River Severn near Chepstow during air firing practice.	1080606 Sgt. D. Machin (k).
24. 7.42.	Douglas Havoc AW410	No.1456 Flight, constant speed unit failed on one engine and the prop' was feathered. Aircraft landed on one engine at Stoke Orchard, but had no brake pressure. Pilot retracted undercarriage to avoid running into a group of workmen.	P/O R.J. Armstrong (pilot).
29. 7.42.	North American B.25 Mitchell FL692	Unit unknown, aircraft crashed on the east west runway at Aston Down with undercarriage trouble. Pilot had previously ordered two ATC cadet passengers to bale out.	925855 F/Sgt. W. Cappleman DFM and crew safe. Both cadets landed safely.
4. 8.42.	Miles Master DL306	No.2 GTS, taxied into an unmarked trench at Little Rissington.	1182665 F/Lt. R.M. Thomasson (pilot).
5. 8.42.	Armstrong Whitworth Whitley Z9432	No.10 OTU, crashed at Home Farm, Hazleton whilst on a cross country training flight at night.	Four killed but Sgt. Venn-Burtt survived after being thrown clear.
5. 8.42.	Avro Anson N5257	No.21 OTU, crashed in a forced landing near Moreton in the Marsh.	
10. 8.42.	Supermarine Spitfire P8377	No.52 OTU, spun into the ground near Stow on the Wold.	Sgt. Callow.

10. 8.42.	General Aircraft Hotspur Glider	No.3 GTS, crashed at Stoke Orchard at 10.00 hours.	Cpl. Masson (i).
12. 8.42.	Airspeed Oxford AT738	No.3 (P)AFU, struck a Married Quarter on take off at 01.00 hours from South Cerney. There was an immediate explosion and both the aircraft and the house were burnt out.	Sgt. Collins (k).
17. 8.42.	General Aircraft Hotspur Glider HH519	No.3 GTS, struck tree after cable release near Stoke Orchard and crashed.	Cpl. McQueen (pupil) (k).
17. 8.42.	Avro Anson DJ814	TFU, crashed near Poulton.	F/O Sellick DFC (pilot) (k). F/O Sellick (Air Gunner) (k). F/Lt. Brown (k). F/O Marsh (k). LAC McCullum (k). AC Umery (k).
19. 8.42.	Vickers Wellington T2903	No.18 OTU, flew into hillside in bad weather at Kingcombe Farm near Chipping Campden.	F/Sgt. S. Dusza (Polish) (pilot) (k). Remainder of crew killed.
19. 8.42.	Airspeed Oxford AB700	No.6 (P)AFU, lost power on take off from Little Rissington and struck tree.	411137 Sgt. Francis (pilot) (Australian) (k).
21. 8.42.	Bristol Beaufort X8935	No.20 MU, caught fire and crashed 2 miles south east of Sapperton.	
22. 8.42.	Miles Master AZ282	No.52 OTU, aircraft struck concrete picketing block whilst taxying damaging tail and tail wheel.	1214321 Sgt. R.P. Fenton.
25. 8.42.	Miles Master DL368	No.3 GTS, after releasing glider the aircraft flew low over Bishops Cleeve Vicarage and dislodged a chimney pot with the trailing tow rope.	1318905 Sgt. J.F. Alexander.
26. 8.42.	Avro Anson DJ181	No.6 AONS, crashed at Stockend Wood, Edge, near Painswick. Flew into hillside in low cloud.	1381973 Sgt. E.C. Perkins (k). 1438259 LAC. L.W. Roper. 630889 F/Sgt. A.G. Richards. 1440292 LAC. B. Cross.
27. 8.42.	Miles Master W8664	No.3 FTS, stalled on approach to Babdown Farm and crashed catching fire. Aircraft came down at Binley Farm. The Severnside Aviation Society examined this site during 1984.	P1901 Cpt. M. Belc (Polish).
28. 8.42.	De Havilland Mosquito DD690	No.23 Squadron, overshot after engine failure and crashed through boundary fence at Moreton Valence.	44070 F/O M.H. Holder.

DATE	'AIRCRAFT TYPE/SERIAL'	DETAILS	
29. 8.42.	Miles Master DL526	No.3 GTS, aircraft stalled on landing at Stoke Orchard and starboard wing struck the ground.	1316009 Sgt. V.D. Howe.
30. 8.42.	Miles Magister	Unit unknown, crashed at New Grounds, Slimbridge.	Two crew safe.
30. 8.42.	Hawker Typhoon R8720	No.9 FPP, in collision with R8756 at Brockworth.	
30. 8.42.	Hawker Typhoon R8756	Unit unknown, see above.	
31. 8.42.	Vickers Wellington R1232	No.1443 Flight, overshot and struck a tree at Moreton in Marsh.	126682 P/O M. Dunn (pupil pilot) (k). 925527 Sgt. B.A. Smith (k). 1375503 Sgt. A. Perret (k). R79302 Sgt. Boyer (i).
4. 9.42.	General Aircraft Hotspur Glider	No.3 GTS, crashed at Boddington after being released from tow.	Cpl. Palmer (k).
4. 9.42.	General Aircraft Hotspur Glider	No.3 GTS, glider struck the ground after dive approach at Stoke Orchard.	Sgt. Howard (i).
5. 9.42.	Supermarine Spitfire X4685	No.52 OTU, crashed in a forced landing near Aston Down.	
6. 9.42.	Vickers Wellington X9942	No.21 OTU, struck a tree shortly after take off from Moreton in Marsh.	
6. 9.42.	Miles Master DL358	No.3 GTS, taxied into a tractor at Stoke Orchard at 10.10 hours.	P/O D. Mogg.
9. 9.42.	Airspeed Oxford N4728	No.3 FIS, caught fire whilst waiting to take-off from Babdown Farm.	
10. 9.42.	Airspeed Oxford V3430	CFS, spun into the ground at Eastington.	
10. 9.42.	Supermarine Spitfire P7834	No.52 OTU, in collision with a second Spitfire and crashed near the Bear Inn at Cirencester.	
11. 9.42.	Miles Master DL532	No.3 GTS, struck a stationary Hotspur Glider HH296 whilst taking-off from Stoke Orchard at 14.35 hours.	J.R. Littlefair (pilot). W.G. Gardiner (Co-pilot).
11. 9.42.	Supermarine Spitfire P7676	No.52 OTU, struck the surface of the River Severn and crashed.	Sgt. Grant (Canadian) (k).
11. 9.42.	Miles Master DL642	No.268 Squadron, struck raised manhole cover while taxying at Staverton and undercarriage leg collapsed.	P/O T.E.D. Mitchell.
12. 9.42.	Armstrong Whitworth Whitley	Unit unknown, crash landed at Windrush after engine failure. Fire in port engine put out by fire crew.	Rear Gunner (i).

13. 9.42.	Supermarine Spitfire X4479	No.52 OTU, crashed in forced landing at Frampton on Severn.	
16. 9.42.	Vickers Wellington BJ728	No.12 OTU, crashed after engine failure at Lower Farm, Upper Milton, Oxfordshire not far from Gloucestershire boundary.	415072 Sgt. R.G. McArthy (New Zealander). 1387312 Sgt. W.J. Ferguson (New Zealander).
19. 9.42.	Miles Master W8723	ECFS, landed with undercarriage retracted at Long Newnton at 16.50 hours.	Maj. G.C. Krummeek (South African) (pilot) safe.
23. 9.42.	Unidentified	Unit unknown, crashed at 22.30 hours during a storm in a field near Kemble. No sign of occupants despite search.	Fragments of body found next day, buried four days later.
26. 9.42.	Supermarine Spitfire X4030	Unit unknown, crashed on landing at Filton at 17.00 hours.	Sgt. Harrison.
26. 9.42.	Supermarine Spitfire R7157	No.52 OTU, dived into the ground near Quedgeley.	
30. 9.42.	Airspeed Oxford AP469	No.3 (P)AFU, crashed in a forced landing after engines cut out near Cirencester.	
2.10.42.	General Aircraft Hotspur Glider BT668	No.3 GTS, crashed after dive approach at Stoke Orchard.	Cpl. Ashworth (k). Pvt. Washington (k).
7.10.42.	Hawker Hurricane BN878	TFU, crashed at Conderton.	Pilot killed.
11.10.42.	General Aircraft Hotspur Glider HH451	No.3 GTS, got tow rope entangled on take-off with that of Hotspur HH591 and crashed Stoke Orchard.	AC2 Carter (k).
13.10.42.	Airspeed Oxford AP401	No.3 FTS, crashed on overshoot at Bibury.	
14.10.42.	Supermarine Spitfire P8381	No.52 OTU, crashed on approach to Babdown Farm.	
14.10.42.	Supermarine Spitfire AR227	No.52 OTU, crashed near Babdown Farm.	
14.10.42.	Miles Master DL325	No.3 GTS, landed with undercarriage retracted at Stoke Orchard.	613110 Sgt. Morton (k). Sgt. Howe.
15.10.42.	Supermarine Spitfire P7966	No.52, OTU, dived into a storage shed at Quedgeley RAF station. A civilian woman was killed and several other persons were injured, shed was set on fire.	P/O Beage (New Zealander) (k).
15.10.42.	Supermarine Spitfire X4059	No.52 OTU, collided with Master AZ364 in the circuit at Aston Down and crashed.	Pilot killed.
15.10.42.	Miles Master AZ364	No.52 OTU, see above.	Pilot killed.

DATE	'AIRCRAFT TYPE/SERIAL'	DETAILS	
17.10.42.	Supermarine Spitfire P7543	No.52 OTU, crashed in bad visibility 1 mile north east of Babdown Farm. Aircraft had been recalled to base due to bad weather.	Sgt. Winther (Norwegian).
28.10.42.	Airspeed Oxford	No.3 (P)AFU, crashed in a field near South Cerney whilst night flying and caught fire.	1456996 Sgt. Wilson (k).
6.11.42.	Airspeed Oxford AP473	No.6 (P)AFU, collided in mid-air with BG551 whilst night flying. Aircraft fell to the ground locked together and burst into flames.	2416472 Sgt. H. Farquharson (New Zealander) (k).
6.11.42.	Airspeed Oxford BG551	See above.	1344537 Sgt. Forrester (k).
8.11.42.	Supermarine Spitfire N3026	No.52 OTU, dived into the ground 3 miles north west of Nailsworth at Street Farm Nympsfield.	
27.11.42.	Airspeed Oxford AB728	No.3 (P)AFU, struck blister hangar on take off from South Cerney.	
29.11.42.	Vickers Wellington LB120	No.1446 Flight, stalled on approach to Moreton in the Marsh.	
30.11.42.	Airspeed Oxford W6624	No.6 (P)AFU, crashed at Windrush.	1127419 Sgt. Crossley (k).
1.12.42.	General Aircraft Hotspur Glider HH596	No.3 GTS, undershot and struck wall at Stoke Orchard.	Cpl. Conlin safe.
7.12.42.	Airspeed Oxford	No.3 (P)AFU, crashed at Barton End Nailsworth.	F/O Spillman (New Zealander) safe. Sgt. Fisher safe.
12.12.42.	Supermarine Spitfire P7442	No.53 OTU, crashed in a forced landing near Cambridge after pilot had reported trouble with the throttle.	Sgt. H.A. Douglas (Australian) (i).
12.12.42.	Miles Magister EM293	No.3 GTS, crashed at Northleach on take off.	Sgt. Williams safe.
14.12.42.	Supermarine Spitfire	No.52 OTU, crashed at Elkstone near Birdlip and burnt out.	Sgt. Joyner (k).
2. 1.43.	Supermarine Spitfire	No.52 OTU, stalled and crashed near the watch office at Aston Down	Sgt. Britto (Trinidadian) (k).
3. 1.43.	Bristol Beaufort L9837	No.301 FTU, crashed on landing at Moreton in Marsh.	
8. 1.43.	Airspeed Oxford	No.3 (P)AFU, crashed at Whiteway Cirencester and burnt out.	P/O R.P. Frayn (Canadian) (k).
13. 1.43.	North American Mustang AL959	No.170 Squadron, flew into the River Severn?	Sgt. Allison (k).

14. 1.43.	Handley Page Halifax W7844	No.5 MU, crashed at Oaksey Woods near Kemble at 12.10 hours.	F/Lt. F.C.B. Harrison (k). F/O H.J. Hamilton (k). 615005 F/Sgt. T.G. Thomas (k). 1029874 Cpl. W.A. Ashworth (k). 1268225 Cpl. H.L. Munsor (k). 1051229 Cpl. F.W. Heywood (k). 1238554 AC L.L. Smith (k). 1411069 AC V.G. Hadrill (k).
17. 1.43.	Hawker Typhoon DN312	No.245 Squadron, crashed in forced landing at Beach Bitton.	Sgt. Clark.
26. 1.43.	Supermarine Spitfire P8207	No.52 OTU, collided with P8208 over the River Severn and made a forced landing on the shore.	Sgt. E.H. Caldwell (k), body never recovered.
26. 1.43.	Supermarine Spitfire P8208	No.52 OTU, see above. Aircraft crashed in the River Severn.	
28. 1.43.	Vickers Wellington X3936	No.115 Squadron, abandoned in bad weather over western Gloucestershire. Aircraft crashed in the River Wye at Brockweir near Chepstow, Gwent.	
29. 1.43.	Vickers Wellington W5705	No.21 OTU, missing from a 'Nickel' raid on Nantes. Later found to have crashed near Stroud at Rushcombe at 23.04 hours.	Sgt. McCausland (k). Sgt. Farren (k). Sgt. Ayres (k). Sgt. Palmer (k). Sgt. Morgan (k).
30. 1.43.	Airspeed Oxford X7261	No.3 FIS, hit haystack on take-off from Babdown Farm.	
6. 2.43.	Supermarine Spitfire	No.52 OTU, aircraft crashed near Sapperton after a Glycol leak which caused the cockpit to fill with fumes.	Sgt. Burden (Canadian).
14. 2.43.	Armstrong Whitley BD285	No.24 OTU, crashed in forced landing at Longborough.	Three injured.
16. 2.43.	Airspeed Oxford V3603	No.3 (P)AFU, caught fire on approach to Bibury and crash landed.	
17. 2.43.	Unidentified	No.6 SFTS, crashed at Signet Hill near Windrush at 01.45 hours.	1315199 Sgt. Llewellyn (k). 1504935 AC Page (k).
17. 2.43.	Miles Master DL538	No.3 GTS, undercarriage collapsed on landing at Northleach.	Sgt. Chattin (pilot).
23. 2.43.	General Aircraft Hotspur HH599	No.3 GTS, undershot and struck trees at Stoke Orchard.	Cpl. Bonome.

DATE	'AIRCRAFT TYPE/SERIAL'	DETAILS	
24. 2.43.	Armstrong Whitworth Whitley EB283	No.5 MU, crashed on take-off for a flight test from Kemble at 17.00 hours.	
7. 3.43.	Supermarine Spitfire	No.52 OTU, struck HT cables whilst low flying at Slimbridge.	R133873 Sgt. J.W. Callinan (Canadian) (k).
10. 3.43.	Avro Anson DJ660	No.6 AOS, struck a hill at Stockend Wood, Edge, south of Staverton at 20.30 hours.	Sgt. J.H. Hammond (pilot). LAC W. Halpern (trainee navigator) plus two other crew.
17. 3.43.	Miles Master DL448	No.3 GTS, struck a fuel bowser whilst taxying at Stoke Orchard.	Sgt. James (pilot).
20. 3.43.	General Aircraft Hotspur HH148	No.3 GTS, undershot landing at Stoke Orchard.	F/O Palmer (instructor). Cpl. Boyle (pupil).
21. 3.43.	Airspeed Oxford	No.6 SFTS, crashed at Fordhill near Bourton on the Water at 11.10 hours.	1436384 Sgt. Wheelhouse (i). 40553 Sgt. Carpenter (New Zealander).
22. 3.43.	De Havilland Tiger Moth R5203	No.2 EFTS, stalled and dived into the ground during a pin point map reading exercise near Moreton in the Marsh.	413475 Sgt. Barber (pilot) (k). R134678 Sgt. Dunn (observer) (k).
23. 3.43.	Avro Lancaster W4879 (AR—D)	No.460 (Australian) Squadron, crashed near South Cerney after being attacked by enemy aircraft (Ju.88). Aircraft caught fire after impact.	Crew safe.
27. 3.43.	Airspeed Oxford	No.6 SFTS, crashed near Windrush at 02.15 hours and caught fire.	1318161 Sgt. Jupp rendered unconscious but escaped injury.
27. 3.43.	Airspeed Oxford	No.6 SFTS, crashed on the perimeter at Little Rissington.	1250518 P/O Bell (i).
3. 4.43.	General Aircraft Hotspur	No.3 GTS, crashed north east corner of Stoke Orchard airfield.	
4. 4.43.	Airspeed Oxford	No.6 SFTS, crashed on top of the MPBW offices at Windrush at 00.05 hours and burst into flames.	1431063 Sgt. Garrett (k). 1314458 Sgt. Green (k).
7. 4.43.	Armstrong Whitworth Whitley K8974	No.8 AOS, blown over in a gale at Aston Down.	
8. 4.43.	General Aircraft Hotspur	No.3 GTS, stalled from 15 feet whilst landing at Northleach with heavy ballast at 16.00 hours. Starboard wing struck the ground and the glider disintegrated.	Sgt. Hulme (pilot) (k). Cpl. Kennedy (i).

10. 4.43.	Airspeed Oxford	No.6 SFTS, incident ? at Windrush at 01.30 hours.	1341390 Sgt. Taylor (k).
16. 4.43.	Hawker Typhoon EK138	No.175 Squadron, collided on landing with Wellington X3595 at Filton.	
19. 4.43.	Vickers Wellington DF734	No.22 OTU, crashed at Staple Farm just west of Withington whilst on a cross-country navigation exercise.	Sgt. J.O. Munro (pilot) (k). F/O H.B. Elliott (k). Sgt. W.C. Scott (k). Sgt. L.E. Lightheart (k). Sgt. A.A. Chambers (k). 3427 Pte. E.A. Bataille (Belgian) (k). 3434 Pte. Depauw (Belgian) (k).
20. 4.43.	Armstrong Whitworth Whitley P4989	No.10 OTU, crashed in a forced landing at Horton near Chipping Sodbury.	One killed and two injured.
29. 4.43.	Avro Anson N5005	No.21 OTU, crashed in a forced landing near Stow on the Wold.	
5. 5.43.	Airspeed Oxford V3908	No.3 (P)AFU, overshot on landing at Southrop.	
5. 5.43.	Vickers Wellington R1242	No.21 OTU, crashed on overshoot at Moreton in the Marsh.	
11. 5.43.	Armstrong Whitworth Whitley EB353	No.24 OTU, struck trees south east of Mickleton and burst into flames following engine failure and loss of height.	Two killed.
14. 5.43.	Miles Master DL456	No.3 GTS, undercarriage collapsed on landing at Stoke Orchard.	Sgt. Chattin (pilot).
21. 5.43.	Miles Master ?	No.3 GTS, landed at Northleach with undercarriage retracted after glider release.	
26. 5.43.	Armstrong Whitworth Whitley LA845	No.24 OTU, crashed Collins Farm, Willersey after engine failure whilst on a training flight.	One killed and five injured.
6. 6.43.	Hawker Hurricane LB596	RAF Kemble, crashed on farmland near Fairford.	
3. 6.43.	Vickers Wellington T2569	No.21 OTU, crashed on take-off from Moreton in the Marsh.	S/Ldr. P.E. Bennet AFC (k).
7. 6.43.	Hawker Hurricane P3458	No.56 OTU, spun into the ground at Broomknow Farm ?	
14. 6.43.	Airspeed Oxford P8969	No.11 (P)AFU, collided with HN724 and crashed Gloucestershire ?	
14. 6.43.	Airspeed Oxford HN724	See above.	
15. 6.43.	Armstrong Whitworth Whitley Z9479	No.24 OTU, forced landing at Chedworth after engine failure.	1203970 F/Sgt. Gillon (pilot).

DATE   'AIRCRAFT TYPE/SERIAL'   DETAILS

DATE	'AIRCRAFT TYPE/SERIAL'	DETAILS	
15. 6.43.	Miles Master DL370	No.3 GTS, undercarriage collapsed on landing at Stoke Orchard.	Sgt. Deasy (pilot).
17. 6.43.	Avro Lancaster ED381	No.1656 CU, following a mid-air collision in the area of Brize Norton airfield in Oxfordshire with Wellington BJ845 the aircraft crashed at Wigstead Farm, Highworth, Wilts.	Crew all killed.
17. 6.43.	Vickers Wellington BJ845	No.27 OTU, see above.	Sgt. Fettell (k), rest of crew parachuted safely.
20. 6.43.	Supermarine Spitfire P7903	No.52 OTU, belly landing at Beckwell Farm Framcote.	
22. 6.43.	Hawker Typhoon R7590	No.8 MU, undercarriage collapsed on landing at Little Rissington.	
22. 6.43.	Miles Master DL520	No.3 GTS, brakes failed on landing at Stoke Orchard and the aircraft ran into a fence.	Sgt. Love (pilot).
4. 7.43.	Supermarine Spitfire P7918	No.52 OTU, crashed following mid-air collision with Mustang AG489 at Nether Lyppiat. Pilot parachuted but chute did not open.	Sgt. Adams (k).
4. 7.43.	North American Mustang AG489	No.20 MU, see above. Aircraft came down at Thrupp after pilot had parachuted.	F/O Cuker (i).
5. 7.43.	Airspeed Oxford V3848	No.6 (P)AFU, crashed on landing at Windrush.	W.O. Dorman (pilot) (i).
5. 7.43.	Vickers Wellington	No.16 OTU, crashed just to the east of Kempsford during a camera gun exercise. Aircraft burst into flames shortly after impact.	
7. 7.43.	General Aircraft Hotspur BT603	No.3 GTS, undershot at Stoke Orchard and hit boundary fence.	
8. 7.43.	Airspeed Oxford	No.3 (P)AFU, crashed at Southrop after engine failure.	Crew safe.
11. 7.43.	Airspeed Oxford	No.3 (P)AFU, crashed near Long Newnton.	
13. 7.43.	Miles Master DL499	No.3 GTS, undercarriage collapsed on landing at Northleach.	
16. 7.43.	Miles Master W8927	No.52 OTU, damaged beyond repair in a taxying accident at Aston Down.	F/O Schurman (Canadian) (k).
18. 7.43.	General Aircraft Hotspur HH264	No.3 GTS, undershot and hit trees on landing at Stoke Orchard.	Sgt. Southwall (k).

19. 7.43.	Miles Master DL491	No.3 GTS, struck telegraph pole on landing at night at Stoke Orchard and crashed.	Sgt. Thorougood (k).
19. 7.43.	Miles Master DL373	No.3 GTS, struck boundary wall at Northleach on landing.	Sgt. Jones (pilot) (i).
26. 7.43.	Miles Master DL467	No.3 GTS, undercarriage collapsed on landing at Stoke Orchard.	Sgt. Smart.
28. 7.43.	Armstrong Whitworth Whitley BD369	No.10 OTU, hit obstruction on landing at Moreton in the Marsh after brake failure.	
31. 7.43.	Supermarine Spitfire	Unit unknown, force landed at Chedworth.	
3. 8.43.	Miles Magister N3893	ATA, crashed on approach to Little Rissington.	
9. 8.43.	General Aircraft Hotspur HH265	No.3 GTS, undershot on landing at Stoke Orchard and struck boundary wall.	
15. 8.43.	General Aircraft Hotspur BT753	No.3 GTS, forcelanded at Stockhill Farm, Birdlip after operating from Northleach.	Cpl. Joyce.
19. 8.43.	Supermarine Spitfire N3121	No.52 OTU, struck by Spitfire BM120 whilst parked at Aston Down.	
20. 8.43.	Supermarine Spitfire JF844	No.6 FPP, crashed in bad weather at Luckley Farm, Stow on the Wold.	
22. 8.43.	Airspeed Oxford	Unit unknown, crashed on the Northleach to Cirencester road.	Sgt. Datson (k).
23. 8.43.	Armstrong Whitworth Whitley T4339	No.42 OTU, dived into the River Severn.	Four crew killed.
31. 8.43.	Miles Master DM404	No.3 GTS, crashed whilst doing aerobatics close to the Farmers Arms pub near Apperley and caught fire.	1322016 Sgt. C.E. Petre (k).
31. 8.43.	North American B-25 Mitchell FR190 ('E')	No.320 (Dutch) Squadron, overshot landing at Long Newnton after cross country training flight. Aircraft ended up in a ploughed field badly damaged at 11.45 hours.	Lt. J.M.A. Collee (Dutch) and crew safe.
10. 9.43.	Airspeed Oxford DF262	No.3 (P)AFU, crashed at Deans Farm Hatherop.	F/O Lister and crew safe.
11. 9.43.	Airspeed Oxford	No.6 SFTS, crashed at Eastleach at 16.50 hours.	137210 P/O Barkworth (k). 1067824 W.O. Renault (k). 163 Cadet 1st. Class Stone ATC (k).
17. 9.43.	Vickers Wellington BK499	No.8 MU, struck pill box on approach to Little Rissington ?, after engine failure.	F/Lt. McDonald (pilot).

161

DATE	'AIRCRAFT TYPE/SERIAL'	DETAILS	
24. 9.43.	Airspeed Oxford	No.3 (P)AFU, crashed on the Bibury to Burford road.	F/Lt. Megget (k). W.O. Freise-Green (k). Sgt. Barker (k).
26. 9.43.	Armstrong Whitworth Whitley Z9428	No.24 OTU, aircraft seen to explode at 5,000 feet over Stoke Orchard at 19.45 hours whilst on a training flight. Came down near Stanley Pontlarge.	Crew of five killed.
26. 9.43.	Airspeed Oxford BG659	No.3 (P)AFU, crashed at Brimpsfield during night training flight.	1454838 Sgt. J. Walker (k).
30. 9.43.	Airspeed Oxford	No.3 (P)AFU, crashed at Windrush at 15.20 hours after catching fire whilst landing.	1029731 Sgt. Fordyce (k).
2.10.43.	General Aircraft Hotspur HH549	No.3 GTS, undershot and struck boundary wall at Northleach.	F/Sgt. Allison and Cpl. Spencer safe.
5.10.43.	Miles Master T8740	No.5 (P)AFU, crashed in a forced landing near Stoke Orchard.	
8.10.43.	Vickers Wellington R1028	No.21 OTU, crashed at Little Rissington after engine failure.	1463377 Sgt. Johnson (k). 1456857 Sgt. Jones (k). 1578285 Sgt. Cox (k). 961005 Sgt. Rees (k). 19907 F/Sgt. Hazeldene (Australian) (k). 1573676 Sgt. J. Smith (i).
17.10.43.	Vickers Wellington	No.82 OTU, tried to land at Little Rissington after engine failure. The second engine then failed and the aircraft crash landed at Windrush and burst into flames.	Sgt. Kirkland (pilot) and crew safe.
19.10.43.	General Aircraft Hotspur?	No.3 GTS, crashed at Northleach.	
20.10.43.	Airspeed Oxford	No.6 SFTS, crashed at Windrush.	Pilot injured. 13327701 Sgt. Lang (k).
21.10.43.	Armstrong Whitworth Albemarle	Hawkesley Ltd., crashed on test flight at Court Farm Brockworth.	ATC Cadet White (k). ATC Cadet Cheriton (k).
27.10.43.	De Havilland Mosquito HX817	No.418 Squadron, struck hangar on take-off from South Cerney and crashed.	F/O H.A. Hague (Canadian) (i). Sgt. Stevenson (Canadian) (i). (Hague later died in hospital).
17.11.43.	Miles Master DL518	No.3 GTS, overshot landing and ran into the boundary hedge at Stoke Orchard.	Pilot safe.
18.11.43.	Miles Master AZ851	No.5 (P)AFU, dived into the ground in bad visibility near Elmore.	151300 F/O H. Walker (instructor) (k). 124815 F/O R. Barr (pupil) (k).

19.11.43.	General Aircraft Hotspur HH556	No.3 GTS, undershot on landing after loss of the canopy at Stoke Orchard.	Pilot safe.
24.11.43.	Miles Master DL520	No.3 GTS, overran landing at Bibury damaging undercarriage and starboard wing.	Sgt. Smart (pilot).
25.11.43.	Airspeed Oxford R6240	No.3 (P)AFU, crashed on approach to South Cerney.	
25.11.43.	Airspeed Oxford L4629	No.6 (P)AFU, crashed in a forced landing just south of Moreton in the Marsh at 10.00 hours.	976674 Sgt. Berry (i). 1575234 Sgt. Hall (i).
26.11.43.	Airspeed Oxford V3592	No.3 (P)AFU, crashed on approach to Bibury after engine failure.	F/O Cunningham (k). Sgt. Mackay (k).
4.12.43.	General Aircraft Monospar X9334 (ex G—AFIV)	No.10 Group Comms. Flight, crashed in a forced landing 1 mile north of Pucklechurch.	
6.12.43.	Bristol Beaufighter T3024	No.63 OTU, crashed on landing at Chedworth.	
17.12.43.	Airspeed Oxford	No.3 (P)AFU, crashed near Little Rissington at 16.00 hours.	150186 P/O Burgess (k). 1316462 Sgt. Jones (pupil) (k).
28.12.43.	De Havilland Mosquito HJ826	No.60 OTU, crashed on approach to Chedworth. Came down near Ablington narrowly missed several houses and caught fire.	F/O Marcus (k). F/O Rogers (American) (k).
1. 1.44.	Bristol Beaufighter R2304	No.63 OTU, abandoned after engine fire near Slimbridge. Aircraft came down at Shepherds Patch on the Berkeley Castle estate at 11.45 hours. Petrol was scattered over a wide area and as a result a horse had its mane and tail burnt off.	143449 F/O D.G. Greville (pilot) (k).
5. 1.44.	De Havilland Mosquito HJ814	No.60 OTU, overshot and collided with an obstruction at Chedworth after engine failure at 13.05 hours.	658552 F/Sgt. K. Davey (pilot).
7. 1.44.	Hawker Typhoon JR426	No.20 MU, crashed in a forced landing 2 miles south west of Stonehouse.	
20. 1.44.	Miles Magister R1955	No.60 OTU, spun into the ground 5 miles to the east of Stoke Orchard.	
2. 2.44.	Miles Master W8822	ECFS, crashed in a forced landing near Acton Turville.	
9. 2.44.	Unidentified	USAAF Filton, crashed 3 miles from the station at Filton.	2nd Lt. A.W. Leeper USAAF (k).
11. 2.44.	Vickers Wellington X3215	No.21 OTU, struck a tree on take-off from Moreton in the Marsh.	

DATE	'AIRCRAFT TYPE/SERIAL'	DETAILS	
14. 2.44.	General Aircraft Hotspur HH605	No.3 GTS, crashed on landing at Stoke Orchard.	
18. 2.44.	De Havilland Mosquito HK225	No.151 Squadron, flew into the ground in cloud 1½ miles north of Tomatin.	10601345 Sgt. R. Smith (American)(k).
21. 2.44.	Miles Master DM441	No.3 GTS, crashed into Cleeve Hill in bad weather.	F/Lt. Sharp (pilot) safe.
24. 2.44.	Vickers Wellington LN596	No.84 OTU, crashed 1 mile north of Long Newnton after engine failure on overshoot. Aircraft was returning from a 'Nickel' raid.	R159445 Sgt. Klunczny (pilot).
28. .2.44.	Curtiss Tomahawk AH852	No.1682 Flight, swung on landing and undercarriage collapsed at Moreton in the Marsh.	
2. 3.44.	Avro Tutor K3319	No.6 OAFU, crashed on landing at Moreton Valence.	
6. 3.44.	Miles Master DL544	No.3 GTS, force landed in a field near Stoke Orchard after engine trouble.	
8. 3.44.	Miles Master DL545	No.3 GTS, crashed on landing at Stoke Orchard.	
15. 3.44.	Miles Master DL433	No.3 GTS, crashed after colliding with stationary Hotspur glider HH591, on take-off from Stoke Orchard.	
23. 3.44.	Airspeed Oxford	No.15 (P)AFU, crashed at Babdown Farm.	P/O Braithwaite (i).
24. 3.44.	Miles Master DL476	No.3 GTS, struck Master DL451 on landing at Stoke Orchard.	
27. 3.44.	Junkers Ju.88A-4 (3E + FT) Werk No.550241	KG.6, crashed in a field at Woodlands Farm, Clapton, near Berkeley. Crashing aircraft set fire to a hayrick and bombs exploded on impact causing a crater 60 feet by 24 feet deep. Crew parachuted, maps recovered showing that Sharpness had been the target. Severnside Aviation Society have visited this site twice and have recovered some parts. Probably shot down by Mosquito night-fighter.	Uffz. W. Tutschek (pow). Gefr. O. Bauch (pow). Uffz. J. Wirth (pow). Obgefr. K. Wiedener (pow).
27. 3.44.	Airspeed Oxford N6403	No.271 Squadron, struck a store building on approach to Little Rissington. Aircraft had been diverted from Down Ampney because of fog.	F/Lt. L.C. Shannon (k). J9499 Sgt. G.W.J. Reynolds (Canadian) (k). 1324162 Sgt. B.H. Dorn (k).
27. 3.44.	Douglas Dakota	No.271 Squadron ?, crashed at South Cerney at 22.15 hours in bad visibility.	

Date	Aircraft	Details	Crew
4. 4.44.	North American Mustang FX881	No.306 (Polish) Squadron, crashed on take-off from Aston Down.	
10. 4.44.	Douglas Dakota KG369	No.512 Squadron, struck trees whilst overshooting at Chedworth. Aircraft was on a night navigation exercise.	152176 F/O Brumwell (pilot) 152147 P/O Teed (k). Sgt. Eastell (k). Sgt. Smith (k).
13. 4.44.	Short Stirling LJ475	No.620 Squadron, stalled and crashed after glider release at Blackford Farm, Kempsford.	
25. 4.44.	Airspeed Oxford	Unit unknown, crashed at Windrush at 04.30 hours.	F/Sgt. Hura Nelson Burns Sgt. Emerl William Tootill (k) 424852 F/Sgt. Cormack (Australian) (i), he died later in the day.
27. 4.44.	Handley Page Halifax EB146	No.1667 HCU, abandoned after engine failure over Marshfield.	4 crew injured, 3 killed including pilot P/O C.D. McIvor (Canadian) (k). J. Crosby-Warren.
27. 4.44.	Gloster F9/40 DG205/G	Gloster Aircraft Co. crashed on a test flight from Moreton Valence. Came down at Minchinhampton after losing aileron.	
4. 5.44.	Percival Proctor Z7217	No.4 RS, broke up recovering from a dive near Coleford.	
7. 5.44.	Airspeed Oxford V3566	No.3 (P)AFU, caught fire taxying at Southrop.	
12. 5.44.	Armstrong Whitworth Albemarle V1612	No.297 Squadron, overshot landing at Windrush.	
19. 5.44.	Short Stirling LJ830	No.620 Squadron, in collision with EF244 over tow rope dropping area and crashed 1 mile west south west of Kempsford.	Pilot F/Sgt. A.B. Haynes RAAF (k) Nav Sgt. G. Powell RAFVR (k) W/OP Sgt. A.T. Franks RAFVR (k) F/Eng. Sgt. J.W. Taylor RAFVR (k) B/A Sgt. R.M. Cotterell RAFVR (k) A/G Sgt. G.P. Jones RAFVR (k)
19. 5.44.	Short Stirling EF244	No.620 Squadron, see above.	
24. 5.44.	Hawker Typhoon MM971	No.84 GSU, crashed at Wickwar quarries near Charfield after engine failure.	
31. 5.44.	De Havilland Tiger Moth R5255	No.14 EFTS, spun into the ground in bad weather near Blockley.	
5. 6.44.	Miles Master DL544	No.3 GTS, struck tractor whilst taxying at Northleach.	
19. 6.44.	Airspeed Oxford V4061	No.15 (P)AFU, overshot and hit Oxford ED139 at Long Newnton.	
19. 6.44	North American Mustang FX981	No.84 GSU, broke up recovering from a dive south east of Stroud and came down at Thrupp.	
20. 6.44.	Hawker Typhoon MN488	No.84 GSU, overshot emergency landing at Aston Down.	

165

DATE	'AIRCRAFT TYPE/SERIAL'	DETAILS
6. 7.44.	Waco CG—4 Glider	RAF Fairford, force landed at Bibury. Cpt. E.I. Slade ATA (k).
13. 7.44.	Vickers Wellington Z1690	No.5 FP, crashed after take-off from Little Rissington and caught fire at 18.00 hours. Sgt. I.J. Flynn (k).
14. 7.44.	Airspeed Oxford AB719	No.3 (P)AFU, spun in from 500 feet near South Cerney village.
14. 7.44.	Hawker Typhoon JR127	No.1 ADF, stalled recovering from a dive and crashed near Aston Down.
16. 7.44.	Miles Magister R1858	FTCCF, hit trees while low flying at Babington Hall?
25. 7.44.	Airspeed Oxford R6280	No.15 (P)AFU, struck a tree and crashed at Horton Court, Chipping Sodbury.
28. 7.44.	North American Mustarg FZ138	No.3 TEU, hit truck on take off from Chedworth and crashed.
28. 7.44.	Vickers Wellington JA147	Unit unknown, made a wheels-up landing at Little Rissington. F/O C.O. Bibby.
29. 7.44.	Supermarine Spitfire JL349	Dowty Rotol Ltd., crashed 3 miles from Staverton, whilst on a test flight. J. Hall (k).
29. 7.44.	North American Mustang FB200	No.3 TEU, undercarriage collapsed on landing at Chedworth. F/O I.G. Wood safe.
30. 7.44.	North American Mustang FX934	No.3 TEU, engine cut just after take-off and aircraft crashed 1 mile north east of Chedworth, near Withington. J35613 P/O J.S. Walsh (k).
30. 7.44.	Handley Page Halifax NA503	No.102 Squadron, struck high ground near Blockley. Seven killed, including F/Sgt. J.E. Hulme (New Zealand). F/Sgt. Luscombe (k). AC.2 Clark (k).
31. 7.44.	Airspeed Oxford HM729	No.3 (P)AFU, crashed shortly after take-off from South Cerney and was burnt out.
4. 8.44.	Hawker Typhoon MN286	No.3 TEU, engine cut on take-off from Aston Down and aircraft crashed through the boundary fence.
5. 8.44.	Hawker Typhoon JR516	No.3 TEU, caught fire in the air and dived into the ground at Tibberton? Severnside Aviation Society visited the site in 1983 but were unable to find anything of consequence. Sgt. Brightwell (k).

166

Date	Aircraft	Details	Crew
10. 8.44.	Avro Lancaster JB716	No.12 Squadron, crashed in Cirencester Park at 03.30 hours after returning damaged from a mining sortie.	F/Lt. G.C. Owens (pilot) (k). F/O G.L. Wiston (k). F/Sgt. E.J.W. Reed (k). Sgt. L.W. Delaney (k). Sgt. W. P. Johnson (k). Sgt. J.G. Robinson (i). Sgt. A.S. Canning (i).
15. 8.44.	Hawker Typhoon R8968	No.3 TEU, swung on landing and undercarriage collapsed at Aston Down.	
16. 8.44.	Airspeed Oxford L4581	No.6 (P)AFU, taxied into a trench and caught fire at Little Rissington.	
19. 8.44.	Airspeed Oxford AT742	No.3 (P)AFU, caught fire whilst in dispersal area at Bibury.	
21. 8.44.	Short Stirling	Probably 620 Squadron, crashed at the end of runway 05 Fairford at 15.00 hours.	Air Gunner (i) and Bomb Aimer (i).
25. 8.44.	Hawker Typhoon JP499	No.3 TEU, landed with undercarriage retracted at Aston Down.	
26. 8.44.	Hawker Typhoon MN207	No.3 TEU, stalled and crashed on approach to Aston Down. Aircraft burst into flames.	F/Sgt. Cameron (k).
26. 8.44.	Handley Page Halifax MZ311	No.78 Squadron, crashed into a quarry on Cleeve Common near Bishops Cleeve. Aircraft was returning from an operational sortie to La Rochelle.	J25977 F/Lt. C.M. Howe (pilot). (Canadian). J28243 F/O E. Freeman (Canadian). J28883 F/O C. McCartney (Canadian). 423759 Sgt. E. Harris. 694019 Sgt. J. McArdle. J36031 F/O J. Glenn (Canadian). R82608 F/Sgt. R. Hamilton (Canadian).
28. 8.44.	North American Mustang FX892	No.3 TEU, disintegrated in the air, location unknown possibly over Aston Down.	W.O. Whyte (k).
28. 8.44.	Airspeed Oxford N6322	No.15 (P)AFU, struck trees whilst on approach to Babdown Farm.	
29. 8.44.	Airspeed Oxford	No.15 (P)AFU, crashed on top of the runway controllers caravan at Babdown Farm, killing the controller.	
3. 9.44.	Hawker Typhoon MM958	No.3 TEU, crashed in a forced landing 1 mile north of Cirencester.	

DATE   'AIRCRAFT TYPE/SERIAL'   DETAILS

DATE	'AIRCRAFT TYPE/SERIAL'	DETAILS	
6. 9.44.	Short Stirling EF296	No.620 Squadron, tyre burst after landing at Fairford, aircraft swung and the port wing was torn off.	Pilot slightly injured.
7. 9.44.	Hawker Typhoon JP537	No.3 TEU, crashed after engine failure near Aston Down. Aircraft struck a haystack and narrowly missed some houses.	
10. 9.44.	Hawker Typhoon EK179	No.3 TEU, tried to land downwind after engine failure, overshoot and landed 'wheels up' in the MU dispersal at Aston Down.	
23. 9.44.	North American Mustang SR414	No.3 TEU, undercarriage collapsed on take-off from Chedworth.	
27. 9.44.	Hawker Typhoon JP904	No.3 TEU, crashed in a forced landing to the east of Aylburton following engine failure.	Pilot injured.
29. 9.44.	Bristol Beaufighter X7941	Unit unknown, crashed outside the airfield boundary at Filton and burnt out.	F/Sgt. Browne (i).
1.10.44.	Airspeed Oxford V3736	No.3 (P)AFU, crashed on overshoot at Chedworth.	
2.10.44.	Hawker Typhoon MN118	No.3 TEU, port tyre burst on take-off and aircraft belly landed at Aston Down.	
3.10.44.	Bristol Buckingham KV432	Bristol Aeroplane Co., crashed on a test flight. Swung on take-off from Filton and crashed into the Test Flight office block.	P/O Porter (pilot).
12.10.44.	Avro Anson AW910	No.15 (P)AFU, overshot on landing and undercarriage collapsed at Babdown Farm.	
30.10.44.	Short Stirling EF177	No.1662 CU, propeller flew off after engine failure and struck a second engine and the fuselage. Aircraft was abandoned and came down at Alveston demolishing a house. The site has been visited by members of the Severnside Aviation Society and some parts were recovered.	Crew all parachuted and three were slightly injured.
10.11.44.	Hawker Typhoon EK151	No.3 TEU, crashed on take-off from Aston Down.	
16.11.44.	Hawker Typhoon MN231	No.3 TEU, engine cut on take-off from Aston Down.	

20.11.44.	Vickers Wellington LN460	No.22 OTU, port engine caught fire over Willersey and the aircraft crashed near Childs Wickham.	D.M. Roy (pilot) and two others killed. Some crew members parachuted, one landing near Broadway railway station.
21.11.44.	Handley Page Halifax LL126	No.1662 CU, crashed after catching fire in the air near Long Ashton. Aircraft dived into the ground and exploded. The resultant fire burnt all night, fuelled by the ammunition and bombs on board. The site has been visited by the Severnside Aviation Society and some parts have been recovered.	Seven man Polish crew all killed.
22.11.44.	Short Stirling EF201	No.1660 CU, crashed out of control after engine trouble on the edge of Northleach airfield at 11.45 hours.	Seven crew killed, two parachuted.
11.12.44.	De Havilland Tiger Moth T8208	RAF Blakehill Farm, crashed in a forced landing at Yanworth.	
17.12.44.	Handley Page Halifax NP752	A&AEE, struck HT cables during unauthorised low flying and made a forced landing at Burnwood.	J20064 F/Lt. F.R. Harris.
23.12.44.	De Havilland Mosquito	654 BS USAAF, crashed at Breakheart Hill south west of Dursley and was burnt out.	Two killed both Americans. J.D. Spear C.B. Bryan
5. 1.45.	North American Mustang KH555	No.20 MU, stalled on take off from Aston Down.	
8. 1.45.	Armstrong Whitworth Albemarle P1651	No.22 HGCU, crashed on landing at Fairford. Starboard undercarriage leg collapsed and port undercarriage unit fell out completely.	1338187 W.O. B. Jacobs. 125589 F/Lt. P.N. Taylor.
14. 1.45.	Hawker Typhoon JP916	No.55 OTU, struck trees and force landed 2 miles east of Aston Down.	
19. 1.45.	Airspeed Oxford L4584	No.6 (P)AFU, struck by Oxford MP403 at Windrush and damaged beyond repair.	
1. 2.45.	Supermarine Spitfire EN915	TFU, abandoned after loss of control due to rudder difficulties. Aircraft came down at Coombe Hill near Tewkesbury.	
10. 2.45.	Supermarine Spitfire NH483	FPP, crashed at Littleton on Severn at 15.20 hours.	
10. 2.45.	Avro Lancaster ME750	No.1666 CU, crashed in flames near Siddington.	F/Lt. Waddell (i) died later. Seven crew killed.
13. 2.45.	Hawker Typhoon EJ951	No.55 OTU, crashed in forced landing just north of Elberton.	

DATE	'AIRCRAFT TYPE/SERIAL'	DETAILS	
13. 2.45.	Hawker Typhoon JR318	No.55 OTU, force landed and caught fire after engine failure just east of Whitfield.	
26. 2.45.	Supermarine Spitfire RM922	No.83 GSU, force landed in a field when low on fuel and turned turtle at Hillfield House Farm Glos.?	
5. 3.45.	Hawker Typhoon MP114	No.55 OTU, struck by JR443 whilst awaiting take-off at Aston Down.	
11. 3.45.	De Havilland Mosquito NT367	No.25 Squadron, overshot single engined landing at South Cerney, ran into a ditch and caught fire at 21.15 hours.	Crew safe.
12. 3.45.	Hawker Typhoon JR212	No.55 OTU, flew into the Severn? whilst recovering from a rocket firing dive.	
13. 3.45.	Armstrong Whitworth Albemarle V2035	No.22 HGCU, crashed on take-off from Fairford.	
15. 3.45.	Avro Lancaster LL902 (EM—A)	No.207 Squadron, crashed at Little Rissington at 02.50 hours.	
18. 3.45.	Hawker Typhoon MN146	No.55 OTU, overshot landing at Chedworth.	
20. 3.45.	Avro Anson DJ471	FPP, collided with Typhoon JP433 on approach to Aston Down.	Two killed.
20. 3.45.	Hawker Typhoon JP433	No.55 OTU, see above.	
23. 3.45.	Airspeed Oxford AS894	No.3 (P)AFU, overshot landing at Overley.	
25. 3.45.	Hawker Typhoon MN236	No.55 OTU, crashed into a Nissen Hut on 'B' site, Aston Down dispersal and burst into flames. A number of airmen and airwomen were trapped inside, two were killed and 15 injured.	Pilot killed.
1. 4.45.	De Havilland Mosquito MM328	PRDU, broke up and crashed after high speed dive Southrop.	
4. 4.45.	Airspeed Oxford DF307	No.3 (P)AFU, crashed after striking tree at Dowdeswell.	Sgt. T.H. Judge (k).
7. 4.45.	Hawker Typhoon MP127	No.55 OTU, crashed at Ashwell Farm, Woolaston near Lydney. Site examined by Severnside Aviation Society and some small items, including the canopy were recovered.	
9. 4.45.	Avro Lancaster PP692	No.46 MU, crashed at Kemble.	

No.	Date	Aircraft	Details	Casualties
11.	4.45.	Hawker Typhoon JP578	No.55 OTU, crashed after tyre burst on take-off from Aston Down.	
15.	4.45.	De Havilland Tiger Moth N6726	No.29 EFTS, abandoned after controls jammed at Mangotsfield.	
17.	4.45.	Hawker Typhoon DN442	No.55 OTU, collided with Mosquito MN285 while taxying at Aston Down.	
22.	4.45.	Hawker Typhoon DN260	No.55 OTU, crashed on overshoot at Aston Down.	
29.	4.45.	Airspeed Oxford DF332	No.3 (P)AFU, hit the brow of a hill at Guiting Power during a hailstorm and disintegrated. Came down near New Barn Farm.	F/Sgt. T. Gould (instructor) (k). F/Sgt. H.B. Montgomery (pupil) (k). F/O Aubrey (passenger) (k).
6.	5.45.	De Havilland Mosquito KB233	PFNTU, pilot lost control possibly due to anoxia and aircraft broke up in the air and crashed on the railway track between Lydney and Gloucester. Severnside Aviation Society visited the site during 1982 but nothing was found as the site had been cleared in 1945.	Crew killed.
8.	5.45.	Airspeed Oxford V4080	No.15 (P)AFU, struck by Oxford LX142 whilst taking-off at night from Babdown Farm.	
12.	5.45.	Airspeed Oxford	Unit unknown, crashed near Shirehampton.	
8.	6.45.	Airspeed Oxford NM299	No.3 (P)AFU, disintegrated in the air over Kemmerton after going into a spin.	F/O T.H. Furlong safe (parachuted).
13.	6.45.	De Havilland Tiger Moth N6714	No.22 EFTS, crashed on landing Broadwell.	
25.	6.45.	Airspeed Oxford V4211	No.295 Squadron, crashed in a forced landing near Moreton in the Marsh.	
25.	6.45.	Airspeed Oxford NJ317	No.3 (P)AFU, dived into the ground after a fire in the starboard wing. Aircraft exploded on impact at Blaisdon.	F/Sgt. Howlet safe (parachuted). F/O K.E. Sutton-Brown (pilot) (k).
25.	6.45.	Armstrong Whitworth Albemarle V2042	No.22 HGCU, brakes failed and the undercarriage was raised to stop the aircraft at Fairford.	
3.	7.45.	Avro Lancaster SW278	No.166 Squadron, crashed in the Bristol Channel?	
11.	7.45.	Armstrong Whitworth Albemarle V1868	No.22 HGCU, crashed on take-off from Fairford.	
		Armstrong Whitworth Albemarle V2047	No.22 HGCU, undercarriage collapsed on landing at Fairford.	

DATE	'AIRCRAFT TYPE/SERIAL'	DETAILS	
27. 8.45.	Avro Lancaster LM681 (G—AHJU)	Flight Refuelling Ltd, overran and crashed through hedge at Staverton, coming to rest in Bamfurlong Road.	Crew of five safe.
4. 9.45.	Vultee Vengeance ??301	Unit unknown, crashed Filton.	
10. 9.45.	Hawker Tempest ??825	Unit unknown, crashed at Filton.	
11.10.45.	Avro Lancaster ND623	Flight Refuelling Ltd, overshot and ran into a ditch and trees at Staverton.	W.O. Davies (pilot) safe. P/O Harris (i) died later.
11.10.45.	Douglas Dakota KG433	No.436 Squadron, undershot, whilst on a night approach to Down Ampney.	

Appendix

Aircraft Incident Log Illustrations

A Miles Magister banking over the camera.

P/O Masterson seen in the cockpit of a Tigermoth Trainer. He was a native of Dublin and only had one hour solo experience on Harvard Trainers when he crashed near Chalford in November 1939. (via Paul Aston)

P/O Noel Masterson who was killed when his Harvard Trainer crashed near Chalford on 21st November 1939. (via Paul Aston)

An interesting view of the Oakridge Ju.88 (July 1940) showing the aftermath of the incident with RAF guard tent pitched nearby. (W. G. Fear – via Paul Aston)

By mid 1940 the Spitfire began to appear on the Gloucestershire casualty list.

The aggressive lines of the Ju.88 are well shown here. This aircraft proved to be one of the most adaptable of the war and was used in a variety of roles. Several aircraft of this type came down in the County.

Burial party of Unteroffizier Walter Theiner killed when Ju.88A 9K+GN of 5/KG51 crashed on 25/07/1940 at Oakridge, Glos. He was buried in Brimscombe Parish Church and later moved to the War Cemetery at Cannock Chase Staffs. *(Severnside Aviation Society)*

The joint grave of Lt. Herbert Holstein navigator of the ill fated Coates Manor Ju.88 and Uffz Ewald Lohrs (note wrong spelling on stone) who died in August 1940 when his Heinkel was rammed by Sgt. Hancock's Anson at Windrush.
(Rennison Collection)

Theiner's grave at Cannock Chase War Cemetery.
(Rennison Collection)

Unteroffizier Herbert Rave of 5/KG27 the observer of Heinkel HeIIIP W.NR 1408, 1G+?T was killed following collision with Sgt. Hancock's Avro Anson.
(Severnside Aviation Society Collection via Frau Else Krombach)

175

The joint grave of an unknown German airman and Luffz Richard Schmidt who died in August 1940 after his Heinkel collided with Sgt. Hancock's Anson at Windrush.

Pilot Officer David Mackintosh Moore Bell of 5 OTU Aston Down who was killed at Tidenham, Glos. on 25th August 1940 in Blenheim 1F L6733 aged 24.

(Severnside Aviation Society)

Two More City Pilots Killed Accidentally In England

Reports of the deaths of two Christchurch pilots in the Royal Air Force at Home have been received. They are:—

Pilot Officer Ronald Stanley Magee, aged twenty-five, son of Mrs C. M. Magee, of 34, Gracefield Avenue, and

Sergeant-Pilot Robert Henry Clifford, aged twenty-four, eldest son of Mr and Mrs H. H. Clifford, of 52, Worcester Street.

Educated at the Reefton District High School and St Bede's College, Pilot Officer Magee took an early interest in flying. He was a member of the Canterbury Aero Club and the Rongotai Aero Club where he obtained his A and B licences. After leaving St Bede's in 1932, he was engaged in surveying. Later, he joined the artillery and, after receiving his training at Trentham, he was stationed at Fort Dorset for two years. It was while in Wellington that he obtained his flying licences, and when he joined the Air Force he had over one hundred hours' flying to his credit.

Pilot Officer Magee left Fort Dorset to join the R.N.Z.A.F. in June last

Pilot Officer R. S. Magee (top), of Christchurch, who has been killed as the result of an aircraft accident in England. Sergeant-Pilot R. H. Clifford (below), also of Christchurch, killed in an accident in England.

year, and he spent three months at Taieri, after which he was transferred to Wigram. He passed out from Wigram on January 15 of this year.

He was married to Miss Shirley Buchanan, of McMillan Avenue, Cashmere Hills, a fortnight before he left for Home. He was a good all-round athlete, being prominent in hurdling, tennis and golf.

Official advice from England stated that Pilot Officer Magee was reported as having lost his life as a result of an aircraft accident on August 26.

Sergeant-Pilot Clifford was educated at Cathedral Grammar School and Timaru Boys' High School. After leaving school he assisted his father in a photography business in Christchurch, later joining the legal firm of H. Cavell and Leitch. At the same time he was taking the legal course at Canterbury College. He was a keen tennis player.

He received his flying training at Wigram and passed out on May 28. He had only been in England about six weeks when the news of his death as the result of an accident was received by his parents.

176

Sgt. George Wilcox (W/Op−AG) and Sgt. Jackie Lane (Observer) were the surviving crew members from Blenheim L8797 of 17 OTU Upwood which crashed at Tuffley, Glos. on the 23rd September 1940.   *(Severnside Aviation Society Collection)*

Bristol Blenheim Mk IV L8797 which crashed at Tuffley, Glos. on 23rd September 1940.   *(Severnside Aviation Society)*

Flight Lieutenant Robert George Coventry aged 30 was killed on 23rd September 1940 when Blenheim L8797 crashed at Tuffley.

(Severnside Aviation Society Collection)

Sgt. Keatley from Norwich was killed when his Oxford N1192 hit high tension cables near Frampton-on-Severn and crashed on the 24th September 1940.

(via Paul Aston)

Sgt. P. Harry (2nd from right, front row) was killed when Oxford N1192 crashed during September 1940.

Oberfeldwebel Johannes Heinrich Tiepelt Pilot of the Messerscmitt 110 shot down at Fishponds Bristol on the 27th September 1940. (Severnside Aviation Society Collection)

P/O R. W. Waine died when his Hurricane (V7190) dived into the ground near Frampton-on-Severn during April 1941. (via Paul Aston)

A Hanley Page Hampden known as the 'Flying Suitcase'. It was an aircraft of this type that broke up in mid air over Highnam during October 1940.

Wellington R1090 (ED−K) of 21 OTU 'pranged' near Moreton-in-Marsh date unknown.

Sgt. E. C. Perkins, a native of Tunbridge Wells was the pilot of Anson DJ181 when it crashed into a hillside near Moreton Valence in August 1942. (via Paul Aston)

LAC (later Sgt.) Basil Jeffery (front centre) pilot of Oxford V3869 of 3 (P) AFO South Cerney who was killed when his aircraft crashed during a landings and training exercise on 5th April 1942 near Lechlade. (RCAF)

Sgt. William John Ferguson (RNZAF) was a member of the crew of the 12 OTU Wellington that crashed close to the Gloucestershire county boundary on the 16th September 1942. (via Paul Aston)

Sgt. Robert George Mcarthy (RNZAF) was the pilot of Wellington BJ728 which crashed at Lower Farm Upper Milton on the 16th September 1942, just over the Gloucestershire border in Oxon. (via Paul Aston)

Sgt. Knut Winter (Norwegian) in training at Little Norway in Canada (extreme right at front) who later died when his Spitfire crashed in 1942. (via Paul Aston)

The remains of Sgt. Winter's Spitfire P7543 of 52 OTU. (via Paul Aston)

Sgt. Knut Winter a Norwegian serving with the RAF who died when his Spitfire crashed near Chavenage on October 17th 1942. (via Paul Aston)

Sgt. Pilot Hector William Farquharson (RNZAF) aged 20 who was killed on 6th November 1942 when Oxfords AP473 and BG551 collided near Little Rissington. (via Paul Aston)

The Hanley Page Halifax was one of the RAF's trilogy of heavy bombers. Several came to grief in Gloucestershire during the war years.

Wireless Operator/Air Gunner Sgt. C. R. Kippen (S. African) was a member of the crew of Wellington LB120 that crashed on the 29th of November 1942 near Moreton-in-Marsh. This picture was taken at Cranwell in 1942.
(via Paul Aston)

Flt. Lt. Harrison Pilot of Halifax H7844 that crashed at Oaksey Wood near Kemble in January 1944.
(via B. Kedward)

A very rare picture of a 'Whitley' V of 24 OTU RAF Honeybourne over Gloucestershire on its was to the Severn Estuary Air Firing Ranges. *(via B. Kedward)*

Flying Officer Robert Barr (centre) with fellow trainee RAF pilots, training in the U.S.A. (They have all awarded themselves USAAF wings!) He was later killed in the crash of Miles Master AZ851. *(Severnside Aviation Society)*

Cadet Stone ATC who died in the crash of a 6SFTS Oxford on 11th September 1943. *(via B. Kedward)*

Flying Officer Robert Barr 5(PAFU (Ternhill) a pupil pilot who was killed at Elmore Glos. in Miles Master II AZ851 on 18th November 1943.

(Severnside Aviation Society)

F/O Tom Brumwell was the pilot of the ill fated Dakota KG369 of 512 Squadron, which came to grief at Chedworth in April 1944.

(Severnside Aviation Society)

Pilot Officer Ronald Teed (Nav) killed at Chedworth in Dakota KG369 on 10th April 1944 while serving with 512 Squadron at Broadwell.

(Severnside Aviation Society)

F/Sgt. Hura Nelson Burns a New Zealander in the RAAF aged 22 was the pilot of Stirling LJ475 of 620 Squadron which crashed near Kempsford, Glos. on 13th April 1944. Five of the crew of six were killed and later buried in Bath (Haycombe) Cemetery; plot 39, sec. H, row B, grave 246.

(Severnside Aviation Society)

Sgt. Emerl William Tootill of 620 Squadron the W/OP on Stirling LJ475 killed at Kempsford on 13th April 1944.

(Severnside Aviation Society)

Sgt. George Whitton Lewis was the Flight Engineer on Short Stirling LJ475 of No. 620 Squadron, Fairford, Glos. He died when the aircraft was involved in a flying accident on 13th April 1944 near Kempsford, Glos.

(Severnside Aviation Society)

Flight Sergeant Arthur Bruce Haynes (Australian) aged 20 was the Pilot of Stirling EF244 of 620 Squadron which crashed at Kempsford, Glos. on 19th May 1944. All crew were killed. He was buried at Bath (Haycombe) Cemetery in plot 51, Sec. H, Row T241.

(Severnside Aviation Society)

F/O Keith Alexander Hills RCAF 620 Squadron. Normally a member of F/Lt Hannah's crew, on 19th May 1944 he had to fly with F/Lt R. O. Francis, as his Navigator was late returning from leave. He was killed when LJ880 collided with EF244 at Kempsford. Keith Hills was a schoolteacher in civilian life and was a very popular individual in the squadron.

(Severnside Aviation Society Collection)

Short Stirling III EF244 of 620 Squadron, Fairford. This aircraft was written off and crew killed in collision with Stirling LJ880 at Kempsford, Glos. on 19th May 1944. The crew members were

        Pilot F/Sgt. A. B. Haynes RAAF
        Nav Sgt. G. Powell RAFVR
        W/OP Sgt. A. T. Franks RAFVR
        F/Eng. Sgt. J. W. Taylor RAFVR
        B/A Sgt. R. M. Cotterell RAFVR
        A/G Sgt. G. P. Jones RAFVR
            (Severnside Aviation Society Collection)

19 year old Sgt. James (Jimmy) Walter Taylor was the Flight Engineer of Short Stirling EF244 (620 Squadron Fairford, Glos.) He was killed when the aircraft was involved in a mid-air collision at Kempsford, Glos. on 19th May 1944.
(Severn. Aviation Society)

During the latter months of the war at least four Mosquito aircraft came down in Gloucestershire.

Part of the trail of destruction wrought by Stirling EF177 when it crashed at Alveston in October 1944.
(Severnside Aviation Society)

A Stirling IV being vacated by its crew following a crash landing at Fairford (date unknown, but prior to D-Day as there are no invasion stripes.)   (Severnside Aviation Society)

185

Bibliography

Action Stations Vol.5; C. Ashworth. (Patrick Stephens)
Action Stations Vol.6; M.J.F. Bowyer. (Patrick Stephens)
Aircraft of the Royal Air Force Since 1918; O. Thetford (Putnam)
Aviation in South West Britain 1910—1979; D. Teague. (Teague-White)
Bomber Squadrons of the RAF.; P. Moyes. (MacDonald)
Bristol Aircraft Since 1910; C.H. Barnes. (Putnam)
Bristol Blitz Diary; J. Dike. (Redcliffe Press)
Bristol Bombed. (F.G. Warne)
Bristol Under Blitz; Ald. T.H.J. Underdown. (J.W. Arrowsmith)
Britain Under Fire. (Country Life)
British Military Aircraft Serials 1911—1971; B. Robertson
Chronology of World War II; Compiled by C. Argyle. (Marshall Cavendish)
Citizens in War and After; S. Spender. (Harrap & Co)
Civil Defence Area 8 Stroud District; P.R. Symonds. (Stroud & Nailsworth Defence Committee)
Fighter Squadrons of the RAF; J. Rawlings. (MacDonald)
Fly and Deliver; H. Bergel. (Airlife Publications)
Front Line. (HMSO 1942)
Gloster Aircraft Since 1917; Derek N. James. (Putnam)
Gloucestershire at War; Ed. D. Archer. (F. Bailey & Son)
Kampfgeschwader 'General Wever' 4; K. Gundelach. (Motor Buch Verlag)
Kampfgeschwader 'Grief' 55; W. Dierich. (Motor Buch Verlag)
Kampfgeschwader 'Legion Kondor' 53; H. Kiehl. (Motor Buch Verlag)
Kampfgeschwader 'Wiking' 100; U. Balke. (Motor Buch Verlag)
Lancaster — The Story of a Famous Bomber; B. Robertson. (Harleyford)
Luftwaffe Encore; K. Wakefield. (W. Kimber)
Men & Machines of the Australian Flying Corps 1914—1919; C. Schaedel.
(Kookabura Tech. Publications)

Night Fighter; C.F. Rawnsley/R. Wright. (Elmfield Press)
Roof over Britain. (HMSO 1942)
Royal Air Force Aircraft K1000 to K9999
Royal Air Force Aircraft L1000 to L9999
Royal Air Force Aircraft N1000 to N9999
Royal Air Force Aircraft P1000 to P9999
Royal Air Force Aircraft R1000 to R9999
Royal Air Force Aircraft T1000 to T9999
Royal Air Force Aircraft V1000 to W9999

Royal Air Force Aircraft X1000 to Z9999
Royal Air Force Aircraft AA100 to AZ999   Air Britain
Royal Air Force in Pictures. (Country Life)
Target England; D. Wood.
The Battle of Britain Then & Now; Ed. W.G. Ramsey. (After the Battle)
The First Pathfinders; K. Wakefield. (W. Kimber)
The Halifax File   Air Britain
The Narrow Margin; D. Wood/D. Demster. (Arrow Books)
The Squadrons of the Royal Air Force. J. J. Halley   Air Britain
The Stirling File   Air Britain
The Typhoon File   Air Britain
Twenty One Squadrons; L. Hunt
Wings Over Rutland; J. Rennison. (Spiegl Press)

PLUS various issues of the following magazines and periodicals; Aeroplane Monthly, Air Pictorial, Air Enthusiast, Air International, Flypast and Aeromilitaria.